Graduate Careers in Context

In a world where there are increasing concerns about graduate underemployment and likely career trajectories, it is not surprising that there is a significant body of literature examining graduate careers in post-industrial societies. However, it has become increasingly evident in recent years that there is a stark disconnect between education and employment researchers and and careers and employability professionals. *Graduate Careers in Context* brings these two separate groups together for the first time in order to provide a better understanding of graduate careers.

The book addresses the problems surrounding the graduate labour market and its relationship to higher education and public policy. Drawing on varied perspectives, the contributors provide a comprehensive examination of current theoretical debates, graduate transitions, and professional and organisational issues, before discussing the benefits of future collaboration between practitioners and academic researchers.

The interdisciplinary focus of this book will make it of great interest to academics, researchers and postgraduate students in the areas of education, sociology, social policy, business studies and career guidance and coaching. It should also be essential reading for practitioners who wish to consider their role and responsibilities within the changing higher education market.

Ciaran Burke is an Associate Professor of Higher Education. His research focuses on access to higher education and graduate employment pathways. Adopting a Bourdieusian theoretical lens, he has published extensively on issues including graduate employment, social justice and social theory.

Fiona Christie is a Careers Consultant, Writer and Researcher. Her experience includes extensive advice and guidance, teaching, and management in Higher Education and she has also worked in Secondary/Further Education. She has recently completed her PhD in Educational Research with a focus on graduate transitions, careers and employability.

Routledge Research in Higher Education

Academics Engaging with Student Writing
Working at the Higher Education Textface
Jackie Tuck

Professional Education at Historically Black Colleges and Universities
Past Trends and Outcomes
Edited by Tiffany Fontaine Boykin, Adriel A. Hilton, and Robert T. Palmer

Articulating Asia in Japanese Higher Education
Policy, Partnership and Mobility
Jeremy Breaden

Global Mobility and Higher Learning
Anatoly V. Oleksiyenko

Universities and the Occult Rituals of the Corporate World
Higher Education and Metaphorical Parallels with Myth and Magic
Felicity Wood

Developing Transformative Spaces in Higher Education
Learning to Transgress
Sue Jackson

Improving Opportunities to Engage in Learning
A Study of the Access to Higher Education Diploma
Nalita James and Hugh Busher

Graduate Careers in Context
Research, Policy and Practice
Edited by Ciaran Burke and Fiona Christie

For more information about this series, please visit: www.routledge.com/
Routledge-Research-in-Higher-Education/book-series/RRHE

Graduate Careers in Context
Research, Policy and Practice

Edited by Ciaran Burke
and Fiona Christie

LONDON AND NEW YORK

First published 2019
by Routledge
2 Park Square, Milton Park, Abingdon, Oxon OX14 4RN

and by Routledge
711 Third Avenue, New York, NY 10017

Routledge is an imprint of the Taylor & Francis Group, an informa business

© 2019 selection and editorial matter, Ciaran Burke and Fiona Christie; individual chapters, the contributors

The right of the editor to be identified as the authors of the editorial material, and of the authors for their individual chapters, has been asserted in accordance with sections 77 and 78 of the Copyright, Designs and Patents Act 1988.

All rights reserved. No part of this book may be reprinted or reproduced or utilised in any form or by any electronic, mechanical, or other means, now known or hereafter invented, including photocopying and recording, or in any information storage or retrieval system, without permission in writing from the publishers.

Trademark notice: Product or corporate names may be trademarks or registered trademarks, and are used only for identification and explanation without intent to infringe.

British Library Cataloguing-in-Publication Data
A catalogue record for this book is available from the British Library

Library of Congress Cataloging-in-Publication Data
Names: Christie, Fiona, editor. | Burke, Ciaran, editor.
Title: Graduate careers in context : research, policy and practice / edited by Fiona Christie and Ciaran Burke.
Description: Abingdon, Oxon ; New York, NY : Routledge, 2018. | Includes bibliographical references.
Identifiers: LCCN 2018013032 (print) | LCCN 2018028284 (ebook) | ISBN 9780203732281 (E-book) | ISBN 9781138301764 (hardback)
Subjects: LCSH: College graduates—Employment. | Education, Higher—Economic aspects. | School-to-work transition.
Classification: LCC HD6277 (ebook) | LCC HD6277 G667 2018 (print) | DDC 331.402/35—dc23
LC record available at https://lccn.loc.gov/2018013032

ISBN: 978-1-138-30176-4 (hbk)
ISBN: 978-0-203-73228-1 (ebk)

Typeset in Galliard
by Apex CoVantage, LLC

Contents

List of figures and tables	vii
List of contributors	ix
Foreword	xi
PAUL REDMOND	

1	Introduction: graduate careers in context – setting the scene	1
	FIONA CHRISTIE AND CIARAN BURKE	

PART 1
Graduate labour market   15

2	'Investing in your future': the role of capitals in graduate employment pathways	17
	CIARAN BURKE AND SARAH HANNAFORD-SIMPSON	

3	Whose employability? Fees, labour markets and the unequal rewards of undergraduate study	29
	ANDREW MORRISON	

4	Regional capital and 'local' graduate employment	41
	TERESA CREW	

PART 2
Graduate careers and transitions   55

5	Graduate labour market myths	57
	CHARLIE BALL	

6	Graduate gap years: narratives of postponement in graduate employment transitions in England	71
	KATY VIGURS, STEVEN JONES, DIANE HARRIS AND JULIA EVERITT	

vi *Contents*

7 Geography, mobility and graduate career development 85
ROSIE ALEXANDER

8 Learning to be employable 96
JANE ARTESS

9 Life in the graduate graveyards: making sense of
underemployment in graduate careers 110
TRACY SCURRY AND JOHN BLENKINSOPP

PART 3
Professional and organisational issues relating to employability 125

10 Organisational responses to the employability agenda in
English universities 127
BOB GILWORTH

11 A new career in higher education careers work 140
SIOBHAN NEARY AND JILL HANSON

12 Contested boundaries of professional expertise in HE
careers and employability services 153
NALAYINI THAMBAR

PART 4
Careers professionals evolving into researchers 165

13 The rise of the practitioner-researcher: how big data
and evidence-based practice requires practitioners with a
research mindset 167
DAVID WINTER

14 Making connections through practitioner research 179
GILL FRIGERIO

15 Conclusion – editorial reflections and a call to action 193
FIONA CHRISTIE AND CIARAN BURKE

Index 197

Figures and Tables

Figures

5.1	Proportion of UK population and workforce with degree or equivalent qualifications (NVQ4+) from 2004 to 2016	59
5.2	Net changes in UK occupational structure 2006–2016	65
5.3	Proportion of UK-domiciled graduates from 2016 working in the UK after six months, who were employed at businesses of different sizes	68
8.1	Selected career education and guidance activities prior to HE by self-rating on clarity of career ideas	102
8.2	Selected career education and guidance activities during the first year of HE by self-rating on clarity of career ideas	104
8.3	Selected career education and guidance activities reported by final year students by self-rating on clarity of career ideas	105
8.4	Selected employment-related outcomes by agreement with the statement 'I have a clear idea of the occupation I hope to have in 5 years' time and the qualifications required to do so'	107
11.1	Careers staff previous roles/sectors	145
12.1	Professional Encapsulation (Thambar, 2016a: 32) representing the work of Ackroyd (1996)	157
14.1	Systems Theory Framework – change over time	180
14.2	Systems Theory Framework – therapeutic system	181

Tables

5.1	Proportion of the UK population with a degree or equivalent qualification at the end of 2016, by age group. Data comes from the APS	60
5.2	Proportion of the English and Welsh population with a degree or equivalent qualification at the end of 2016, by urban area. Data comes from the APS	61

viii *Figures and Tables*

6.1 Number of students in the sample (n74) planning a
graduate gap year   74
6.2 Type of graduate gap year by participant   76
6.3 A comparison of pre-university and graduate gap year types   81
11.1 Comparison of staffing levels between 2008 and 2016   141

Contributors (listed as they appear in book)

Dr Paul Redmond – Director of Student Experience and Enhancement, University of Liverpool

Dr Fiona Christie – Careers Consultant, University of Salford and PhD graduate, University of Lancaster

Dr Ciaran Burke – Associate Professor, International Centre for Guidance Studies, University of Derby

Dr Sarah Hannaford-Simpson – Independent Scholar

Dr Andrew Morrison – Senior Lecturer in Education, Sheffield Hallam University

Dr Teresa Crew – Lecturer in Social Policy, Bangor University

Dr Charlie Ball – Head of Higher Education Intelligence, Graduate Prospects

Dr Katy Vigurs – Associate Professor, International Centre for Guidance Studies, University of Derby

Dr Steven Jones – Senior Lecturer, School of Environment, Education and Development, University of Manchester

Dr Diane Harris – Researcher, School of Environment, Education and Development, University of Manchester

Dr Julia Everitt – Researcher, International Centre for Guidance Studies, University of Derby

Rosie Alexander – Researcher, Lecturer, Careers Adviser and Manager – based in Orkney, Scotland

Jane Artess – Visiting Research Fellow, International Centre for Guidance Studies, University of Derby

Dr Tracy Scurry – Senior Lecturer, Newcastle University Business School

Professor John Blenkinsopp – Professor of Management, Newcastle Business School at Northumbria University

x *Contributors (listed as they appear in book)*

Dr Bob Gilworth – Director of The Careers Group, University of London

Dr Siobhan Neary – Associate Professor, International Centre for Guidance Studies, University of Derby

Dr Jill Hanson – Researcher, International Centre for Guidance Studies, University of Derby

Dr Nalayini Thambar – Director of Careers and Employability, University of Nottingham

David Winter – Head of Research and Organisational Development, The Careers Group, University of London

Gill Frigerio – Principal Teaching Fellow, Centre for Lifelong Learning, University of Warwick

Foreword

These are challenging times for universities and, in particular, their careers services. Technology, globalisation and changing social attitudes are rapidly transforming the once elitist world of higher education. Within the space of a lifetime, the sector has expanded beyond all previous parameters. More than 2.2 million students are currently enrolled at Britain's universities, making being a student the most populous occupation in the country (UUK, 2017). For today's undergraduates, going to university has become almost a mainstream activity, becoming accessible to more people, at more locations, in more venues, than any time in the sector's history.

But with scale has come almost halogen-light levels of scrutiny. Like all public institutions, universities have to justify themselves in ways which would have been unthinkable to previous generations. Concerns over value for money, contact hours, quality of teaching, the student experience, levels of managerial pay, have led to the introduction of numerous checks and balances – from the Teaching Excellence Framework (TEF) to the National Student Survey (NSS) – to be presided over by the newly created regulator, the Office for Students.

And at the forefront of the higher education debate is the subject of employability.

Tracing the link between universities and employability is complex, and it is timely that it should be explored further in this book. As will become clear in the following chapters, at the heart of employability is an implied commitment to autonomy and self-reliance: of acquiring the skills and know-how to manage and pilot one's own career. Employability, as an ex-CEO of the Association of Graduate Recruiters (AGR) once noted, implies much more than 'just' having a job. It's about being able to 'get a job, keep a job and, if the need arises, get another job.'[1]

I believe there are three reasons why employability has become so ubiquitous in today's universities. First, as numerous studies suggest, improving future career prospects is a major motivational factor behind prospective students' decisions to enrol at university. Focusing on employability helps universities address students' concerns; it also illustrates how far universities have moved in recent years from their classical, Victorian vision. Cardinal Newman defined the idea of xii *Foreword*

the university as the 'alma mater' who knew 'all her children by name.' Today, at the very least, she would be expected to offer them a work placement.

Second, employability has become a powerful measure against which universities are now measured – locally, nationally and internationally. Until now, the measurement for this was the Destinations of Leavers survey (DLHE), which, somewhat ironically, given the unintended consequences that it subsequently triggered, was invented by university careers services in the 1970s. That this prototype 'first destination survey' would one day morph into DLHE then Graduate Outcomes was an 'outcome' few could have anticipated.

Third, and perhaps most significant of all, there is a growing awareness that due to technology and Artificial Intelligence, the world of graduate jobs is evolving, with immense implications for thousands, if not millions, of traditional graduate careers.

Admittedly, as regards this third point, we've been here before. Since the First Industrial Revolution, technology has led to the forging of new jobs and the destruction of others. Previously, however, there has been an important difference. Those jobs which have vanished have tended to require low-level skills and knowledge. Jobs requiring higher-level skills and, in particular, higher education qualifications, have remained safe; in many cases, they have thrived.

Hence why, in the West, this seemingly immutable law of the job market led to the emergence in the 1990s of the idea of the 'knowledge worker' – the 'smart' worker who earns a living trading on his or her knowledge, skills and contacts. Rather than being tied to one job or employer, like an in-demand actor, the knowledge worker moves between assignments and projects in an opportunity-rich, symbolically analytical economy, trading and exchanging data, deciphering information, building and disseminating contacts (Reich, 1992).

The idea of the knowledge worker was expressed evocatively in Joe Klein's 1996 novel, *Primary Colors*. Based on Bill Clinton's 1992 presidential campaign, Klein recounted a scene in which his fictitious candidate, Jack Stanton, addresses a meeting of angry factory workers, who have just been laid off. Breaking with tradition, he tells them the harsh truth about the new world of knowledge jobs in which they will have to exercise their brains, not their physical strength as they have done in their 'muscle jobs'. Since the 1990s, this idea of the end of 'muscle jobs' and the rise of 'knowledge jobs' – which in turn call for higher qualifications – has driven the expansion of Western higher education. Even now, it's an idea that holds powerful sway in universities.

But all this may be about to change. It turns out that Klein was wrong. Knowledge jobs are no more resistant to economic forces than were muscle jobs. The difference, however, is that knowledge jobs aren't being lost to people in other countries. In fact, people hardly come in to it.

According to research by Deloitte and the University of Oxford, over the next twenty years just over one third of current jobs in the UK are at high-risk of being lost to computerisation (Osborne & Frey, 2015). Many of these jobs, according to researchers, are likely to be in white-collar professional occupations, such as chartered accountancy, marketing, financial services and business analysis. In the next decade alone, robots and Artificial Intelligence are expected to cause the loss of over 12 million US jobs, many of them in roles and functions once reserved exclusively for those with university-level qualifications (CNBC 2016).

The onset of this 21st century industrial revolution provides the backdrop against which this book should be read. The following chapters provide a fascinating and expert glimpse into a rapidly changing world – a world in which ideas about work, careers, professional identities, careers services and higher education are being reconsidered.

As we approach the third decade of the 21st century, the time has come for universities and career professionals to rethink and reimagine the graduate career and, equally as important, the idea of the careers service itself. Research should underpin such reimagining and the contributions in this book are a welcome addition to such rethinking and serve to question many established ideas.

Paul Redmond
University of Liverpool

Note

1 In 2017, AGR was renamed the Institute of Student Employers.

References

CNBC (2016). *The Robots Set to Disrupt White Collar Work.* (online) available from: www.cnbc.com/2016/07/07/the-robots-set-to-disrupt-white-collar-work.html

Klein, J. (1996). *Primary Colors.* New York: Random House.

Osborne, M., and Frey, C. (2015). "The Future of Employment: How Susceptible are Jobs to Automation". (online) available from: www.oxfordmartin.ox.ac.uk/downloads/academic/The_Future_of_Employment.pdf

Reich, R.B. (1992). *The Work of Nations.* New York: Vintage Books.

Universities UK (UUK) (2017). *Higher Education in Facts and Figures 2017.* (online) available from: www.universitiesuk.ac.uk/facts-and-figures

1 Introduction
Graduate careers in context – setting the scene

Fiona Christie and Ciaran Burke

Summary of book

Once an institution that existed on the fringes of the economy, the university now plays a central role in economic and social policy and, in many countries, higher education is charged with the responsibility to meet the demands of the knowledge economy and to provide value for money for students (Case, 2014). Varied commentators including the media, universities, employers and government give increasing attention to the careers of graduates, with fears of a mismatch between the supply and demand of graduates. In addition, work from the UK government's own *Social Mobility Commission* has consistently shown how elitism prevails in the graduate labour market, very clearly illustrated by the predominance of privately educated graduates in the most sought after professions. Similar inequalities persist across many recent and established post-industrial countries (OECD, 2017).

Since the great financial crash of 2008, a significant body of academic literature has grown in response to these issues, most recently from the sociology of education and labour market studies which depict the challenges that current graduates face (Tomlinson and Holmes, 2016; Tholen, 2014). Meanwhile professional university staff have been increasingly tasked with providing careers and employability services to individual students and graduates, providing practical expertise about graduate careers and the labour market. Professional practice in this field tends to have been dominated by organisational and policy demands with a focus on fostering individual employability amongst students.

It has become increasingly evident that there are few points of interaction between practitioners and sociologically oriented academic researchers, although they share mutual interests in growing knowledge and expertise about graduates and the labour market. *Graduate Careers in Context* brings together these perspectives – including authors who are academic researchers as well as those whose writing originates from experiences in policy/practice, and some who straddle both. This is the first time such a collection of writing has been brought together, introducing a range of topics which illuminate the context of graduate careers in today's world. Initially, the book was born out of conversations between editors and authors following a UK research conference for careers and employability practitioners which highlighted an appetite to explore issues of mutual interest. This book is situated

2 *Fiona Christie, Ciaran Burke*

in the UK context, drawing authors from England, Scotland, Wales and Northern Ireland; however, the issues it raises are of relevance to other nations in what is quickly becoming a global knowledge economy.

Drawing on diverse perspectives, this book provides an examination of a variety of issues surrounding the graduate labour market and its relationship to higher education and public policy. The book includes chapters from researchers which address debates about how theory can stimulate new ways of thinking about careers and employability. It goes on to writing which explores graduate transitions into the job market and how these are changing. It then moves on to chapters from authors working in careers services which illuminate professional and organisational responses to demands for universities to support the employability of their students, before moving on to final chapters which consider how professional (non-academic) staff are becoming more research active themselves, and why this is important.

Situating the book

Research and scholarship of relevance to graduate careers has been historically diverse, and there is a strong argument for a more holistic approach to the consideration of issues around careers which can add value to research, policy and practice in these fields.

Broadly, we would argue the following schools of thought have influenced the context of graduate careers and the work of practitioners and researchers who are the authors/editors of this book. Labour market commentary addresses large-scale trends influencing graduate career paths and their subsequent prospects. Management literature seeks to describe how careers are less linear and depicts what can make individuals flourish or not in dynamic and uncertain contexts. Employability literature addresses issues related to individual employability and the policy imperative upon universities in facilitating this. Sociologists consider the thorny topic of what agency individuals really can have in the development of their careers and the social factors that impinge upon people. Finally, literature associated with career guidance and development tends to have focused on theory that may have a practical application in supporting those tasked with helping individuals with their careers.

In practice, theories about careers are often tacit and partially formed, consciously and unconsciously drawing upon existing ideas. We would argue that for both practitioners and researchers, more holistic and rigorous thinking about subjects associated with careers and employability can contribute to more meaningful understanding of current contexts in which many of the taken-for-granted assumptions about the labour markets in OECD nations are being questioned.

Diversity and uneven returns in the graduate labour market

Labour market literature traces trends in the structure of the labour market which illustrate changes in the number and nature of work opportunities for graduates, with a growth of diverse outcomes (e.g., Behle et al., 2015; Elias et al., 1999; Elias and Purcell, 2013; Purcell and Elias, 2004). It raises questions about normative definitions of what a successful graduate outcome really is, and whether having a degree can help insure against the worst parts of an uncertain job market. In a context of mass higher education participation, it questions the optimism of human capital theory (Becker, 1994) and effectively casts doubt upon public policy which is based on simplistic economic benefits of getting a degree (Green and Henseke, 2016; Green and Zhu, 2010). Other questions are raised with regard to factors that contribute to different outcomes for graduates in transition; these include location, social class and subject studied. In explicitly sociological analysis of the labour market graduates are variably positioned as winners and losers (Bradley, 2005) in difficult job markets, evoked as victims and responsible agents by Tholen (2014). Other analysis also highlights how there are serious shortages of graduates for certain careers, e.g., nursing, teaching, construction and engineering (Ball, 2015).

The growth of the individual career actor

The twin concepts of boundarylessness (Arthur, 1994; Arthur and Rousseau, 1996; Defillippi and Arthur, 1994; Gubler et al., 2014; Rodrigues et al., 2014) and the protean career (Baruch, 2014; Hall, 2004; Waters et al., 2014) have been significant in influencing contemporary attitudes to careers and approaches to employability in universities, though rarely referenced explicitly. Much literature which draws upon boundaryless and associated protean career orientations is individualistic and psychological, and considerable assumptions of individual agency are apparent, while organisational careers are in decline. Successful career seekers are positioned as flexible and chameleon-like. Specific personal orientations are itemised and evaluated. The development of questionnaires and instruments that can measure and test orientations are commonplace. Such instruments are developed with a target audience that is responsible for human resource management, career counselling and occupational psychology so there is perhaps a pragmatic and implicit emphasis on what action can be taken and what individuals can control rather than what may be outside of their control (i.e., the world economy and inequality therein). In general, it does appear that such approaches risk downplaying the wider socio-economic factors that impact on individual careers. An extrapolation of these theories also connects to what many have depicted as a neo-liberalist emphasis on the individual as the source of securing a meaningful career (Duckworth, 2016; Gershon, 2017) which sociological writing argues against.

Employability in higher education

Employability is broadly the predominant driver of careers and employability policy and practice in universities. This exerts considerable pressure on the direction of university careers services in particular. Government policy has increasingly required higher education to focus on its role in preparing graduates for

4　*Fiona Christie, Ciaran Burke*

employment (BIS, 2011, 2015; Wilson, 2012). The increase in student tuition fees has been defended by government as justifiable due to the potential graduate premium with an implicit assumption that individuals will be aware of the potential return on their specific degree subject (Britton et al., 2016). A clear sign of the increasing relationship between higher education and employment has been the inclusion of graduate employment outcomes in the recently introduced UK Teaching Excellence Framework. Ironically, the policy emphasis on employability is not married to any tradition of industrial or labour market-informed planning of higher education provision. Provision of courses can often be in response to student demand which in the past has resulted in commentary which argues that there is an over-supply of certain graduates and an under-supply of others. In addition, there has been a steady growth of literature illustrating the practical implications and issues of careers provision within UK higher education (Artess et al., 2017; Tomlinson and Holmes, 2016).

Prevailing approaches in universities do tend to focus on the development of individual employability (via skills and attributes) rather than a consideration of structural challenges to employability probably due to the difficulty of doing the latter in an uncertain socio-economic landscape. There is also an emerging focus which explores issues of identity which offers an alternative to dominant ideas about skills (Holmes, 2015; Tomlinson et al., 2017). The tradition of writing about employability which critiques the evolution of it into something that is focused on individual employability rather than acknowledging the combination of individual factors, personal circumstances and external factors which influence likely success (Brown et al., 2004; McQuaid and Lindsay, 2005) has not gained much interest in either government or university policy contexts.

In summary, employability literature is wide-ranging and does raise questions about the prevailing focus on individual employability in universities. However, policy approaches do tend to give priority to the individual capacity to develop employability, and practical approaches to encouraging students to consider the contingent nature of their likely career success are scarce. As such employability in universities is arguably very much influenced by ideas from management and psychology which emphasise the individual career actor.

The social nature of graduate careers

Recent literature that broadly originates from the sociology of higher education draws upon the work of Bourdieu (1979, 1977) and focuses on social class as a lens to explore the careers of students and graduates. In doing so it reveals how some of the notions already discussed of being employable or having a suitably boundaryless or protean career orientation can be bound up with social background, individual habitus and an ability to draw upon valuable capitals. The significance of social background is evident in the labour market research of the Warwick Institute for Employment Research. The findings of the longitudinal Futuretrack study (Purcell et al., 2013) indicate that socio-economic background

Introduction 5

may have a greater significance than age, gender or ethnicity in likelihood of participation in activities and lifestyle that can enhance career prospects and the subsequent chance of securing a graduate level role later on.

Sociological literature makes an important contribution to reflections on graduate careers. This literature has shifted from a traditional/stereotypical perception of sociological commentary which depicts destinies as largely socially determined (Roberts, 1977; Willis, 1977) to a context that is drawn by recent literature that explores barriers but also how agency may be manifest or not. New ideas have emerged which depict individual careers in deeply relational terms, and warn of the dangers of individual responsibilisation in a context in which any notion that the job market is meritocratic is illusory (Bathmaker et al., 2013; Burke, 2015; Finn, 2015). The challenge of such literature is that in its depiction of unequal social contexts it risks what Holmes (2016) has described as a 'counsel of despair'.

Career guidance theory and responses to uncertain contexts

Career theories associated with the UK professional careers advisory community have developed for over a century. Savickas (2008, 2011, 2012) has partially traced this history which has tended towards a more psychological orientation; from Parsons's (1909) original ideas of trait theory and vocational choice, to Holland's matching approach (1997), to Super's (1983) ideas of developmental stages. More recently Krumboltz and Levin's (2010) theory of happenstance and Savickas and Porfeli's (2012) theory of career adaptability have considered how individuals respond to environments where uncertainty is endemic. However, despite contextual framing, the underlying philosophy of both these latter theories remains psychological and individualist in orientation. This strong tradition between career guidance and psychology, which tends to have been influenced by US writers, is something that has long been criticised by left-leaning sceptics of careers guidance in the UK (Roberts, 1977, 2013). Much classic career development theory is prefaced by an assumption that a professional infrastructure such as a university careers service with suitably expert staff exists to support individuals in utilising or acting upon ideas.

Other schools of thought associated with careers advice have been more willing to grapple with sociological and political issues that may affect guidance theory and practice. It is perhaps no accident that much such theory has originated from the UK context in which careers work has been subject to the twin forces of strong policy pressures and an enduring social class system. Some British writing on career development is more transdisciplinary in its heritage, drawing upon a balance between psychology and sociology, individual agency and social circumstances (Bimrose and Hearne, 2012; Gothard et al., 2001; Hodkinson, 2008; Law, 2009; McCash, 2008). With regard to policy issues, Tony Watts provided a socio-political analysis of secondary level guidance to depict the political aspect

6 *Fiona Christie, Ciaran Burke*

of careers guidance, a perspective which has gained little traction in the higher education careers professional community:

> Careers education and guidance is a profoundly political process. It operates at the interface between the individual and society, between self and opportunity, between aspiration and realism. It facilitates the allocation of life chances. Within a society in which such life chances are unequally distributed, it faces the issue of whether it serves to reinforce such inequalities or to reduce them.
>
> (Watts, 1996: 351)

Career development practices in UK universities are influenced more by employability outcome measures and metrics than by the application of any kind of career development theoretical framework, whatever its origin. Theoretical frames have been squeezed and perhaps found wanting in a context in which practice is dominated by marketised pressures to prepare graduates to be suitably employable for employers in competitive and crowded job markets. UK career studies literature for higher education (McCash, 2008, 2016) does encourage a critical approach to employability which advocates that students are educated to consider issues of professionalism, identity and the contingent nature of their future career prospects. However, the drive to being responsive to market pressures has led to an approach to career development support which draws upon an eclectic range of theories and ideas, and is arguably in some cases atheoretical as services are reactive to contexts.

It does appear that the tradition of psychologically based career theory, which has historically informed the guidance profession, may not be fit for purpose in current organisational and uncertain labour market contexts. This assertion is supported by more recent appeals which call for a new approach to career theory that can support practice more meaningfully with a strong social justice narrative. A theory that can be sensitive to psychological, sociological and political contexts could have a significant practical application (Hooley, 2015; Hooley et al., 2017; Hooley et al., 2012; Patton and McMahon, 2006; Sultana, 2014; Watts, 1996). There are signs of a demand for a new approach to career theory which can build upon the breadth of career studies heritage in a meaningful way.

Weaving diverse perspectives

It is in this context of varied and competing perspectives on careers and employability that our authors in this book find themselves as they write about issues that surround the graduate labour market. Our book is structured around theoretical debates, graduate transitions, professional and organisational responses, and finally looks forward to how practitioners may develop their practice by becoming more research-active and using new approaches to theory, policy and research. In so doing, we also challenge academic researchers to consider that it is only by meaningfully engaging with practitioners that they can really claim that their work has real impact.

Introduction 7

Graduate labour market: theoretical debates

The opening section of the text begins with Burke and Hannaford-Simpson's *'Investing in your future': the role of capitals in graduate employment pathways,* where they provide a discussion on the prominence of capitals within graduate attributes frameworks. The authors voice concern of uncritically applying a term which carries a lot of theoretical weight. Through a thorough discussion of Bourdieu's operationalisation and application of capitals the authors discuss the range of influences capitals have in directing individuals' trajectories. Their point is further illustrated through presenting contrasting life histories of graduates and unpacking the role of capitals.

In chapter three, *Whose Employability? Fees, labour markets and the unequal rewards of undergraduate study,* Morrison presents a social justice informed examination of graduate employment. Firstly, he interrogates what we mean by graduate employability and illustrates the continuing disparity in graduate pathways and incomes by various socio-economic metrics. He then goes on to explore these inequalities through the lens of Nancy Fraser's theory of two-dimensional participatory justice

In chapter four, *Regional capital and 'local' graduate employment,* Crew writes from the Welsh context and presents fascinating conclusions about how specific capitals such as the ability to speak Welsh and to own your own transport are of enormous significance in Wales. In so doing she highlights the limitations of discussions about employability which ignore more fundamental issues which are crucial for individuals in starting their careers. Her writing raises wider questions about regional diversity in job markets and the requirements for them.

Graduate careers and transitions

In chapter five, *Graduate labour market myths,* Ball firmly rebuffs some popular myths about the graduate labour market, i.e., 'everyone has a degree nowadays', 'there aren't enough jobs for graduates', 'all the graduate jobs are in London' and 'graduates all work in big business'. He utilises macro-level data from a number of national sources to make his argument in defence of the importance of graduates to the labour market, but also acknowledges that universities and society can't be complacent. Notably, he illustrates that while some graduates may struggle to find their place in the job market, there are still many roles for which there is an under-supply of graduates. Ball is able to expertly manipulate quantitative data sources to make an argument that will be reassuring to many policy-makers about the value of higher education and the relatively better position of graduates over non-graduates in the job market. What he cannot do with such data is explore more individual experiences of different graduates. However, his chapter does serve to reveal the flawed myths of much media reportage, which appears politically motivated and associated with wider criticism of the university sector.

In contrast to Ball's macro-level analysis of the labour market, in chapter six, *Graduate gap years: narratives of postponement in graduate employment transitions in England,* Vigurs et al. explore the early career experiences of graduates.

Their work spans 2014 and 2015 graduates (the latter being the first cohort in England to graduate with higher tuition fee debt). They trace increasing complexity and postponement in how graduates narrate their transition evoked by the concepts like taking a 'Gap Year' which historically was associated with a preuniversity experience.

In chapter seven, *Geography, mobility and graduate career development*, Alexander questions assumptions of geographical mobility in graduate careers. She writes from her unique perspective as a careers manager in a remote Scottish island community. Her research illustrates that dominant individualistic ideas that exhort individuals to be geographically mobile do not reflect how individuals really make career decisions, and that some graduates purposefully integrate a desire to stay in their island home, rather than to move away. Alexander reflects upon how careers practitioners respond to these different perspectives and uses the typology of mobilisers and integrators to describe contrasting approaches. Her typology raises powerful questions about ideological positions about mobility that advisers may draw upon, which go beyond the remote location of her own research.

In chapter eight, *Learning to be employable*, Artess discusses hitherto unreported data from the large-scale Futuretrack research study conducted by Warwick's Institute for Employment Research. She traces responses to questions about career clarity from respondents before, during and after university (2006–12) which indicate that engagement with a range of career development activities can positively support employability by contributing to individual ability to have confidence in their future career direction. Her findings raise interesting questions about how universities embed employability, suggesting that approaches need to factor in the space for students to consider issues of career identity, values and preferences which risk being ignored in employer-centred approaches to employability, which emphasise moulding students to become employable.

Scurry and Blenkinsopp in chapter nine, *Life in the graduate graveyards: making sense of underemployment in graduate careers*, depict the lived experiences of graduate underemployment with a focus on call centres in the Midlands of England. Their findings illustrate the uncomfortable adjustments and rationalisations (notably on occasion both symbolic and/or humorous) that occur for graduates as they reflect upon their career situations and prospects.

Professional and organisational issues relating to employability

Chapter ten, *Organisational responses to the employability agenda in English universities*, sees Gilworth drawing upon his own Doctorate of Business Administration (DBA) research and work as a director of university careers services, as well as his national role as AGCAS Director of Research and Knowledge. He describes how different universities respond to the employability agenda and the role of university careers services within this using an analytical typology born out of his research. He shines a particular light on how managers of careers services navigate this highly political environment.

In chapter eleven, *A new career in higher education careers work*, Neary and Hanson report on research conducted with the HE career development workforce and focus on careers advisers who have moved into the field within the last five years. Their research illustrates a highly dedicated and satisfied workforce demonstrating a strong set of values. Predominantly, most have moved from other roles in education/higher education or HR and recruitment. They raise questions about the highly gendered nature of careers work which is dominated by women; as they suggest, unsurprisingly given how many caring jobs are still associated with a female workforce. Their chapter supports what Thambar goes on to depict in her chapter about the dedicated nature of careers advisers.

In chapter twelve, *Contested boundaries of professional expertise in HE careers and employability services*, Thambar focuses upon the challenges of university careers services in establishing their position in contemporary universities. In particular she explores the changing role of the careers adviser which has historically been the dominant role in careers services. She describes the irony that the growth in importance of employability has not necessarily resulted in a growth in the core professional role of careers adviser that has historically been expert in careers. She documents the expanding and fragmenting of roles in careers services and subsequent uncomfortable adjustment undertaken by staff, running in parallel to a growing interest amongst academics who may question the value of a careers service. She argues that careers advisers need to adapt to organisational demands, but that professional managers in careers services also need to more confidently champion their careers advisers' expertise within university contexts or risk the careers service being seen as unimportant. She argues that this may require greater mutual understanding of all parties within careers services, and recommends that a successful evolution of the professional identity of careers advisers can contribute to organisational demands.

Careers professionals evolving into researchers

The final section of the book opens with chapter thirteen, *The rise of the practitioner-researcher. How big data and evidence-based practice requires practitioners with a research mindset*. Winter describes a large-scale research project called Careers Registration that has been conducted across sixteen universities, led by careers services. The project has collected data about career readiness and work experience amongst student populations and has secured HEFCE Learning Gain funding due to its ability to trace movement of career and employability readiness over time. Already the project has identified some surprises; e.g., over 40% of final years can be considered still in the "Deciding" phase of career readiness, a finding which contradicts any received wisdoms that students choose degrees with clear career ideas. Winter argues that the growth of Big Data available to careers services does mean that practitioners need to be better able to manage and interpret it. Such a development extends what university careers personnel have been accustomed to do and is perhaps a territory in which they

10   *Fiona Christie, Ciaran Burke*

can collaborate further with academic researchers in presenting research findings which can generate practical recommendations.

In chapter fourteen, *Making connections through practitioner research*, Frigerio reflects on her own learning about how theory, research and practice can inform each other. She draws upon three case studies based on her own experience as a careers manager, a researcher and a teacher of research to career practitioners. In particular, she argues for the value of a Systems Theory Framework perspective about careers, drawing upon the work of Patton and McMahon. Interestingly, this theoretical approach is not one that has gained much traction in practitioner contexts, certainly in the UK, and Frigerio's chapter invites wider questions about the accessibility of theory, which can lie dormant in academic books. Frigerio argues for the contribution to professional identity and practice that can be stimulated by engagement in theory and research.

References

Artess, J., Hooley, T., and Mellors-Bourne, R. (2017). *Employability: A Review of the Literature 2012–2016.* (online) available from: www.heacademy.ac.uk/resource/employability-review-literature-2012-2016.

Arthur, M.B. (1994). "The boundaryless career: A new perspective for organizational inquiry", *Journal of Organizational Behavior, 15*(4): 295–306.

Arthur, M.B., and Rousseau, D.M. (1996). *The Boundaryless Career: A New Employment Principle for a New Organizational Era.* New York: Oxford University Press.

Ball, C. (2015). *Our Response to the CIPD's Report on Overqualification and Skills Mis-match.* (online) available from http://hecsu.blogspot.com/2015/08/our-reponse-to-cipds-report-on.html.

Baruch, Y. (2014). "The development and validation of a measure for protean career orientation", *The International Journal of Human Resource Management, 25*(19): 2702–2723.

Bathmaker, A.-M., Ingram, N., and Waller, R. (2013). "Higher education, social class and the mobilisation of capitals: Knowing and playing the game", *British Journal of the Sociology of Education, 34*(5–6): 723–743.

Becker, G.S. (1994). Human capital revisited. In: *Human Capital: A Theoretical and Empirical Analysis with Special Reference to Education (3rd Edition).* Chicago: The University of Chicago Press.

Behle, H., Atfield, G., Elias, P., Gamblin, L., Green, A., Purcell, K., . . . Warhurst, C. (2015). "Reassessing the employment outcomes of higher education", In: Huisman, J., and Case, J. (Eds.), *Investigating Higher Education: International Perspectives on Theory, Policy and Practice.* Oxon, NY: Routledge Press, pp. 114–131.

Bimrose, J., and Hearne, L. (2012). "Resilience and career adaptability: Qualitative studies of adult career counseling", *Journal of Vocational Behavior, 81*(3): 338–344.

Bourdieu, P. (1977). *Reproduction in Education, Society and Culture.* London: Sage.

Bourdieu, P., and Passeron, J.-C. (1979). *The Inheritors: French Students and their Relation to Culture.* Chicago: University of Chicago Press.

Bradley, H. (2005). "Winners and losers: Young people in the 'new economy'", In: Bradley, H., and van Hoof, J. (Eds.), *Young People in Europe: Labour Markets and Citizenship.* Bristol: Policy Press, pp. 99–114.

Britton, J., Dearden, L., Shephard, N., and Vignoles, A. (2016). *How English Domiciled Graduate Earnings Vary with Gender, Institution Attended, Subject and Socioeconomic Background – Executive Summary.* (online) available from: www.ifs.org. uk/publications/wp.

Brown, P., Hesketh, A., and Williams, S. (2004). *The Mismanagement of Talent: Employability and Jobs in the Knowledge Economy.* Oxford. New York: Oxford University Press.

Burke, C. (2015). *Culture, Capitals and Graduate Futures: Degrees of Class.* London: Routledge.

Case, J. (2014). *Researching Student Learning in Higher Education.* London: Routledge.

Defillippi, R.J., and Arthur, M.B. (1994). "The boundaryless career: A competency-based perspective", *Trends in Organizational Behavior, 15*(4): 307–324. doi:10. 1002/job.4030150403.

Department of Business Innovation and Skills (BIS). (2011). *Higher Education: Students at the Heart of the System.* London: UK Government, HMSO.

Department of Business Innovation and Skills (BIS). (2015). *Fulfilling Our Potential: Teaching Excellence, Social Mobility and Student Choice.* (BIS/15/623). London: UK Government, HMSO. (online) available from: www.gov.uk/government/ publications.

Duckworth, A. (2016). *Grit: The Power of Passion and Perseverance.* New York: Simon and Schuster.

Elias, P., McKnight, A., Pitcher, J., Purcell, K., and Simm, C. (1999). *Moving On: Graduate Careers Three Years After Graduation.* (online) available from: www. hecsu.ac.uk/moving_on.htm.

Elias, P., and Purcell, K. (2013). *Classifying Graduate Occupations for the Knowledge Society.* Futuretrack Working Paper No. 5. (online) available from: www2.warwick. ac.uk/fac/soc/ier/futuretrack/findings/elias_purcell_soche_final.pdf.

Finn, K. (2015). *Personal Life, Young Women and Higher Education: A Relational Approach to Student and Graduate Experiences.* London: Palgrave Macmillan.

Gershon, I. (2017). *Down and Out in the New Economy: How People Find (or Don't Find) Work Today.* Chicago: University of Chicago Press.

Gothard, B., Mignot, P., Offer, M., and Ruff, M. (2001). *Careers Guidance in Context.* New York: Sage.

Green, F., and Henseke, G. (2016). *Should Governments of OECD Countries Worry about Graduate Over-education.* (online) available from: www.researchcghe.org.

Green, F., and Zhu, Y. (2010). "Over qualification, job dissatisfaction, and increasing dispersion in the returns to graduate education", *Oxford Economic Papers-New Series, 62* (4): 740–763.

Gubler, M., Arnold, J., and Coombs, C. (2014). "Organizational boundaries and beyond: A new look at the components of a boundaryless career orientation", *Career Development International, 19*(6): 641–667.

Hall, D.T. (2004). "The protean career: A quarter-century journey", *Journal of Vocational Behavior, 65*(1): 1–13.

Hodkinson, P. (2008). *Understanding Career Decision-making and Progression: Careership Revisited.* Paper presented at the John Killeen Memorial Lecture, Woburn House, London.

Holland, J.L. (1997). *Making Vocational Choices: A Theory of Vocational Personalities and Work Environments.* Psychological Assessment Resources.

12 Fiona Christie, Ciaran Burke

Holmes, L. (2015). "Becoming a graduate: The warranting of an emergent identity", *Education and Training*, 57(2): 219–238.

Holmes, L. (2016). "Graduate employability: Future directions and debate", In: Tomlinson, M., and Holmes, L. (Eds.), *Graduate Employability in Context*. London: Palgrave Macmillan, pp. 359–369.

Hooley, T. (2015). *Emancipate Yourselves From Mental Slavery: Self-actualisation, Social Justice and the Politics of Career Guidance*. (online) available from: http://derby.openrepository.com/derby/handle/10545/579895.

Hooley, T., Sultana, R., and Thomsen, R. (2017). *Career Guidance for Social Justice: Contesting Neoliberalism*. London: Routledge.

Hooley, T., Watts, A.G., Sultana, R.G., and Neary, S. (2012). "The 'Blueprint' framework for career management skills: a critical exploration", *British Journal of Guidance and Counselling*, 41(2): 117–131.

Krumboltz, J.D., and Levin, A.S. (2010). *Luck Is No Accident: Making the Most of Happenstance in Your Life and Career*. California: Impact Publishers.

Law, B. (2009). *Community Interaction and Its Importance for Contemporary Careers Work*. (online) available from: www.hihohiho.com/memory/cafcit.pdf.

McCash, P. (2008). "Career studies handbook: career development learning in practice", In: Yorke, M. (Series Ed.), *Learning and Employability Series*, pp. 1–48. (online) available from: www2.warwick.ac.uk/study/cll/about/cllteam/pmccash/mccash_hea_career_studies_handbook.pdf.

McCash, P. (2016). "Employability and depth psychology", In: Tomlinson, M., and Holmes, L. (Eds.), *Graduate Employability in Context*. London: Palgrave Macmillan, pp. 151–170.

McQuaid, R., and Lindsay, C. (2005). The Concept of Employability. *Urban Studies*, 42(2): 197–219.

OECD (2017). *Education at a Glance: 2017*. (online) available from: www.oecd-ilibrary.org/docserver/download/9617041e.pdf?expires=1516959542&id=id&accname=guest&checksum=3B4C3B9A080894B3E65244BA62C48011.

Parsons, F. (1909). *Choosing a Vocation*. Houghton Mifflin.

Patton, W., and McMahon, M. (2006). "The systems theory framework of career development and counseling: Connecting theory and practice", *International Journal for the Advancement of Counselling*, 28(2): 153–166.

Purcell, K., and Elias, P. (2004). *Seven Years On: Graduate Careers in a Changing Labour Market*. Warwick: HECSU.

Purcell, K., Elias, P., Atfield, G., Behle, H., Ellison, R., Luchinskaya, D., . . . Tzanakou, C. (2013). *Futuretrack Stage 4: Transitions Into Employment, Further Study and Other Outcomes*. (online) available from: www.hecsu.ac.uk/assets/assets/documents/Futuretrack_Stage_4_Final_report_6th_Nov_2012.pdf.

Roberts, K. (1977). "The social conditions, consequences and limitations of careers guidance", *British Journal of Guidance and Counselling*, 5(1).

Roberts, K. (2013). "Career guidance in England today: Reform, accidental injury or attempted murder?" *British Journal of Guidance & Counselling*, 41(3): 240–253.

Rodrigues, R., Guest, D., and Arthur, M.B. (2014). "The boundaryless career at 20: Where do we stand, and where can we go?" *Career Development International*, 19(6): 627–640.

Savickas, M. (2008). "Helping people choose jobs: A history of the guidance profession", In: Athanasou, J.A., and Esbroeck, R. (Eds.), *International Handbook of Career Guidance* (pp. 97–113). Dordrecht: Springer Netherlands.

Savickas, M. (2011). "The centennial of counselor education: Origin and early development of a discipline", *Journal of Counseling and Development, 89*(4): 500–503.

Savickas, M. (2012). "The 2012 Leona Tyler Award Address: Constructing careers: Actors, agents, and authors", *The Counseling Psychologist, 41*(4): 648–662.

Savickas, M., and Porfeli, E. (2012). "Career adapt-abilities scale: Construction, reliability, and measurement equivalence across 13 countries", *Journal of Vocational Behaviour, 80*(3): 661–673.

Sultana, R.G. (2014). "Pessimism of the intellect, optimism of the will? Troubling the relationship between career guidance and social justice", *International Journal for Educational and Vocational Guidance, 14*(1): 5–19.

Super, D.E. (1983). "Assessment in career guidance: Toward truly developmental counseling", *Personnel and Guidance Journal, 61*(9).

Tholen, G. (2014). *The Changing Nature of the Graduate Labour Market: Media, Policy and Political Discourses in the UK*. London: Springer.

Tomlinson, M., and Holmes, L. (2016). *Graduate Employability in Context: Theory, Research and Debate*. London: Springer.

Tomlinson, M., McCafferty, H., Fuge, H., and Wood, K. (2017). "Resources and readiness: The graduate capital perspective as a new approach to graduate employability", *Journal of the National Institute for Career Education and Counselling, 38*(1): 28–35.

Waters, L., Briscoe, J.P., Hall, D.T., and Wang, L. (2014). "Protean career attitudes during unemployment and reemployment: A longitudinal perspective", *Journal of Vocational Behavior, 84*(3): 405–419.

Watts, A.G. (1996). "Socio-political ideologies in guidance", In: Watts, A.G., Law, B., Killeen, J., Kidd, J.M., and Hawthorn, R. (Eds.), *Rethinking Careers Education and Guidance: Theory, Policy and Practice*. London: Routledge, pp. 351–363.

Willis, P.E. (1977). *Learning to Labour: How Working Class Kids Get Working Class Jobs*. Farnham: Ashgate.

Wilson, T. (2012). *Review of Business-University Collaboration*. (online) available from: www.gov.uk/government/uploads/system/uploads/attachment_data/file/32383/12-610-wilson-review-business-university-collaboration.pdf.

Part 1

Graduate labour market

Theoretical debates

2 'Investing in your future'
The role of capitals in graduate employment pathways

Ciaran Burke and Sarah Hannaford-Simpson

Introduction

The rise of post-industrialisation and, with it, the knowledge economy has firmly placed education as the primary tool of social mobility. As such, the university is seen to be the central institution to provide this social mobility – so much so that the 'success' of a university graduate is measured not by their degree classification but by the employment they are able to secure upon leaving higher education. A direct and clear consequence of this human capital discourse of 'access equals success' is that there are more and more individuals reading for degrees in UK Higher Education Institutions. As a result, there are increasingly fewer graduate jobs than graduates, leading to a devaluation of educational capital and graduate underemployment. It is within this context, coupled with the continuing destructuring of the labour market, that this chapter considers what other forms of capital influence graduate employment trajectories – in particular, social, cultural and economic. This chapter will provide a review of contemporary research, examining the classed pathways/barriers university graduates face, and consider the application of various sociological theories. It will, then, unpack findings based on primary research to offer close qualitative accounts of these experiences.

Skills, attributes and capitals

Within Daniel Bell's (1973) seminal text *The Coming of Post Industrialisation*, a central facet of our new society was a knowledge economy. As we left the confines of the factories and the shackles of heavy modernity behind, individuals, irrespective of social background and natal environment, had the opportunity to 'succeed' and become socially mobile. The origin of this great equaliser was education; the central market requirement was no longer based on birthright or borough but graft and determination. In the UK, as is the case in many other parts of the world (Case, 2014; Mullen, 2010; Li, 2015), there is an established relationship between participation in higher education and entry into the graduate labour market. Again, as is the case in many post-industrial nations, this relationship is growing in terms of levels of participation (OECD, 2017) and expectation. The last twenty years of UK higher education policy has witnessed an increased reliance on the HE sector to provide graduates who are not only well versed in their specific disciplines but are employable and able to meet market demands. Three particularly significant moments in UK higher education have been the introduction and gradual increase in university tuition fees through:

- *Teaching and Higher Education Act (1998)*
- *The Future of Higher Education (2003)*
- *Students at the Heart of the System (2011)*

Within these documents, a common theme emerged: a university education provides entry to the graduate labour market, so those individuals attending university should meet the financial requirements for attendance. In other words, UK higher education policy was organised and operated on a not so subtle human capital basis. Echoing Schultz's position that 'knowledge is our most powerful engine of production' (1971: iv), higher education was the great equaliser that Bell prophesised in the early 1970s. Mediating human capital assumptions and market requirements/realities has been a strong focus on skills. Stemming from the *Dearing Report* (1997), UK HEIs had a responsibility to provide academic knowledge as well as transferable skills – in particular, communication, numeracy, IT and learning how to learn (Morrison, 2014). The rationale from *Dearing* and subsequent skills policies was that graduates equipped with discipline-specific knowledge and adaptable skills would be suitable for the contemporary graduate market and for markets to come. However, UK HE skills policy has faced heavy criticism (Wolf, 2007; Archer and Davison, 2008, Tholen and Brown, 2018). A lasting issue has been a mismatch of skills provided and skills required; the British Chambers of Commerce reported (2014) that over half of graduate employers voiced concern on the preparedness of graduates for the graduate labour market. These issues have led recent government reports (BIS, 2012; Milburn, 2012) and legislation to call for a closer tie to industry, informing skills provision and curriculum design.

To meet the increasingly expanded skills set and the required ability to adapt to unseen and unknown futures, there is a focus on graduate attitudes or attributes. Artess et al. (2017) provide a review of graduate attribute frameworks. While reminding their audience that attributes will differ by region and industry, there are a number of attributes recurring throughout these frameworks:

- Aspiration
- Critical thinking
- Resilience
- Opportunity awareness
- Social intelligence
- Autonomy

An essential feature in supporting these attributes, Artess et al. suggest, is the development of networking and social capital. The rationale is that increased social capital provides increased understanding and more avenues to pursue, allowing the graduate to be adaptable. The primacy of social capital is evident within a number of individual university graduate attributes frameworks. One particular institution whose framework gained media interest is Queen Mary University of London. Here, the university places a great deal of focus on developing future graduates' social capital (QMUL, 2017), echoing Artess et al.'s (2017) rationale of increasing opportunities for career trajectory but also as a form of social justice, rebalancing the levels of non-scholastic capitals students possess and exchange. In the context of greater reliance on social capital to generate graduate employment opportunities and social mobility, there has been increased focus on co-curricular and extra-curricular activities (Milburn, 2012; Bridge Group, 2017). Previous studies (Bathmaker et al., 2016; Tomlinson, 2008) have demonstrated the importance of such activities in fostering skills and experiences required by the graduate labour market as well as the development of long-term social networks.

Bourdieu: the complication of cashing in

It is in the context of the increasingly casual use of the term 'social capital' that I am reminded of Geoff Payne's (2012) cutting rebuke of the conflation between the academic operationalisation of social mobility and government measurements. Payne's argument is that concepts and theories developed by the academy often have a particular meaning and are steeped in a strong philosophical tradition, and, while these terms often have a lay understanding, we must not let this replace the academic definition nor be hijacked by policy makers. In a similar tradition, it would be prudent to reiterate what we mean by social capital and how it is understood to operate in an abstract context. While Robert Putnam's (2000) seminal work *Bowling Alone* has provided a hugely influential commentary on the societal benefits of increased social networks and groups, the form of social capital advocated by Pierre Bourdieu (2004) has surpassed Putnam's form in terms of influence and application. As such, it is essential to outline what Bourdieu meant by social capital and where it fits within his larger social theory to reflexively consider the role of social capital on graduate employment trajectories.

The work of the French philosopher and social commentator Pierre Bourdieu has been applied in a range of disciplines, including politics, anthropology and cultural studies. However, it is higher education and graduate employment though which his concepts have perhaps enjoyed the greatest dissemination, in part due to the shift toward an increasingly neo-liberal knowledge economy and Bourdieu's own continued focus on education and higher education (1977, 1979). Bourdieu's particular theory of practice was formed in 1960s France, where, at the time, competing accounts of society advocating the primary role of structure (Levi-Strauss, 2011) or agency (Merleau-Ponty, 1963) dominated sociological debate. It was in this binary context that Bourdieu's structural constructivist model was developed, which examined and demonstrated the influence and presence of both structure and agency. In an effort to put this theory into

20   Ciaran Burke, Sarah Hannaford-Simpson

practice, Bourdieu developed a number of thinking tools, expressed in the formula [(habitus) (capital)] + field = practice (1984: 101).

Perhaps the best known of the thinking tools – and at times problematically overused (Reay, 2004) – is habitus (Bourdieu, 1977). At its most basic definition, the habitus can be understood to be comprised of norms, values and dispositions. There are a number of sources influencing the composition of habitus; however, the family and early school experiences are seen as being formative in terms of the initial habitus construction as well as how an individual would assess and perhaps opt out of experiences contrary to its initial dispositions. In many ways, the habitus is understood to form the basis of choices, practices and imposed limits/barriers – what Bourdieu described as 'regulated improvisations' (1977: 78). While habitus has been the main site of critique and the basis for charges of structural determinism (Jenkins, 2002), the permeable nature of habitus (Reay, 2004) is open to new experiences and influences; however, in contrast to Baudrillard's (1994) hyper-reality model of society, a departure from our natal environment significant enough to alter habitus is unlikely (Bourdieu, 1992).

The second thinking tool – and the focus of this chapter – is capital. In an effort to move beyond a Marxist and Weberian model of power and status, Bourdieu developed forms of capital: economic, social and cultural (2004). For Bourdieu, capital has three central roles: to act as currency to exchange for a range of things, to plot an individual's position within social space and to direct an individual's levels of expectations – what Bourdieu termed the 'field of the possibles' (1984: 110). While it is important to unpack how these forms work, it is equally necessary to outline what they are. Economic capital illustrates the clearest influence of Marx in that this form of capital refers to financial resources – namely, savings, stock portfolios and property. Social capital refers to social networks and connections; in contrast to Putnam's (2000) model, such connections are hierarchal and often used as a way to informally reproduce social inequalities. For Bourdieu, it is not enough to simply have social connections, as the end result of their investment will illustrate the level of social capital an individual enjoys. Cultural capital – best described as cultural competency – is formed of a range of activities, practices and knowledge. Cultural capital can be sub-divided into three forms: institutional capital, where cultural capital is gained through association with a prestigious institution, very often a university; objective cultural capital, demonstrated through artefacts such as owning a classical instrument or an extensive library collection; and embodied cultural capital, where an individual can express a level of cultural competency through their body.

The final thinking tool is field, often understood as the arena in which habitus and capital interact. However, similar to the differences between a basketball court and tennis court, different fields have different rules and will reward various resources and abilities accordingly. In addition, fields are dynamic and often change their rules and requirements without consultation. As such, individuals and groups must re-calculate how they navigate these spaces. An example of the temporal value of capitals in the face of changing fields is the graduate labour market; Bourdieu (1979, 1984) criticises the continuing assumption that, in an inflated graduate labour market, there is the belief from some that educational capital will still lead to a graduate job and increased life chances.

Graduate trajectories: putting empirical meat on the conceptual bone

As C. Wright Mills (1959) argued in his discipline-defining text *The Sociological Imagination*, a solely theoretical argument, like a helium balloon, tends to wander into unintended and unhelpful locations. The solution, Mills suggests, is to pair theoretical arguments with empirical findings, requiring theory to be grounded in real life. While theory will lose its sharp edge through such an exercise, the practical applications and long-term commentary on social issues is worth blunting our (thinking) tools. In this section of the chapter, I will introduce an empirical study examining graduate employment pathways and present the pathways of two respondents, illustrating the importance of capitals – in particular, social capital.

The research in question was based in Northern Ireland. Driven by the research question 'are strategies that graduates use to secure employment influenced by social class?', biographical narrative interviews (Miller, 2000; Schütze, 2008) were conducted with 27 respondents. All respondents had attended a Northern Irish university to read for a degree in a non-vocational subject between two and 10 years before the research was carried out. The research sample was further stratified by social class, calculated using the NS-SEC self-completion questionnaire, gender and institution attended. Two universities formed the basis of my research sample; 'Southern' was a pre-1992 university and a member of the elite Russell Group of UK universities, and 'Northern' was a teaching-focused post-1992 university.

The general findings of the study (Burke, 2016) reported five different conceptual groups of graduates. Within the middle-class sample, two distinct groups emerged: the strategic middle class, a group of graduates who had demonstrated a continued ability to successfully negotiate various levels of education and the graduate labour market; and the entitled middle class, a group of graduates who had successfully negotiated secondary and higher education but, stemming from inverted symbolic violence (Burke, 2017), were unable to translate these successes into the graduate market. Within the working-class sample, three distinct groups emerged: the strategic working class, a small group of respondents who, through a combination of educational credentials and social gate-keepers, were able to successfully enter the graduate labour market; the static working class, a group who, while having successfully entered higher education, were unable to repeat this transition into the graduate labour market and remained in low status/insecure jobs; and, finally, the converted working class, a group of respondents who were able to make the successful transition to the graduate labour market based on a very specific social contact whose connection could only be used once, thereby limiting their navigational capabilities within the labour market. While there was a range of conceptual groups, a general binary model did also present itself. The majority of middle-class respondents fell into the strategic middle-class group, and the majority of working-class respondents were in the static working-class group.

Phil, a member of the strategic middle class who read for a degree in English Literature and Film at 'Southern', demonstrated a habitus typical of his conceptual group: quite high levels of aspirations and expectations, both in terms of various stages of education and subsequent employment. His habitus presented a strong 'feel for the game' and a confidence to navigate and combine contrasting paths without the insecurity of presenting as a failed attempt. There was a clear influence on his habitus from his family of professionals and university graduates, who, in part, illustrated the myriad of trajectories available to graduates and the need to be proactive in the labour market in the face of a devalued degree. As a result of his habitus, Phil demonstrated a strong and agile graduate employment trajectory. At time of interview, he had had a number of jobs within the media, including in set design, as a runner on television and film productions and as a writer, and, more recently, had gained a TEFL qualification.

Phil outlines how he has manoeuvred quite successfully within an increasingly unstructured labour market. He outlines how he entered his profession and the importance of making the most of opportunities:

> *I was working in [part time job] the day before my graduation, and some of the other guys were moving a table for someone. That someone was a producer for a TV company down the street, and they were setting up their offices on the top floor of the building to film a series. She asked them if they knew anyone who would want to be a trainee. My friend said me, and then I asked her some details. She said I could come in about two weeks as a runner or come in next week in the art department painting sets.*

While this opportunity could be described as lucky, he understands it to be more than luck:

> *I mean, the way it happened to me – because I didn't expect it to happen – when it did happen, I just had to harness it 110% every day. If you blow that one chance, sure, you send out C.V.s, but that's the opportunity.*

The informal series of events which led Phil to his first position were reminiscent of the industry he was trying to enter. I asked him whether interviews were more informal chats:

> *Yeah, well, that's been my experience. [I] don't know if it's like that across the board. I've never heard of a formal interview with three people sitting at a desk with a set of questions.*

On a number of occasions throughout his graduate life, Phil demonstrated an ability to adapt to the current graduate labour market environment. After

'Investing in your future'   23

working on several short media projects after graduation, Phil learned that production work is often seasonal, leading to long periods of limited opportunities. However, he adapts well to this new and unforeseen situation:

> *After that the work dried up for a while, it appeared to me how lucky I had been for the first few months of my career, like, and I just had to do what everyone here does: you do stuff for free. So I keep on working in [part time job], which was helpful because they were really flexible, so, for the rest of that year, I was just doing short films and not really a lot – maybe one a month. When April rolled around, work started up again.*

Again, later in his career, Phil adapted to the effects of the financial crisis on his industry:

> *I was chatting to the story producer, and he said 'send in a script'. And I did, and he liked it, and [. . .] then the recession hit. There were going to be 15 episodes – then it got reduced to 10 – so, instead of hiring new writers, they were firing old ones [. . .] so I found myself in that situation a couple of times, like where people would sort of like my work but wouldn't take risks or couldn't get shows made. It was a bit frustrating. So I looked into doing a TEFL course [. . .] that's where I am now, waiting to go [away].*

This aptitude to adapt to new labour market situations further illustrates his ability to foster his own particular career path, understanding his combination of production work and teaching as managing a volatile and unpredictable market:

> *Having a backup qualification – my trade can be difficult, [as] it can be floods and droughts – to have something else would be good. To have this kind of work, you have to be self-employed. If things go dry, I can teach English. There's enough of an immigrant community now that there's money to be made. It's all about branching out with the different ways to make a living.*

Crucial to Phil's trajectory was the role of capital – in particular, social capital. Within his preferred form of employment, having close social connections was fundamental to initial entry into the profession and, then, to support a continued trajectory. Phil highlights the importance of social connections in an unstructured market:

> *Because the freelance community here is relatively small and close knit, more work kinda transpired immediately, like.*

Increased levels of social capital provided Phil with opportunities which would otherwise not be available:

> *Another time, if I hadn't known [friend], I wouldn't have known to send in a C.V. for that show. It's always who you know and who you're talking to, like.*

24 *Ciaran Burke, Sarah Hannaford-Simpson*

In contrast to the value he placed on social networks, Phil is quite disparaging toward bespoke industry training schemes. For him, working in the media industry requires much more than credentials:

> *These training schemes that everyone is applying for – it seemed slightly futile, in a way. There's no guarantee or qualifications to work on a set – certainly not one that could guarantee work.*

Returning to Bourdieu, the field or sub-field of the graduate profession Phil has entered and navigated since graduation can be described as a volatile, informal environment where practical work-based experience is valued above educational credentials, regardless of their vocational character. Within this field, the accumulation of social capital has allowed Phil to reside within a confident position within this social space. In addition, social capital has allowed Phil to expand his horizons and pursue pathways which would not have been open to him previously. Importantly, the application of his social capital is supported by his habitus and, in particular, his practical understanding of the general graduate labour market and lack of insecurity with creating a career rather than following a structured/linear path associated with his university degree subject. Phil's willingness to ask for assistance and use his social contacts echoes Abraham's (2017) findings on the classed disparity between using social contacts. Here, she argues that middle-class graduates are more comfortable relying on a range of capitals including social capital to aid in their trajectory in contrast to working-class graduates.

Fergal, a member of the static working class who read for a degree in English Literature at 'Northern', demonstrated a habitus typical of his conceptual group which had quite low levels of aspirations and expectations, both in terms of various stages of education and subsequent employment. His habitus presented a limited 'feel for the game' and low levels of confidence to navigate the graduate labour market. In contrast to Phil, as a first-generation university graduate, he had limited access to familial support in terms of practical advice. As a result of his habitus, Fergal demonstrated a limited graduate employment trajectory, characterised by a lateral trajectory into a range of part-time and/or insecure non-graduate employment positions. At time of interview, he had had many jobs in retail and the service industry.

During our interviews, Fergal expressed quite a negative attitude to the graduate labour market and, in particular, the likelihood of a successful transition:

> *I'm starting to become pretty disillusioned with the work world because I'm finding it quite hard to find jobs [. . .] I suppose, at the minute, I've been thinking a lot about the future – where I'll be in five years' time – and it's hard to . . . any job I do get will be fairly low level and something quite low paid probably in, em, a big chain again, maybe in retail or the service industry.*

Fergal has had quite a few jobs working in retail, as a cleaner and a local music promoter. While his portfolio may appear to be a bespoke combination of various industries, similar to Phil's, each shift toward a different profession or the cessation of a role has been due to redundancy rather than a self-led trajectory. Fergal recalled his attitude to his first job after graduating:

> *I got a job in [retail shop], which I intended to be very temporary [. . .] I stuck with that some two years. Eventually, I was made redundant due to staff cuts in the company.*

Fergal explained that a similar process happened at his next position:

> *The time there [retail position] came to a natural end. I was on a temporary contract, and my contract ran out so . . .*

Subsequently, Fergal took on a position at a cleaning company working full time as an office cleaner. He continued to work there until his position was no longer tenable:

> *That summer, the company was going out of business.*

Facing unemployment, Fergal began to apply for numerous jobs before securing a position at the first retailer he worked for after graduation. This last employment offer completed his lateral trajectory from non-graduate position to non-graduate position before returning to his first non-graduate job. Alongside these positions, Fergal was also a local music promoter; this attracted limited success and, similar to other roles, this did not end from his own volition:

> *I realised, well, I've put quite a lot of money into this [music promotion], and I haven't got much back. Then, the bar closed down, and I realised that I didn't want to do it anywhere else, and I was sick of doing it.*

Fergal is quite frustrated at his current employment prospects, and he struggles to effectively align his degree to market demands, citing the non-vocational character of his qualifications:

> *I think I'm qualified to do a lot of jobs, but, eh, employers can be picky enough to find someone who seems to always be built for the job they're looking for, and, having done an English degree, I'm not well-built for any particular job for employers anyway.*

While Fergal's trajectory has been driven by uncertainty and frustration and led to quite a negative outlook on his future life chances, social capital has still played a role in his post-graduation life. When I asked Fergal about the process he went through when looking for employment, it was clear that, similar to Phil, he relied on social network. In the case of his cleaning job, he explained:

> *I knew someone who knew the boss. They told me that I should go and ask. I was hired on the spot. It was a family run business.*

Even in the case of returning to his first retail employer, a company with more bureaucratic recruitment policies, he explained:

ended up getting my old one back at [retail shop] though sheer nepotism.

The contrast between Phil and Fergal's return on their social capital demonstrates the need to think quite carefully about how capital operates. Capital needs to be appreciated in terms of volume, composition and current market value (Atkinson, 2010). In addition, Fergal appears frustrated at the limited buying power of his educational capital. His comments here demonstrate the classed nature of which capitals students invest in when at university. Previous research (Reay et al., 2009a, 2009b) has discussed the tendency for working-class students to continue to favour the human capital narrative of access to higher education bringing increased life chances, and, as such, it is another source of the reproduction of social position/inequalities before entering higher education and upon graduation.

It is difficult to pinpoint a particular sub-field of the graduate labour market Fergal occupied. Rather, he was attempting to navigate the general field, which is characterised by increased competition, reduced structures/progression opportunities and an ever-changing list of sought-after skills and capitals. Within this context, Fergal's low levels of social capital affected his position within the field, leaving him in a frustrating and precarious position. His limited social networks led to reduced opportunities and affected his adaptability, most clearly seen through the return to his first employer after a succession of short-term positions. Finally, in contrast to Phil, his levels of expectations – in part directed by capitals (Bourdieu, 1984) – are reduced and capped. After years in the graduate labour market and the succession of lateral moves, Fergal expects to follow a similar trajectory for the foreseeable future.

Conclusion

The rationale behind this chapter has been to identify a growing feature of higher education practitioner literature – social capital – and provide a pause to consider the theoretical roots of this concept to better inform what it is that we mean when we say it and the far-reaching implications social capital has. To reiterate, within the Bourdieusian model, capitals do three things: act as resources which can be exchanged for a range of things, chart an individual's or group's position within social space/hierarchy and direct levels of expectations. Through following Phil and Fergal's contrasting trajectories and demonstrating the role of social capital on their pathways, this chapter has highlighted the importance of social capital and, in particular, how it goes beyond influencing levels of adaptability (Artess et al., 2017) and is at the centre of graduate resilience (Burke, *forthcoming*). It is very encouraging that social capital has gained increased interest in debates concerning graduate attributes, but we must be careful to ensure that the ubiquity of the term does not dilute our understanding and, therefore, our ability to effectively provide and measure its development.

References

Abrahams, J. (2017). "Honourable mobility or shameless entitlement? Habitus and graduate employment", *British Journal of Sociology of Education*, *38*(5): 625–640.

Archer, W., and Davison, J. (2008). *Graduate Employability: The View of Employers*. London: Council for Industry and Higher Education.

Artess, J., Hooley, T., and Mellors-Bourne, R. (2017). *Employability: A Review of the Literature 2012–2016*. York: Higher Education Academy.

Atkinson, W. (2010). *Class, Individualisation and Late Modernity: In Search of the Reflexive Worker*. Hampshire: Palgrave MacMillan.

Bathmaker, A.-M., Ingram, N., Abrahams, J., Hoare, T., Waller, R., and Bradley, H. (2016). *Higher Education, Social Class and Social Mobility: The Degree Generation*. London: Palgrave.

Baudrillard, J. (1994). *Simulacra and Simulation*. Michigan: University of Michigan Press.

Bell, D. (1973). *The Coming of Post-industrial Society: A Venture in Social Forecasting*. New York: Basic Books.

Bourdieu, P. (1977). *Outline of a Theory of Practice*. Cambridge: Cambridge University Press.

Bourdieu, P. (1984). *Distinction: A Social Critique of the Judgement of Taste*. London: Routledge and Kegan Paul.

Bourdieu, P. (2004). "The forms of capital", In: Ball, S.J. (Ed.), *The RoutledgeFalmer Reader in Sociology of Education*. London: RoutledgeFalmer, pp. 15–29.

Bourdieu, P., and Passeron, J.-C. (1977). *Reproduction in Education Society and Culture*, 2nd ed., London: Sage.

Bourdieu, P., and Passeron, J.-C. (1979). *The Inheritors: French Students and their Relation to Culture*. Chicago: University of Chicago Press.

Bourdieu, P., and Wacquant, L. (eds) (1992). *An Invitation to Reflexive Sociology*. Cambridge: Polity Press.

Bridge Group (2017). *Social Mobility and University Careers Services*. London: UPP Foundation.

British Chambers of Commerce (BCC) (2014). "BCC Workforce Survey". (online) Available from: www.britishchambers.org.uk/policy-maker/policy-reports-and-publications/workforce-survey-infogaphic.html.

Burke, C. (2016). *Culture, Capitals and Graduate Futures: Degrees of Class*. London: Routledge.

Burke, C. (2017). "Graduate blues: Considering the effects of inverted symbolic violence on underemployed middle-class graduates", *Sociology*, *51*(2): 393–409.

Burke, C. (forthcoming) "Maybe it is for the likes of us. . .: Reconsidering classed higher education and graduate employment trajectories", In: Stahl, G., Wallace, D., Burke, C., and Threadgold, S. (Eds.), *International Perspectives on Theorizing Aspiration: Applying Bourdieu's Tools*. London: Bloomsbury.

Case, J. (2014). *Researching Student Learning in Higher Education*. London: Routledge.

Department for Business, Innovation and Skills (BIS) (2012). "A review of Business-University collaboration: The Wilson review". (online) Available from: www.gov.uk/government/publications/business-university-collaboration-the-wilson-review.

Jenkins, R. (2002). *Pierre Bourdieu*, revised edn, London: Routledge.

Levi-Strauss, C. (2011). *Tristes Tropiques*. London: Penguin Books Ltd.

Li, H. (2015). "Moving to the city: Educational trajectories of rural Chinese students in an Elite University", In: Costa, C., and Murphy, M. (Eds.), *The Art of Application: Bourdieu, Habitus and Social Research*. London: Palgrave MacMillan, pp. 126–151.

Merleau-Ponty, M. (1963). *The Structure of Behaviour*. Boston: Beacon Press.

Milburn, A. (2012). *University Challenge: How Higher Education Can Advance Social Mobility*. (online) available from: www.gov.uk/government/uploads/system/uploads/attachment_data/file/80188/Higher-Education.pdf.

Miller, R.L. (2000). *Researching Life Stories and Family Histories*. London: Sage.

Mills, C.W. (1959). *The Sociological Imagination*. Oxford: Oxford University Press.

Morrison, A.R. (2014). " 'You Have to be Well Spoken': Students' views on employability within the graduate labour market", *Journal of Education and Work*, 27(2): 179–198.

Mullen, A.L. (2010). *Degrees of Inequality: Culture, Class and Gender an American Higher Education*. Baltimore: The Johns Hopkins University Press.

OECD (2017). *Education at a Glance: 2017.* (online) available from: www.oecd-ilibrary.org/docserver/download/9617041e.pdf?expires=1516959542&id=id&accname=guest&checksum=3B4C3B9A080894B3E65244BA62C48011.

Payne, G. (2012). "A new social mobility? The political redefinition of a sociological problem", *Contemporary Social Science: Journal of the Academy of Social Sciences*, 7(1): 55–71.

Putnam, R. (2000). *Bowling Alone*. New York: Simon and Schuster.

QMUL (2017). *Social Capital: the New Frontier in Widening Participation at Universities.* (online) available from: www.qmul.ac.uk/media/news/items/200043.html.

Reay, D. (2004). "It's all becoming a habitus: Beyond the habitual use of habitus in educational research", *British Journal of Sociology of Education*, 25(4): 431–444.

Reay, D., Crozier, G., and Clayton, J. (2009a). " 'Fitting In' or 'Standing Out': Working-class students in UK higher education", *British Educational Research Journal*, 32(1): 1–19.

Reay, D., Crozier, G., and Clayton, J. (2009b). " 'Strangers in Paradise'? Working-class students in Elite Universities", *Sociology*, 43(6): 1103–1121.

Schultz, T.W. (1971). *Investment in Human Capital: The Role of Education and of Research*. New York: The Free Press.

Schütze, F. (2008). "Biography analysis on the empirical base of autobiographical narratives: How to analyse autobiographical narrative interviews Part I", EU Leonardo da Vinci Programme. (online) available from: www.biographicalcounselling.com/download/B2.1.pdf.

Tholen, G. and Brown, P. (2018). "Higher education and the myths of graduate employability", In: Waller, R., Ingram, N., and Ward, R.M. (Eds.), *Higher Education and Social Inequalities*. London: Routledge, pp. 153–167.

Tomlinson, M. (2008). " 'The Degree is Not Enough': Students' perceptions of the role of higher education credentials for graduate work and employability", *British Journal of Sociology of Education*, 29(1): 49–61.

Wolf, A. (2007). "Round and Round the Houses: The Leitch Review of Skills", *Local Economy*, 22(2): 111–117.

3 Whose employability?

Fees, labour markets and the unequal rewards of undergraduate study

Andrew Morrison

Introduction

Drawing upon a broad range of literature, this chapter takes a critical view of both the concept and empirical reality of graduate employability as it relates to working-class undergraduates and graduates in England. Graduate employability is a subject of central concern to higher education (HE) in England. For example, it was a key rhetorical thread of both the 2011 and 2016 HE white papers for England (DBIS, 2011; 2016) where it was linked to the government's social mobility agenda. The political salience of the issue may be judged by the fact that, following the 2017 Higher Education and Research Act, graduate employment destinations now form a key component of the Teaching Excellence Framework (TEF). This chapter addresses the issue of graduate employability in two principal sections.

In the first, I interrogate the concept of graduate employability. I begin by outlining the dominant policy-led approach wherein employability is typically seen to be an essentially supply-side issue. I then move to briefly considering some key critiques of this view from academic researchers. However, the key focus of this first section will be to argue that graduate employability needs to be seen, at least in part, as the sum of the differential between a student's financial investment in acquiring a degree and the monetary returns they may expect to see upon their investment through their labour market earning power. This conception of graduate employability is now of increased importance in light of the tripling of tuition fees in England and of evidence to indicate that graduate earning power varies significantly by a range of key metrics (socio-economic background and gender) and also by other measures which are widely accepted to broadly map onto student socio-economic categories (type of institution attended, type of subject studied) (Britton et al., 2016). Moreover, while the rewards for degree-level study may be differentially distributed, the costs to students in terms of fees are largely the same in England. This is essentially a matter of social justice, and here I turn to the second section of the chapter.

In the discussion section, I explore these tensions in a more philosophical way through the lens of Nancy Fraser's theory of two-dimensional participatory justice. Fraser is a critical social philosopher of international significance whose work in social justice is starting to be employed more widely within educational research, and the application of her theory to the problematic of graduate employability represents a key contribution of my chapter. The theory offers two analytically separable forms of justice: distribution (economic) and recognition (cultural). A later development of this theory incorporated a third dimension of *representation*. For the purposes of this chapter, however, I shall limit discussion to Fraser's original two dimensions. I draw upon the work of Fraser and a range of other sources to argue that, in general, working-class (under)graduates confront a number of economically rooted and culturally rooted inequalities in the competition for graduate employment. These inequalities lead, in turn, to both forms of injustice.

The problematic of graduate employability: the context

Graduate employability has been a *leitmotif* running through higher education policy discourse in England for at least the past two decades. It was, for example, a key trope of the New Labour administrations of 1997–2010 where it served to mark out discursive boundaries between Tony Blair's Third Way policies and those of his Conservative predecessors. Thus, following a well-rehearsed political rhetoric, the globalisation of financial markets, advances in communications technologies and the growth of transnational corporations, were all held to signify a need to move away from the traditional mass production of standardised goods, and move instead towards a new competition based on knowledge-based innovation and creativity (Brown et al., 2003: 112).

New Labour's faith in the economic value of education does, of course, need to be seen in its wider context. As Rizvi and Lingard (2010) observe, the globalisation of capitalism has resulted in a re-framing of the ways in which policies, including education ones, are developed and implemented. Where public policies were once the exclusive domain of nation states, they are now increasingly framed by, and within, a multi-layered global 'system' of international and supranational bodies. Among the key organisations in this new global complex of policy actors are the Organisation for Economic Cooperation and Development (OECD), the World Bank and (despite the recent Brexit) the European Commission. Crucially, the policy values of these organisations reflect those of the global neo-liberalist order whereby the value of education is seen to reside primarily in its potential to produce human capital and to ensure national economic competitiveness. In consequence, as Rizvi and Lingard (2010: 16) argue, economic restructuring has now become the 'metapolicy' by which all policy for educational reform is framed. Thus, given the hegemony of this international political order, it should be of little surprise that a later Conservative-Liberal Democrat coalition government of ostensibly different political stripes to those of New Labour should espouse remarkably similar rhetoric (see DBIS, 2011), and that the present Conservative administration should do the same.

The importance attached to graduate employability in current policy discourse may be seen in the fact that the employment outcomes of graduates from each institution in England, as measured by the Destinations of Leavers from Higher Education (DLHE) survey form, one of the core metrics of the Teaching Excellence Framework (TEF). This, in turn, is linked to institutions' ability to charge different fee levels for undergraduate courses. Graduate employment outcomes are thus a key element in the inter-institutional competition that characterises an increasingly marketised sector. In policy discourse, however, the success of an institution's record on developing graduate employability is to be judged not just in relation to employment outcomes *per se* but to the rather more problematic concept of what constitutes a 'graduate-level' occupation. This is a key point because the growth of the HE sector in England has been predicated upon the promise of a reward to young people of highly skilled, well-paid employment. There is, though, no universally agreed measure of graduate-level occupations. The DLHE survey employs a coding frame called SOCDLHE2010. This was devised by Elias and Purcell (2013) and is itself a development of the Standard Classification of Occupations (SOC, 2010) which is used by the Office for National Statistics (ONS).

Employability is, then, a key discourse running through English higher education policy in which much importance is attached to graduate employment outcomes. But it is more than that; it is also discursively constructed as a set of necessary skills or attributes. For example, the representative body of graduate-recruiting employers, the Institute of Student Employers (or ISE but known previously as the Association of Graduate Recruiters), may be regarded as a key actor and influence on policy thinking. This organisation has identified nine employability skills. These include 'soft' skills related to intra-personal and inter-personal capacities but the predominant emphasis is placed upon commercial and entrepreneurial acumen (AGR, 2016: 12). If we turn, though, to the Higher Education Academy (HEA) – the body with a consultative and regulatory remit in relation to HE teaching and learning, a key element of which includes the embedding of employability within HE curricula – we see a rather different picture. In line with its educative remit, the HEA sees '21st-century skills' in more generic terms, as organised into the following categories: literacies (literacy, numeracy, citizenship, digital, media); competencies (critical thinking, creativity, collaboration); and character qualities (curiosity, initiative, persistence, resilience, adaptability, leadership) (HEA, 2017). There are, then, some differences in approach between these two key policy-level approaches to graduate employability. What they both have in common, however, is that they reflect a general tendency to see graduate employability as essentially a supply-side issue: a pedagogised process of *becoming* by which an individual develops a set of skills and attributes that will enable them to navigate the vagaries of highly competitive and unpredictable labour markets in which there is no promise of a 'job for life'.

For Brown, Hesketh and Williams (2003), the singular attention devoted to supply-side issues reflects the predominance within policy-level discourses of what they term the 'absolute' aspect of employability. The absolute aspect refers to individuals' possession of the relevant skills and qualities valued by employers, the development of which may be fostered through education and training.

32 *Andrew Morrison*

As Brown, Hesketh and Williams (2003: 110) argue, this aspect is certainly important with regard to an individual's employability since high-skilled work requires high-level knowledge, skills and an appropriate range of attributes. However, they go on to argue that the emphasis placed upon the absolute dimension of employability within policy-related discourse has had the effect of obscuring what they term the 'relative' dimension: the reality that an individual's employability is contingent upon the laws of supply and demand within the labour market (Brown et al., 2003: 110). And, as Brown, Lauder and Ashton (2011) argue, one of the key weaknesses of the UK economy is its relatively *low* demand for graduate-level skills, a problem which is manifested in an apparent over-supply of graduates to the labour market (see also, Keep and Mayhew, 2014). Of course, academics' views are by no means monolithic on this point. For example, in an early paper, Elias and Purcell (2013) took issue with the influential analysis produced by Brown, Lauder and Ashton (2011) which they regarded as overly pessimistic and insufficiently grounded in an empirical understanding of the UK labour market.

There seems to be support for the position of Elias and Purcell (2013) if we look at the evidence for the 'graduate premium' – the difference between what an individual can earn as a graduate compared with what they can earn with secondary level qualifications. Here, research suggests that the financial value of a degree has held up. A government-commissioned study found that female graduates may earn an extra £252,000 over their lifetime while male graduates may earn an extra £168,000 (DBIS, 2013). Other recent studies have come to broadly similar conclusions (Britton et al., 2016). However, a critical view would say that a graduate premium is not in itself evidence of a healthy demand for graduates. As Lauder, Brown and Tholen (2012: 60) note, the graduate premium may be produced by a decline in the earnings of non-graduate labour if graduates were employed in work previously performed by non-graduates. On this point, it is interesting to note that, in a more recent paper, Elias and Purcell, with colleagues, now sound a less optimistic note than their previous analyses in observing that graduate entry into previously non-graduate employment appears likely to remain a structural characteristic of the UK labour market for the foreseeable future (Behle et al., 2016: 125).

It is in this context that we encounter the reality of class inequalities. Individuals most likely to be unemployed or to work in lower paying non-graduate level jobs are those from lower socio-economic backgrounds (HEFCE, 2015) and also those who studied at 'low-tariff' institutions where students from lower socio-economic backgrounds tend to be concentrated (Behle, 2016). More generally, students from lower socio-economic backgrounds can expect, on average, to earn less than their more advantaged counterparts. A recent large-scale study found that male graduates from higher income households can earn up to about 60% more than their peers from lower-income households with an equivalent figure of 45% for females, and that even allowing for differences in the subjects studied or institutions attended there remained a significant gap of around 10% at the median (Britton et al., 2016: 55). Clearly, then, the financial benefits of higher education study are not equitably distributed, and here graduate employability becomes an issue of social justice as I indicated in the introduction. This has two facets. Even if we were to put aside tuition fees as an aspect of social justice (i.e., if university were free), structural inequalities in graduate labour market outcomes would still be indefensible. If meritocracy means, as a bare minimum, that an individual's material success should be judged by the single benchmark of IQ plus effort then the evidence we have on the relationships between graduate earnings and social class points strongly to some deep-seated problems with this ideal. However, tuition fees do exist and this is the second facet. Being currently capped at £9,250 per year for England-domiciled students, they are the highest of any country in the OECD, including the USA (OECD, 2016: 3). And while they are the same for most students in England no matter what their employment outcomes, the average debts with which students emerge from university are not equally shared across the social classes. The removal of maintenance grants and their replacement by loans in 2015 now means that graduates from the poorest 40% of families build up average debts of £57,000 as compared with an average of £43,000 for graduates from the richest 30% of families (Belfield et al., 2017: 17).

It is not difficult to see, then, a class-based inverse (one may even say perverse) relationship between the financial investment made in a degree and the financial gains from it. Of course, it could be argued that any question of social injustice is tempered by the knowledge that most undergraduates are eligible for up-front public loans to cover tuition fees while, at the time of writing, graduates do not begin to repay those loans until they earn at least £25,000 per year, with monthly repayment amounts being linked to average annual earnings. While this may be a mitigating factor it does not, though, displace the issues that I have outlined above as key social justice concerns. It is my argument, therefore, that the measure of graduate employability should be not simply the extent to which an individual is able to develop skills and attributes of value to the labour market – a supply-side model – but, additionally, the extent to which the labour market distributes its employment opportunities and related financial rewards on an equitable basis across key categories such as class, 'race' and gender. In the following section, I shall take a critical view of barriers to working-class graduate employability by looking through the lens of Nancy Fraser's theory of two-dimensional participatory justice.

The problematic of graduate employability: a critical social justice perspective

Nancy Fraser is an American radical social philosopher whose theories of social justice have attracted wide critical attention (Lovell, 2007; Olson, 2008). Fraser's theory of two-dimensional participatory justice offers us a valuable theoretical lens through which to better understand the issues of inequality and injustice in relation to graduate employability that I have outlined. The founding premise of Fraser's theory lies in her critique of what she perceives to be two different but interrelated forms of justice claims: redistribution and recognition.

34 *Andrew Morrison*

Thus, redistribution justice claims are usually directed towards the amelioration or cessation of economic practices or structures that exploit particular social groups. Demands to end working practices which discriminate against women or minority ethnic communities would be examples of this type. Here, the emphasis is upon a 'group-blind' approach to justice because resource distribution (wages, conditions of employment, etc.) is made without reference to particular group membership. In contrast, recognition justice claims are normally an attempt to seek equal respect and value for group differences that are subject to historical and continuing modes of inferiorisation in relation to dominant societal norms and values (Fraser, 1995: 80). This form of justice is, then, 'group-sensitive' as it seeks validation of rights based around group membership and identity and, according to Fraser (1995: 82), the logic of its claims would appear to lead to the opposite conclusion to that of redistribution justice. And the tensions between these two distinct forms of justice claims represent the 'dilemmas of justice' in what Fraser (1995) terms our 'post-socialist' age.

The solution for Fraser (1995) is a two-dimensional theory of justice in which redistribution and recognition are understood to be analytically separable but also closely interrelated in concrete empirical circumstances. And this, in turn, is rooted in Fraser's key conceptual distinction between economy and culture as different but interrelated forms of social process and social relations in late capitalist societies (Fraser, 1999). Following this type of 'dual-systems' heuristic framework, Fraser (1999) proposes that we view key social categories such as class, 'race' and gender as what she terms 'bi-valent': injustices related to these categories are rooted in both material social arrangements, which point towards redistribution justice claims, and in the cultural-valuational social order, which point towards demands for recognition justice. To address the conceptual distinction but close concrete interrelationship between economic-related and culturally related injustices, Fraser (1999: 43) argues for a 'perspectival dualism'. Following this form of analysis, all social practices are to be viewed as being composed of *both* economic and cultural dimensions (although not always to equal degrees) and therefore require both redistribution and recognition justice. By retaining these analytical distinctions, perspectival dualism allows us to discern culturally related injustices in what may usually be regarded as the economic sphere and to locate the economic aspects of what are normally determined to be cultural-valuational processes (Fraser, 1999: 45).

In more specific terms this translates as a two-dimensional critically normative theory of justice, premised upon two 'objective' preconditions and one 'intersubjective' precondition which, when all met together, constitute what Fraser (1999) terms 'parity of participation'. The three key preconditions are: (a) legal equality; (b) distribution of material resources; and (c) 'intersubjective equality' (Fraser, 1999: 37). Legal equality and equitable distribution of material resources are the 'objective' preconditions of participatory parity. The third precondition is 'intersubjective' parity which insists that, at a societal level, all groups and individuals be accorded equal respect and enjoy equal opportunities for the achievement of social esteem (Fraser, 1999: 37). In line with Fraser's dual-systems approach, full participatory parity means that both the objective and the intersubjective pre-conditions need to be met as neither alone is sufficient. How then can we apply Fraser's theory to place the employability inequalities alluded to above within a critical social justice framework? To do this, I first want to examine, by reference to recent literature, some of the key cultural and material drivers of graduate socio-economic disadvantage within contemporary labour markets. The focus of this body of research has been largely, although not exclusively, upon social class, and that shall be the object of my critique within the remainder of this chapter; I recognise, though (as do the authors of these studies), the independent effects of other key variables such as gender or 'race' and their cross-cutting, intersectional relationship with social class.

An influential starting point from which to explain working-class graduate cultural and material positional disadvantage is the work of Phillip Brown and colleagues. In line with his view that the UK economy is characterised by a relatively low-level demand for graduates in relation to supply, Brown (2013) argues that twenty-first century graduates are experiencing all the negative effects of 'social congestion': too many graduates chasing too few graduate-level jobs in an economy that has failed to deliver on the 'opportunity bargain' of well remunerated professional employment. The result of this congestion has been that big, highly selective employers are placing an increasing premium upon 'soft' skills and certain behavioural competencies such as drive, resilience and personal charisma (Brown and Hesketh, 2004: 33). These latter conclusions might appear to be congruent with that of key policy actors such as the ISE or the HEA which, as discussed previously, argue for the importance of soft skills in the development of graduate employability. Where analyses sharply diverge, however, is in Brown and colleagues' critical view that such soft skills are essentially socially classed skills – a case of large elite-entry corporations rewarding candidates with the closest 'social fit' to the recruiters themselves (Brown and Hesketh, 2004: 225). Here, then, working-class candidates may find themselves disadvantaged in lacking sufficient levels of what, in Bourdieusian terms, are the dominant forms of embodied cultural capital (Bourdieu, 1997) within the field of fast-track graduate recruitment. Inequality does not stop here, however. Cut-throat competition for jobs means that even those with the 'right' forms of cultural capital and class membership cannot simply rely upon them to open the door: scholastic, cultural, social and experiential assets have to be actively packaged up into a performative 'narrative of employability' – the self told as a life story replete with productive promise (Brown and Hesketh, 2004: 36).

In short, the rules of the employment game have changed, and the general effect of this has been to exacerbate the cultural and material inequalities with which working-class graduates are faced as a growing body of research has shown. One area of inequality relates to the extent to which working-class undergraduates and graduates are aware that the rules have changed. Of course, we should be careful not to homogenise working-class orientations towards graduate labour markets as research reveals evidence of intra-class differences. Nevertheless, studies that have made a direct comparison of working-class and middle-class (under)

36 *Andrew Morrison*

graduates have indicated that their working-class subjects were more likely than their middle-class counterparts to play by the rules of the old game and to focus upon enhancement of scholastic capital rather than acquisition of experiential assets through the development of ECAs or internship work (Burke, 2016; Bathmaker, Ingram and Waller, 2013), a finding also echoed in a study by Greenbank and Hepworth (2008) that focused particularly upon final-year working-class undergraduates.

However, even when working-class (under)graduates are aware of the new rules of the game, a lack of suitable economic and social assets may inhere to further their positional disadvantage. Bathmaker, Ingram and Waller (2013) found that their working-class subjects generally lacked the social contacts to obtain internships in high-status fields such as law or banking while lower levels of economic capital meant that unpaid internships in different geographical locations were a much less realistic option for them. Other studies have found that lower levels of economic capital have meant that working-class graduates have been under pressure to obtain any kind of paid employment, usually within their local community of origin and often not ostensibly commensurate with their paper qualifications, with the result that they lack time to engage in strategic job hunting (Burke, 2016; Furlong and Cartmel, 2005). There is also evidence that working-class undergraduates and graduates tend be more geographically limited in their search for employment than their middle-class peers (Burke, 2016; Furlong and Cartmel, 2005; Perryman et al., 2003). Levels of economic and social capital, as alluded to above, are key factors in this but so too are cultural factors that revolve around an (under)graduate's 'sense of place' within the labour market (Furlong and Cartmel, 2005; Morrison, 2014)

We need now to return to the work of Nancy Fraser to locate these disadvantages within a critical social justice framework. If we first consider the economic inequalities, it seems clear that the maldistribution of resources which they represent constitutes a breach of Fraser's (1999: 37) 'objective' condition of participatory parity which ' precludes forms and levels of material inequality and economic dependence that impede parity of participation.' Critics, though, may argue that I have misinterpreted Fraser here, as she goes on to note that this condition of participatory parity thus precludes 'social arrangements that institutionalize deprivation, exploitation, and gross disparities in wealth, income and leisure time, thereby denying some people the opportunity to interact with others as peers' (Fraser, 1999: 37). At first sight, working-class economic disadvantage of the sort that I have discussed within this chapter does not, perhaps, represent the 'gross disparities in wealth' as Fraser intended them to be understood. However, in an endnote to her definition of objective participatory parity, Fraser (1999: 50) herself acknowledged that it was a moot point how much economic inequality could be congruent with full parity of participation, and that where the limit lay was a question for investigation. We know that the UK is characterised by deep and enduring economic inequalities (Social Mobility Commission, 2017) and these are reflected, at least to some extent, in the economic resources to which working-class (under)graduates have access and consequently (as the literature reviewed above indicates) their capacity to enjoy full parity of participation with their more privileged middle-class peers in the competition for jobs.

The culturally rooted disadvantages encountered by many working-class (under)graduates that I have discussed above are complex and encompass, in the Bourdieusian sense, both subjective and objective cultural constraints (Bourdieu, 1984). What they all have in common, however, is that they fail to meet Fraser's (1999: 37) precondition of 'intersubjective' parity which insists that society accord all groups and individuals equality of respect and equal opportunities to achieve social esteem. For Fraser, this breach of intersubjective parity constitutes an act of misrecognition, that is, '. . . an institutionalized pattern of cultural value [which] constitutes some social actors as less than full members of society and prevents them from participating as peers' (2000: 114). James (2015) makes the valid point that Fraser's conceptualisation of misrecognition is very different from that of Bourdieu with whom the term is more commonly associated. This is true as Fraser's (2000) status model is framed primarily around material sources of subordination – government policies and juridical and administrative practices. These are not the origins (at least, not directly) of the cultural disadvantages I have outlined above. Yet Fraser (2000: 114) goes on to argue that status subordination by misrecognition can also be perpetrated more informally through ingrained social practices of civil society. The labour market is a key institution of the civil society of all late modern capitalist societies and, as the literature previously discussed indicates, the new rules of the labour market game are rigged against many working-class (under)graduates from the start. And herein lie Fraser's processes of cultural misrecognition and status subordination: what Fraser (2000: 114) terms 'institutionalized patterns of cultural value' mean that not everybody's cultural knowledges or social resources hold equal worth in an over-competitive jobs market.

Concluding remarks

This chapter has taken a critical view of graduate employability. Drawing upon a range of literature, I have argued that dominant supply-side models fail to acknowledge the deep-seated cultural and economic inequalities with which many working-class graduates are faced in competing within an over-crowded labour market. The principal contribution of this chapter to graduate employability research has been the application of Nancy Fraser's theory of two-dimensional participatory justice. This model, which is premised upon an economy-culture perspectival dualism, has been employed as a lens through which to tease apart the origins of the two different kinds of injustice that attend working-class (under)graduate employability. This analytical dualism has, therefore, much to offer research into graduate employability as it permits the researcher to abstract the different forms of injustice from the complexity of individuals' concretely lived experiences. This, in turn, is important because as Sayer (2005: 92) argues, the task of abstract theory is to identify the necessary conditions of the existence of objects as opposed to their contingent associations. Abstraction facilitates this

38 *Andrew Morrison*

by focusing upon a particular variable among others within which it is embedded, for example the economic injustices of class caught up within culturally related forms of disadvantage. Having established through such abstraction that economic capital has causal powers independent from those of cultural and social capital, the task of concrete analysis is then to examine how the three variables contingently interact, possibly producing emergent effects (Sayer, 2005: 92).

This is important to analysis because, although I have discussed economic and cultural injustices within this chapter as analytically separable areas, as Fraser (1995) maintains, in all real life circumstances, they are mutually inter-connected. This is clearly so in the case of working-class (under)graduates, as the literature reviewed within this chapter has indicated the co-constitutive nature of the economic and cultural inequalities which they face in relation to the labour market. Furthermore, if the origins of injustices are analytically separable but complexly intertwined in real-life, so too are their associated forms of restorative justice because, as Fraser (1999) herself reminds us, all redistribution claims have implications for recognition justice and vice versa. Thus, employability is centrally concerned with factors perceived to affect access to employment and, consequently, it is clearly concerned with matters of distribution justice. However, as Fraser (1995) notes, equitable distribution justice implies a claim of moral worth on the part of the claimant, and thus a more level playing field in the competition for graduate jobs can never be just about employment and earning power *per se* but also strongly reflects the social esteem which working-class (under)graduates enjoy and their capacity to function as peers within society.

References

Association of Graduate Recruiters (AGR) (2016). *The AGR 2016 Annual Survey.* London: AGR.

Bathmaker, A., Ingram, N., and Waller, R. (2013). "Higher Education, Social Class and the Mobilisation of Capitals: Recognising and Playing the Game", *British Journal of Sociology of Education*, 34(5–6): 723–743.

Behle, H. (2016). *Graduates in Non-Graduate Occupations.* Higher Education Funding Council for England [HEFCE]/Society for Research in Higher Education [SRHE]

Behle, H., Atfield, G., Elias, P., Gambin, L., Green, A., Hogarth, T., and Warhurst, C. (2016). "Reassessing the employment outcomes of higher education", In: Case, J., and Huisman, J. (Eds.), *Researching Higher Education: International Perspectives on Theory, Policy and Practice.* London: Routledge, pp. 114–131.

Belfield, C., Britton, J., Dearden, L., and van der Erve, L. (2017). *Higher Education Funding in England: Past, Present and Options for the Future.* IFS Briefing Note BN211. London: Institute for Fiscal Studies.

Bourdieu, P. (1984). *Distinction: A Social Critique of the Judgement of Taste.* London: Routledge.

Bourdieu, P. (1997). "The forms of capital", In: Halsey, A., Lauder, H., Brown, P., and Wells, A.S. (Eds.), *Education, Culture, Economy and Society.* Oxford: Oxford University Press, pp. 46–58.

Britton, J., Dearden, L., Shephard, N., and Vignoles, A. (2016). *How English Domiciled Graduate Earnings Vary With Gender, Institution Attended, Subject and Socio-Economic Background*. IFS Working Paper W16/06. London: Institute for Fiscal Studies.

Brown, P. (2013). "Education, opportunity and the prospects for social mobility", *British Journal of Sociology of Education, 34*(5–6): 678–700.

Brown, P., Lauder, H., and Ashton, D. (2011). *The Global Auction: The Broken Promises of Education, Jobs and Incomes.* Oxford: Oxford University Press.

Brown, P., and Hesketh, A. (2004). *The Mismanagement of Talent: Employability and Jobs in the Knowledge Economy.* Oxford, New York: Oxford University Press.

Brown, P., Hesketh, A., and Williams, S. (2003). "Employability in a knowledge-driven economy", *Journal of Education and Work, 16*(2): 107–126.

Burke, C. (2016). *Culture, Capitals and Graduate Futures.* Abingdon: Routledge.

Department for Business, Innovation and Skills (BIS) (2011). *Higher Education: Students at the Heart of the System.* London: HMSO.

Department for Business, Innovation and Skills (BIS) (2013). *The Impact of University Degrees on the Lifecycle of Earnings: Some Further Analysis.* London: HMSO.

Department for Business Innovation and Skills (BIS) (2016). *Fulfilling Our Potential: Teaching Excellence, Social Mobility and Student Choice.* London: HMSO.

Elias, P., and Purcell, K. (2013). *Classifying Graduate Occupations for the Knowledge Society* HECSU/IER.

Fraser, N. (1995). "From redistribution to recognition? Dilemmas of justice in a 'Post-Socialist' age", *New Left Review, 212*: 68–93.

Fraser, N. (1999). "Social justice in the age of identity politics: Redistribution, recognition, and participation", In: Ray, L., and Sayer, A. (Eds.), *Culture and Economy After the Cultural Turn.* London, Thousand Oaks, New Delhi: Sage, pp. 25–52.

Fraser, N. (2000). "Rethinking recognition", *New Left Review, 3*: 107–120.

Furlong, A., and Cartmel, F. (2005). *Graduates From Disadvantaged Families: Early Labour Market Experiences.* Bristol: The Policy Press.

Greenbank, P., and Hepworth, S. (2008). *Working Class Students and the Career Decision-Making Process: a Qualitative Study.* HECSU: UK.

Higher Education Academy (HEA). (2017). *21st Century Skills.* (online) Available from: www.heacademy.ac.uk/knowledge-hub/21st-century-skills.

Higher Education Funding Council for England (HEFCE). (2015). *Differences in Employment Outcomes: Equality and Diversity Characteristics.* HEFCE.

James, D. (2015). "How Bourdieu bites back: Recognising misrecognition in education and educational research", *Cambridge Journal of Education, 45*(1): 97–112.

Keep, E., and Mayhew, K. (2014). "Inequality – 'Wicked Problems', labour market outcomes and the search for silver bullets", *Oxford Review of Education, 40*(6): 764–781.

Lauder, H., Brown, P., and Tholen, G. (2012). "The global auction model, skills bias theory and graduate incomes: Reflections on methodology", In: Lauder, H., Young, M., Daniels, H., Balarin, M., and Lowe, J. (Eds.), *Educating for the Knowledge Economy? Critical Perspectives.* Abingdon: Routledge Falmer, pp. 43–65.

Lovell, T. (Ed.) (2007). *(Mis)recognition, Social Inequality and Social Justice: Nancy Fraser and Pierre Bourdieu.* Abingdon: Routledge.

Morrison, A. (2014). 'You have to be well spoken': Students' views on employability within the graduate labour market', *Journal of Education and Work, 27*(2): 179–198.

40   *Andrew Morrison*

Office for National Statistics [ONS] (2010). *Standard Occupational Classification 2010: Volume 1: structure and descriptions of unit groups*. Basingstoke, UK: Palgrave Macmillan.

Olson, K. (Ed.) (2008). *Adding Insult to Injury: Nancy Fraser Debates Her Critics*. London: Verso.

Organisation for Economic Co-operation and Development (OECD) (2016). *Education at a Glance 2016: United Kingdom*. New York: OECD.

Perryman, S., Pollard, E., Hillage, J., and Barber, L. (2003). *Choices and Transitions: A Study of the Graduate Labour Market in the South West*. Exeter: HERDA/IES.

Rizvi, F., and Lingard, B. (2010). *Globalizing Education Policy*. Abingdon: Routledge.

Sayer, A. (2005). *The Moral Significance of Class*. Cambridge: Cambridge University Press.

Social Mobility Commission (2017). *State of the Nation 2017: Social Mobility in Great Britain*. London: HMSO.

4 Regional capital and 'local' graduate employment

Teresa Crew

> *The Welsh [higher education] sector makes a significant contribution to the economy – £3 billion a year in gross expenditure to the Welsh economy, employing 24,600 people and having an annual turnover of £1.3 billion.*
> *(Welsh Assembly Government, Policy Statement on Higher Education).*

Introduction

Higher education (HE) has been a devolved matter for the Welsh Government since devolution in 1999. This means that devolved nations have the power to make legislation relevant to the area. Welsh universities, public institutions funded by the Welsh Government through the Higher Education Funding Council for Wales (HEFCW), charge tuition fees, capped at £9,000 per year for UK and EU students on undergraduate courses providing they can demonstrate a commitment to widening access. Wales differs from England as Welsh students have their fees partly subsidised[1] irrespective of the location of their higher education institution. This progressive policy, with a nod to social justice, recommended in the Diamond Review of Higher Education in Wales, 2016, means that Welsh students face a significantly lower average level of debt on leaving university than English-domiciled students (HEFCW, 2015). Despite distinct approaches to HE policy and funding, a common theme is employability.

Defining employability is complex as there is little consensus over its meaning. Up until the 1940s 'unemployability' referred to *defects of character*. Following World War II there was a more sympathetic approach due to large scale unemployment (Komine, 2004). The concept was repositioned in 1980s with the individual being seen as responsible for his or her own employability. Today we see multiple stakeholders involved in the business of employability. An employable graduate is vital to the UK's economic growth whilst employers desire the specialist knowledge that a graduate brings. A track record in graduate employability enhances an institution's reputation, which in turn attracts students mindful of a rise in tuition fees, whereas students are encouraged (by the other stakeholders) to see university as a choice that will enhance their employability (Artess et al., 2017). The Higher Education Academy (HEA) framework for employability describes the key aspects of employability as: graduate behaviours; experience and networks; enterprise and entrepreneurship; internationalisation; reflection and articulation; and career management (cited in *ibid*: 10). Arguably, with its focus on skills acquisition, the concept lends itself to a neo-liberal vision of the 'ideal graduate'. This is problematic as the graduate labour market is an arena where some are more advantaged.

An explanation for these advantages can be found by applying Pierre Bourdieu's three central concepts of habitus, capital and field to graduate employment. Habitus are the 'norms and dispositions' (Burke, 2015: 9) linked to our social biography (family, school, peer groups, etc.) (Burke et al., 2017). Habitus is not static, and is 'modified over the life course. Yet despite its transformative quality, habitus can influence one's "field of the possible"' (Burke, 2015: 11), so much so that 'working class' graduates may have a different sense of what is available to them, in terms of employment, (*ibid*) compared to those from middle-class backgrounds. For instance, whilst there is financial support[2] for students to gain international experience – an influencing factor in higher graduate salaries – participation from those with disadvantaged backgrounds has remained low (7 per cent among students whose parents were in professional occupations to 2 per cent among those whose parents had never worked or were long-term unemployed [UK Higher Education International Unit, 2015]). If habitus is accumulated history, capital could be described as accumulated labour. A store of capital, i.e., 'economic' (money); 'social' (social networks); and 'cultural' (prestige), makes life less of a lottery (Bourdieu, 1986). These can be transferred from one arena to another. Using the example of a gap year, the parent's economic capital 'buys' both the enhanced social status gained from being well travelled (cultural capital) and access to other, privileged graduates (social capital). These advantaged networks bring the potential for higher earning opportunities. The final concept is field. A field is a *competitive social space* (Bourdieu, 1984: 245) that represents a network of positions that has its own rules and patterns of behaviour. Those who have a suitable habitus and the greatest store of capital will reproduce their privilege (Burke, 2015: 16). Large cities and smaller regions are a sub-field of the field of graduate employment. This chapter uses the case study of North Wales to argue that graduates need additional resources to successfully navigate a regional graduate employment field.

Regional capital

Interest in the geography of graduate labour is growing, particularly in relation to the ability of the smaller regions to attract and retain graduates. Traditional graduates tend to be strategic in their choices (Bathmaker et al., 2013) choosing red brick universities located in larger cities, and then staying or moving to capitalise on the elite employment opportunities this institutional capital brings. This mobility, often seen as part of the graduate trajectory, should be considered within the context of possession of capital. Due to a lack of economic capital, the atypical graduate is more inclined, or expected, to return to or stay in small

Regional capital and 'local' graduate employment   43

towns that have may have limited opportunities for graduates (Christie, 2016: 56). Wales is a net exporter of graduates retaining high numbers of graduates (in comparison to many English regions) as there is a clear pull of 'home' for those who have left the region to study elsewhere (Bristow et al., 2011). Location is important as it influences the options available to graduates (Christie, 2016). North Wales does not offer the same variety of graduate roles when compared with those living in London or other large cities. Many graduate opportunities in North Wales are temporary employment within the local authorities and the voluntary sector (Crew, 2015). The HEA framework provides a comprehensive list of the skills graduates are expected to attain, yet there is little mention of locally based forms of capital. Regional capital draws upon habitus, capital and field to argue that there are factors that may interact in complex and nuanced ways, in different geographical fields, to confer degrees of advantage or disadvantage on graduates in the labour market and beyond. As capital is influenced by its field, regional assets are cashable only in the immediate local context.

Cymraeg (the Welsh language) is a particularly 'visible' example of 'capital' in the 'field' of Wales (Coupland, 2012). But this wasn't always the case. During the 1800s, Cymraeg was the language of the private sphere with English being the language needed for social mobility (Hodges, 2011: 304). The Welsh Language Act 1993 put the Welsh language on an equal footing with the English language in Wales with regard to the public sector. Concerns of local people about countless managerial vacancies going to English speakers from outside of the local area led to local authorities designating some front facing, customer led roles as being 'Welsh essential' (Morris, 2010). Despite a small drop in the 2011 census, over half of the population in some areas of North Wales speak the Welsh language and there is concerted action by the Welsh Assembly Government to double the number of Welsh speakers to one million by 2050 (Welsh Assembly Government, 2017). This is timely as 71 per cent of employers in Wales stated Welsh was desirable for jobs in their companies, and there is a shortage of bilingually skilled staff in graduate occupations such as nursing and in the tourism industry (Careers Wales, 2010). Despite Cymraeg being one of Europe's most robust minority languages, having survived despite its close proximity to one of the most dominant world languages (English), the Welsh language is less likely to be considered a form of capital outside of Wales.

The ability of jobseekers to develop and use their social capital to gain information about forthcoming employment opportunities and personal recommendations for jobs is a key aspect of employability in the modern labour market. In other words, 'It's not what you know, it's *who* you know'. Longitudinal research by the Paired Peers team found that it is middle-class students who are far more able to draw upon family resources to help them to get work experience and internships (Bradley et al., 2013). In North Wales, the Welsh language is a potent but complex consideration in relation to social networks in Wales (Coupland et al., 2006). For many, Cymraeg is the only obvious symbol of Welsh identity (Day, 2002). The language spoken at home is a 'major determinant of the Welsh-language density of the young people's social networks' (Morris, 2010). Yet these

44   Teresa Crew

locally based networks are less likely to be useful if the recipient moves from the local area. New networks would be needed.

Transport policy has traditionally focused on the needs of the motorist, with the location of essential services such as employment opportunities, schools, hospitals and retail outlets being planned on the assumption that everyone has access to their own personal transport. North Wales is a mixture of small urban towns and rural areas where jobs and services are widely dispersed. As such, a car is a useful form of cultural capital. In 2014, 73 per cent of adults aged 17 and above held a driving license (Department of Transport, 2016), with women on low incomes, lone parents and carers being less likely to have a car (Crisp et al., 2017). Research by Mahieux and Mejia-Dorantes (2013) reveals that no car often equals no job. Those relying on public transport may experience difficulties regarding the frequency of public transport and range of places they are able to travel to. This is less likely to be a necessity in large urban areas as transport links tend to be strong, plus taking a car can bring added stresses like high parking tariffs. As barriers relating to car use transcend North Wales, there will be less of a focus on this issue.

Research methods

The research was undertaken in two phases:

> *Phase one*: Secondary analysis of semi structured questionnaires and interviews from Crew (2015). The aim being to answer the following research question:
> *What skills do graduates need to gain employment within North Wales?*

Twelve respondents who graduated 2008–2011 from two HEIs in north Wales were chosen from the overall sample of 66 graduates as they explicitly discussed aspects of employability outside of that outlined in HEA Framework. Nine respondents were female, three were male, all were 'mature' graduates (aged 25 and over) and all but one was white British. All respondents described themselves as Welsh: two respondents were 'first language Welsh'; five were 'Welsh learners'; the remaining five spoke English only. All but two had access to their own transport.

> *Phase Two* consisted of informal conversations with nineteen employers at two business networking events[3] All employers were asked:
> *What skills do you look for in graduates?*

The data from both phases was transcribed and recorded in a Microsoft Excel spreadsheet. Three examples of regional capital were identified.

Limitations. My findings should be seen in the context of my lack of bilingual Welsh language skills. Two respondents spoke Welsh as their first language, and

Marinez (2016) points out that interviews may be hindered when respondents are not interviewed in their mother tongue

Situating the researcher

McDowell (1992: 409) writes that we must recognize our own position, and include this in our research practice. Presenting my own account is paramount as the genesis of the idea originated in my own search for graduate employment. Whilst the traditional, more mobile graduate may focus on their ideal employment my 'regional stickiness', the emotional connections that affect decision-making (Finn, 2015), meant that my main requirement was to be close to home for various caring responsibilities. My mobility was further impeded after being diagnosed with epilepsy. After much deliberation, a manageable commute via public transport centred around the North Wales area. My use of public transport jarred with my graduate identity as interviewers focused less on my graduate attributes and more on how I travelled into work. On a number of occasions employers stated that my mode of transport did not match my professional ambitions. Why I did not drive [my health condition] was less of a concern in comparison for apparent need for employers that I 'look the part'.

When searching for suitable roles I would match the person specification except when bilingual English/Welsh communication skills were required. As I moved to Wales towards the end of my compulsory education I had only picked up basic phrases in Welsh. Similar to the experiences reported in Hodges and Prys (2017), I felt uncomfortable attempting to speak Welsh in the work environment. Despite these barriers, I developed effective local professional networks. The financial downturn of 2008 led to many permanent graduate roles in North Wales becoming project based employment. This was advantageous for my career as the employment agencies in England (where they were advertised) were ignorant to bilingual language requirements. The high-level nature of the projects meant that I built local professional networks across the region. Working now as Lecturer in an HEI, I am at the frontline, seeing it as my responsibility to embed employability into my teaching practice. I do this diligently despite having an uncomfortable sense that this will not stop advantaged graduates remaining advantaged. I will return to this theme again.

Findings and discussion

Bilingual (English/Welsh) language skills

The Welsh Assembly Government have been active in protecting and encouraging the Welsh language through policies promoting bilingualism. The business case for companies to use the language is that it improves the quality of your customer service, attracts more business and it's a way of engaging more closely with

46   *Teresa Crew*

customers (Welsh Assembly, 2017). These messages have been successful as all but one of the local employers spoken to as part of this study stated that bilingual written and oral communication skills were essential for business related reasons which included respect, integration, goodwill and loyalty:

We live in Wales, so our graduates should speak the language (Respect).
It's about fitting in. Everyone speaks Welsh in the office (Integration).
We like to offer a service to everyone (Goodwill and Loyalty).

Graduates also mentioned the importance of Welsh language skills:

Where I work everyone speaks Welsh . . . it is quicker to communicate [Lucy].
I have applied for jobs such as Family Support Officer but you need bilingual skills [Anna].

This supports Mann's (2011) research for the Wales Institute of Social & Economic Research, Data & Methods (WISERD) which highlighted the importance of Welsh–English bilingual skills for public employment. The public sector is a key employer throughout Wales, accounting for at least a quarter of total employment in each unitary authority (Drinkwater et al., 2011: 8). Alongside this, the voluntary sector plays an increasingly important role in providing services and employment for people in Wales, particularly in care, advocacy and advice, where communication is a core part of the service. In recent years there has been an emphasis on the use of Welsh in the private sector with Marks & Spencer, HSBC, and John Lewis having worked with the Welsh Language Board to develop services (Agored Cymru, 2015).

Whilst Welsh is seen as *a skill that will help gain employment in Wales* [Lucy], respondents who were born in Wales reported there being a closer connection to their place of birth through the language. Mann (2007: 216) expands on this in his research with adult learners. Respondents felt there was a sense of 'missing something' in being Welsh but not speaking Welsh. Mann speculated that the 'civic orientated discourse' is more prominent amongst the in-migrant Welsh learner while Welsh-born learners articulated a personal sense of obligation. Interviews with my own respondents support this as migrant Welsh learners (of which there were two) talked about learning the language to support their ambitions to work in the public sector, whilst respondents who were born in Wales had a more emotional tie to Cymraeg.

I want to 'feel' like I am Welsh [Louise].
Being Welsh means speaking the language [Ben].

One interviewee expanded on this, noting:

When I use my Welsh in my everyday life, I am part of protecting the language and helping it to thrive [Abby].

This is similar to the views of participants in McAllister et al. (2013), who referred to the role of the Welsh language as part of the nation's heritage and the nation itself. Cymraeg adds to the distinctiveness of Wales.

All five of the respondents who were learning Welsh talked of having a lack of confidence in their language abilities, citing interviews as being an example of where they would struggle – similar to findings reported in Hodges and Prys (2017). Consistent with Mann (2011), economically disadvantaged Welsh speakers in this study self-excluded from using Welsh in the workplace as they felt that the Welsh they spoke at home was not the same as the more formal Welsh needed for employment purposes:

> *I can certainly carry out a conversation in Welsh, write quite well but I wouldn't want to write a report in Welsh, give a presentation or even speak for any length of time. It's not about my Welsh, it's about writing in Welsh in a professional manner* [Abby].

Further questioning revealed Abby's concerns about the 'type' of Welsh she spoke, feeling that it was too 'common'. The meanings given to language are rooted in the power relationships. People's positioning in power relationships affects their opportunities to claim legitimacy as speakers of the language (Mann, 2011). As Welsh in the workplace has been affiliated with the traditional middle class of Wales, i.e, teachers, preachers and public servants (Day, 2002), the graduates I spoke to, including Abby, who had Welsh as their first language did not conceive that they spoke the 'right' type of Welsh suitable for a graduate position. When their habitus encounters a field with which it is not familiar, insecurity and uncertainty can ensue (Reay et al., 2001).

Local networks

Community is a social and spatial concept with contrasting definitions. For some it infers shared lives and views of the world (Clark, 2007), or local networks of kinship and friendship (cited in *ibid*). Interviews with employers and graduates referred to the need for local connections – whether it be family, friends or 'friends of friends'. All respondents spoke well of their parents and close friends and the emotional support they received when looking for work, yet advantaged graduates had an awareness of the social capital they possessed and were predisposed to use it by pulling strings and capitalising on favours (Bathmaker et al., 2013: 11): playing the game and playing to win (Burke, 2017: 396). For instance, Lucy spoke of how her uncle and grandfather had worked for the local council, so:

> *It was a given that I would work there.*

'James' revealed that his initial entry into the company where he had worked since graduation had been due to his father being friends with its director.

> *My father has lived in the local community all his life, so a lot of the contacts I have are down to him, they are his community contacts.*

James went on to say how he was able to capitalise on these contacts and gain employment because he was 'Emrys's lad'.

Communities are often portrayed as tight-knit networks, yet not all members of the community will 'know the right people' who can provide access to employment opportunities. The interviews with 'Sean' and 'Jenny', graduates from disadvantaged backgrounds, highlight this:

> *My friends and family would not know about the jobs I am looking for so would not be able to recommend me* [Sean].
> *I have people who could support me, but these are people from where I live, my parents, my family: they are not the decision makers* [Jenny].

Further questioning revealed that like most graduates from their background, they tended to socialise with those they enjoyed spending time with as opposed to 'contacts' who could help them most in the labour market. Whilst Lucy and James 'knew' the right people', Jenny and Sean recognised that their contacts would be limited if called upon to provide practical job searching advice, mainly because their parents had no experience of the graduate labour market and the types of roles that they would be applying for.

Interviews revealed some feel excluded from their community.

> *I don't feel 'local'. It's difficult when you are explaining it but people born here have advantages that I don't – they speak the language, they have friends that I don't have and they will use them to gain jobs* [Hannah].

Hannah's views are unsurprising as nationhood is often based on the criteria of birthplace, residence, parental links and so on. Furthermore, Morris (2010) found that monoglot English-only speakers were more socially isolated in comparison to bilingual Welsh-English speakers. Respondents in this study who spoke only English (all described themselves as being Welsh) were least likely to cite local connections as helping them gain employment or other opportunities. For Hannah, finding employment in North Wales meant battling against individuals with the perceived advantages she didn't have, e.g., speaking Welsh as their first language, and having friends who were born in the area. Generally, English language graduates, and two out of five of the Welsh learners, reported that the difficulties they faced when looking for graduate employment were primarily due to their insufficient language skills and secondly, by not being born in the area, i.e., they were not 'proper Welsh' [Abby]. Whilst this is a sweeping explanation for employment barriers, there was a presumed:

hierarchy, with those who are first language Welsh 'at the top' so to speak, and the English languishing in the nether regions [Sean].

That Cymraeg can be divisive within Wales (Day, 2002: 221) is unsettling as language is about inclusion. The English language graduates embraced the Welsh language (even if they did not speak it), and reported pride in Wales, but expressed desire for diversity in definitions of Welshness, so that national identity extends beyond the idea that Welsh as a first language affords a stronger Welsh identity (Coupland et al., 2006).

Driving license and access to own transport

The Higher Education Funding Council for Wales's (HEFCW) 2015 Insight into Employability conference stated that it was important for a graduate to have access to a driving license and a car. All employers within this study agreed, stating that a driving license was vital. One employer, referring to the rural location of her business said:

> *unless he/she knew someone at the company, they would need to drive.*

References to rurality and the need to drive is understandable as North Wales has a rural landscape, with small towns on the periphery. The 'rural idyllic', a popular narrative of rural life, ignores an ageing and cumbersome public transport system. Driving from Holyhead (in the north-west) to Wrexham (in the north-east) takes approximately 90 minutes, increasing to almost three hours if travelling via train, and five and a half hours by bus. It is quicker to travel to London. However, an employer, located centrally in the region, alongside a frequent bus route, stated that the ability to drive was needed to travel between offices. This emphasis on a graduate with their own transport indirectly discriminates against those who do not drive due to medical reasons.[4] Emma, a graduate with a medical condition that affected her spatial awareness, had attempted to learn to drive but her condition meant that it was more challenging for her to pass her test. Although she outlined her condition in job applications when the requirement was a driving license so that the employer knew there was a reason why she did not drive, she did not get shortlisted. Emma felt she did not get the job due to her inability to drive as she felt she was suitable in every other way. The problem with the focus on a driving license is that a lack of geographical mobility increases the probability of graduates being underemployed. Both Emma and Zoe had experienced temporary employment and had periods of unemployment whilst waiting to start new employment.

One employer reiterated a comment familiar to me during my early career:

> *It's an image. We can't expect our managers to travel by bus.*

As the number of graduates have increased, advantaged graduates have been able to mobilise different forms of 'capital' to enhance their positioning (Bathmaker

50　*Teresa Crew*

et al., 2013). The car in this case is an example of objectified cultural capital, the type which is in keeping of the status that a graduate role brings. Alongside this, a survey by the Arts Council England (2014) included 'a family car for transport when you need it' as being an example of economic capital. Having your own transport is seen as being important in order to engage with arts and culture. Alongside this, Schwanen et al. (2015) links transport disadvantage with social exclusion, and a lack of social capital. It would be useful to evaluate if 1. driving license/ownership of a car are a requirement for graduate roles in similar regions, or in larger cities, and 2. if this is based on practical concerns, or related to retaining an image of a graduate.

Recommendations for further research and conclusion

This chapter has sought to provide a geographical understanding of employability using the case study of North Wales, the overall argument being that bilingual Welsh–English language skills, locally based networks and access to own transport are needed in order to gain graduate employment in the 'field' of North Wales. Moving forward, a recommendation is that there should be further research into what might comprise regional capital in different locations, across the UK, Europe and outside of the EU. For instance, Irish is the national and first official language of the Republic of Ireland, and Scotland has a statutory duty under the Gaelic Language (Scotland) Act 2005 to promote Gaelic. It would be interesting to observe if employers cite these skills in advertisements for employment across Ireland and Scotland, and, taking this further, to examine the specific language requirements needed for graduates in European and non-EU countries. There are thirty-six minority languages in the European Union, spoken by twenty million people (Sierp, 2008) – are these minority languages an asset for employment? In North Wales, the Welsh language is at the heart of these social networks, and further research should evaluate what is a focal point of such networks needed in other regional economies.

'Employable identities'

Burke (2016: 157) rightly asked if we should we be encouraging disadvantaged graduates to acquiesce and build 'employable identities'. My response is that this is difficult because, despite effort by careers services, universities and the graduates themselves, those with advantaged backgrounds are always one step ahead of the 'game'. Why? Because the 'ideal graduate' is middle class. Whilst this chapter identifies regional capital, i.e., skills that are useful in a local capacity, the aim is not to suggest that all graduates should add them to the never-ending list of skills and attributes that they are expected to have/gain or learn. Instead there needs to be an uncomfortable conversation with those who demand such skills. Whilst employability is based on replicating a middle-class disposition, disadvantaged graduates will always fall short. Social justice permeates Welsh higher education, so here is the place to start a new way of looking at employability. One that does

Regional capital and 'local' graduate employment   51

not see some graduates in deficit, and instead, recognises the financial, academic and social hurdles that non-traditional students have had to climb to become graduates. The public and voluntary sectors (most often graduate employers in North Wales) born out of the need to serve societies' responses to social need, may be well served by the atypical graduate. Further to this, as the future of the Welsh language resides with those who currently do not speak Welsh (Day et al., 2010), the Welsh Government's long-term vision to encourage more people to use Welsh language skills in a work situation is the perfect opportunity for inclusiveness. Encouraging employers in the region to be more welcoming to Welsh learners, and where possible, consider graduates from disadvantaged social backgrounds (whether they speak Welsh or not) is an ideal start. Focusing on the infrastructure, i.e., language technologies and translation facilities, rather than the individual (WAG, 2017) will ensure that there are fewer graduates who feel like a 'fish out of water'.

Notes

1 Students can apply to Student Finance Wales for a tuition fee loan, which will cover the first £4,046. They can then apply for a fee grant, which will pay the balance of £4,954.
2 The Erasmus Scheme
3 Federation of Small Businesses (FSB), North Wales Policy Conference, Wed, 12 Jul 2017; FSB Wales Education and Skills Summit, 25 September 2015 in Llandudno.
4 Under the Equality Act 2010 alternatives should be offered, i.e., employer paying for a taxi (as opposed to mileage).

References

Agored Cymru (2015). *Welsh in a Bilingual Society.* (online) available from: www. agored.org.uk/getfileQuartz.aspx?fileid=5270775&unitid=1336179.
Artess, J., Hooley, T., and Mellors-Bourne, R. (2017). *Employability: A Review of the Literature 2012–2016.* York: Higher Education Academy.
Arts Council England. (2014). *Cultural Capital Quantitative Survey.* (online) available from: www.anewdirection.org.uk/asset/1688/download?1415980291.pdf.
Bathmaker, A., Ingram, N., and Waller, R. (2013). "Higher education, social class and the mobilisation of capitals: Recognising and playing the game", *British Journal of Sociology of Education, 34*(5–6): 723–743.
Bourdieu, P. (1986). "The forms of capital", In: Richardson, J. (Ed.), *Handbook of Theory and Research for the Sociology of Education.* Westport, CT.
Bourdieu, P. (1984). *Distinction: A Social Critique of the Judgement of Taste.* Cambridge, MA: Harvard University Press.
Bradley, H., Abrahams, J., Bathmaker, A., Beedell, P., Hoare, T., Ingram, N., Mellor, J., and Waller, R. (2013). *The Paired Peers Project Year 3 Report: A Degree Generation.* University of Bristol (online) available from: https://www.bristol.ac.uk/media-library/sites/spais/migrated/documents/report.pdf.
Bristow, G., Pill, M., Davies, R., and Drinkwater, S. (2011). *Stay, Leave or Return? Understanding Welsh Graduate Mobility.* The Wales Institute of Social and Economic Research, Data & Methods.

52 Teresa Crew

Burke, C. (2015). "Bourdieu's theory of practice: Maintain the role of capital", In: Thatcher, J., Ingram, N., Burke, C., and Abrahams, J. (Eds.), *Bourdieu: The Next Generation: The Development of Bourdieu's Intellectual Heritage in Contemporary UK Sociology*. London: Routledge.

Burke, C. (2016). *Culture, Capitals and Graduate Futures: Degrees of Class*. London: Routledge.

Burke, C. (2017). " 'Graduate Blues': Considering the effects of inverted symbolic violence on underemployed middle class graduates", *Sociology*, *51*(2): 393–409.

Burke, C., Scurry, T., Blankinsopp, J., and Marsh-Davies, K. (2017). "Critical perspectives on graduate employability", In: Tomlinson, M., and Holmes, L. (Eds.), *Graduate Employability in Context: Theory, Research and Debate*. London: Palgrave Macmillan.

Careers Wales. (2010). *Dewis da – Why Choose Welsh?* (online) available from: www.careerswales.com/en/tools-and-resources/dewis-da-why-choose-welsh/.

Christie, F. (2016). *Uncertain Transition: Exploring the Experience of Recent Graduates*. Manchester: Higher Education Careers Service Unit.

Clark, A. (2007). *Understanding Community: A Review of Networks, Ties and Contacts: Real Life Methods Working Papers: Understanding Community*. University of Manchester.

Coupland, N. (2012). "Bilingualism on display: The framing of Welsh and English in Welsh public spaces", *Language in Society*, *41*: 1–27.

Coupland, N., Bishop, H., and Garrett, P. (2006). " 'One Wales?' Reassessing diversity in Welsh ethnolinguistic identification", *Contemporary Wales*, *18*: 1–27.

Crew, T. (2015). *Beyond Graduation: The Trajectories of Graduates in North Wales: People, Place and Policy*. 9(1). 29-47 (online) available from: http://extra.shu.ac.uk/ppp-online/wp-content/uploads/2015/04/beyond-graduation-north-wales.pdf.

Crisp, R., Gore, T., and McCarthy, L. (2017). *Addressing Transport Barriers to Work in Low Income Neighbourhoods*. Sheffield: Centre for Regional Economic and Social Research, Sheffield Hallam University.

Day, G., Davis, H., and Drakakis-Smith, A. (2010). " 'There's one shop you don't go into if you are English: The social and political integration of English migrants into Wales", *Journal of Ethnic and Migration Studies*, *36*(9).

Day, G. (2002). *Making Sense of Wales: A Sociological Perspective*. Cardiff: University of Wales Press.

Department of Transport. (2016). *National Travel Survey: 2016*. (online) available from: www.gov.uk/government/uploads/system/uploads/attachment_data/file/633077/national-travel-survey-2016.pdf.

Drinkwater, S., Blackaby, D., and Murphy, P. (2011). *The Welsh Labour Market Following the Great Recession*. Cardiff: Wales Institute of Social and Economic Research, Data and Methods.

Finn, K. (2015). *Personal Life, Young Women and Higher Education: A Relational Approach to Student and Graduate Experiences*. London: Palgrave Macmillan.

The Higher Education Funding Council for Wales. (2015). *About the Higher Education Sector in Wales*. (online) available from: www.hefcw.ac.uk/about_he_in_wales/he_policies_and_partners/about_he_sector_in_wales.aspx.

The Higher Education Funding Council for Wales (2015). *Insight into Employability: How Welsh Universities Hone Graduate Skills*. Insight into Employability Conference.

Hodges, R. (2011). "'Towards the Light/ Tua'r Goleuni?' Welsh-medium education for the non-Welsh-speaking in south-Wales: A parent's choice", In: *International Conference of Minority Languages Tartu, Estonia 2009 Conference Proceedings Esuka-Jeful 2–1*.

Hodges, R., and Prys, C. (2017). *A Toolkit for Promoting the Welsh Language in the Community*. Bangor: Bangor University.

Komine, A. (2004). "The making of Beveridge's unemployment (1909): Three concepts blended", *The European Journal of the History of Economic Thought, 11*(2): 255–280.

Marinez, E. (2016). "Methodological and ethical issues in research interviewing with a multicultural group of university students: Are there dos and don'ts?", In: Pawlak, M. (Ed.), *Classroom-oriented Research: Reconciling Theory and Practice*. London: Springer.

Mahieux, A., and Mejia-Dorantes, L. (2013). *The Impacts of Public Transport Policies on a Non-Mobility Area: French Study Case in the North of France*. Working Paper 2013–35. (online) available from: http://hal.univ-lille3.fr/hal-01006684/document.

Mann, R. (2011). *Welsh Speakers and Welsh Language Provision Within the Public Sector*. The Wales Institute of Social and Economic Research, Data & Methods. (online) available from: https://wiserd.ac.uk/publications/welsh-speakers-and-welsh-language-provision-within-public-sector.

Mann, R (2007). "Negotiating the politics of language: Civic identity and language learning in Wales", *Ethnicities, 7*(2): 208–224.

McAllister, F., Blunt, A., and Prys, C. (2013). *Exploring Welsh Speakers' Language Use in Their Daily Lives*. Beaufort Research Report.

McDowell, L. (1992). "Doing gender: feminism, feminists and research methods in human geography", *Transactions, institute of British Geographers, 17*: 399–416.

Morris, D. (2010). *Welsh in the 21st Century*. Cardiff: University of Wales Press.

Reay, D., David, M., and Ball, S. 2001. "Making a difference?: Institutional habituses and higher education choice", *Sociological Research Online*.

Schwanen, T., Lucas, K., Akyelken, N., Solsona, D.C., Carrasco, J.A., and Neutens, T. (2015). "Rethinking the links between social exclusion and transport disadvantage through the lens of social capital", *Transportation Research Part A: Policy and Planning*.

Sierp, A. (2008). "Minority language protection in Italy: Linguistic minorities and the media", *Journal of Contemporary European Research, 4*(4): 303–321.

UK Higher Education International Unit (2015). *Gone International: Mobile Students and Their Outcomes*. UK Higher Education International Unit. (online) available from: http://go.international.ac.uk/sites/default/files/Gone%20International%20mobile%20students%20and%20their%20outcomes.pdf.

Welsh Assembly Government (2017). *Cymraeg 2050: A Million Welsh Speakers*. (online) available from: www.assembly.wales/laid%20documents/gen-ld11108/gen-ld11108-e.pdf. http://go.international.ac.uk/sites/default/files/Gone%20International%20mobile%20students%20and%20their%20outcomes.pdf

Part 2

Graduate careers and transitions

5 Graduate labour market myths

Charlie Ball

Misconceptions about education and about graduates have existed as long as there has been a higher education system. Often, they have been fed by an apparent remoteness between universities and their student bodies and academic staff, and the rest of the population. In the modern era, as higher education has become more common and has attained a higher social, economic and political profile, few influencers in politics, business or media are without an opinion on the university system and its perceived effects or value, and whilst many of these opinions are well-informed, it is inevitable in a media and cultural environment that values quick, eye-catching comment, that some myths are promulgated and become common.

This chapter examines a few of the more prominent myths about graduates and their relationship with the labour market, and gives data and evidence about them. It is not an exhaustive list of every current misconception about graduate employment. Some of these myths are very old indeed; some have become much more prominent of late. Nor are all of the statements that are examined completely wrong. Indeed, most have a kernel – or more – of fact at their heart. But all are widespread, commonly repeated in one form or another, and influence the current debate on higher education.

'Everyone has a degree nowadays'

It is often stated or paraphrased that 'there are too many graduates'. The 'too many graduates' theory is an exceptionally old one, and one that particularly recurs in the aftermath of significant changes to the higher education sector. It was encapsulated in a much-quoted piece by the writer Kingsley Amis, when he wrote in *Encounter* (1960), at the prospect of the expansion of higher education that eventually took place in that decade (the 'Robbins expansion'), about 'the pit of incapacity and ignorance into which British education has sunk since the war'. Inevitably, 'more will mean worse'. Amis was hardly the first commentator to bemoan a decline in standards that has occurred since they left education, and the current debate on higher education often looks and sounds as if it has not moved on at all. But, after a significant expansion of higher education in the last 25 years and in the aftermath of the UK's first recession of the 21st

58 *Charlie Ball*

century, it is not wise to immediately discount this old cliché in the current UK labour market. Few pieces of academic research on the graduate labour market are complete without a section on underemployment or job mismatch – difficult though that can sometimes be to definitively demonstrate. At the same time, there are clearly shortages of graduates in many crucial disciplines and specialities. The most judicious reading of the situation would suggest that although it is not immediately clear that we have too many graduates, it is clear that the UK is not using the stock of graduates it does have as effectively as it could and that the pipeline of supply of graduate skills to the economy is not working quite as anyone would like.

However, some of the supplementary arguments about how there are too many graduates stem from a flawed notion that 'everyone has a degree nowadays'. This is not usually meant in a strictly literal sense, but more as a general expression of the perceived ubiquity of higher education qualifications. The reality is somewhat different. It is true that many people have degrees in the UK, but hardly 'everyone'.

Fifty years ago, in 1966, the UK in general and higher education in particular were rather different. Bobby Moore's England had just won the World Cup. It would not be for another three years that Neil Armstrong would make a giant leap for mankind. Some of the crucial juggernauts of modern employment had not yet been founded – neither Microsoft nor Apple would be created until the middle of the '70s. The UK had recently agreed to accept the provisions of the Robbins Report and expand the higher education sector to the point where the student population was anticipated to be well over 200,000 in the middle of the 1970s.

It was in this context that 32,166 first degrees were awarded in the UK in 1966 (UGC, 1966). Fifty years later, the 2015/16 Destinations of Leavers from Higher Education (DLHE) dataset from the Higher Education Statistics Agency (HESA) shows that 382,095 first degrees were awarded by UK institutions, 82.9 per cent to UK citizens, in 2016. This is clearly an extremely substantial increase and has led to an increase in the prevalence of higher education qualifications in the UK. But this must be kept in proportion.

One way to examine the facts is using Annual Population Survey (APS) data from the Office for National Statistics (ONS). This can be accessed through a public tool, NOMIS,[1] and this is how the data that follows has been produced. Any reader of this book can therefore check the data for themselves and draw their own conclusions. The basic data is unambiguous. APS data shows that at the end of 2016, 38 per cent of the UK working age population, and 43.5 per cent of the workforce, held a degree or equivalent qualification. This is plainly a far cry from 'everyone' having a degree – higher education is (and is likely to remain) a minority sport in the UK. But what is more interesting is how this belief may have come about.

Delving into the data a number of things become plain. Firstly, and most obviously, is that the proportions have increased over time. Figure 5.1 demonstrates that change between 2004 and 2016.

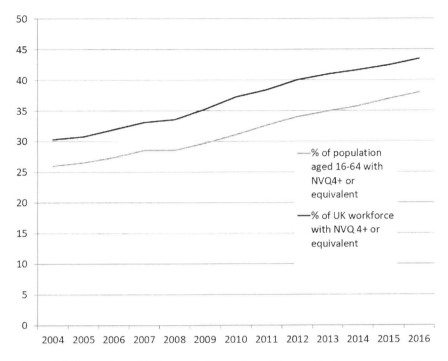

Figure 5.1 Proportion of UK population and workforce with degree or equivalent qualifications (NVQ4+) from 2004 to 2016

The figures clearly show a rise from 30.3 per cent of the workforce and 26 per cent of the working age population in 2004 to the figures we see today. The rate of increase in prevalence of higher education qualifications accelerated during the recession; perhaps surprising to those embedded in higher education who remember the recent recession as a difficult time for the sector, but of course less of a shock when one considers that the less well-qualified always fare worse in recessions. So to the observer it is clear that degrees have become more prevalent in the last decade. But it is still the case that significantly fewer than half of the UK has one.

The next argument to examine is that older members of the population do not have degrees, but higher qualifications are much more common amongst the young. 'Everyone' therefore applies to people who have recently left education. Table 5.1 examines the proportion of the population with a higher education or equivalent qualification by age group.

Although it is clear that younger people are more likely to have degrees and that nearly half the population aged 30–39 have a higher education or equivalent qualification, this is not even a majority of any age group, let alone anything that looks like 'everyone'.

60   Charlie Ball

Table 5.1 Proportion of the UK population with a degree or equivalent qualification at the end of 2016, by age group. Data comes from the APS

Age	Proportion of UK population with HE or equivalent qualification at the end of 2016
20–24	29.8
25–29	46.1
30–39	48.7
40–49	43.1
50–64	35.6

Perhaps there is another factor? Geography gives us much the biggest steer. 49.3 per cent of workers in Scotland had degrees at the end of 2016. Indeed, 57.8 per cent of the Scottish population aged 30–39 had a degree. This is clearly a majority, although it is difficult to really imagine that the national conversation is being driven by one Scottish age cohort (the equivalent figure for England is 48.3 per cent – still not a majority). But when we look at data by urban area, then some of the genesis of this myth may start to emerge.

Table 5.2 shows the data for major English and Welsh urban areas for the workforce and for that section of the population most likely to have a degree – the 30 to 39 year olds.

The population of affluent cities in the south of England (and a few strong regional economies with large university sectors, notably Manchester and Cardiff) is often predominantly graduate. Nearly two thirds of the London population in their 30s has a degree – and when you look by borough, this figure ranges from 38.9 per cent in the outer East London borough of Havering to 86 per cent in Richmond and 89 per cent in Wandsworth. Three quarters of the population in their 30s in Oxford or St Albans have a degree. Thus we can start to form a picture. If one is from an affluent town or city in London or the south of England, then it is quite possible that nearly everyone you meet or know has been to university. This is, not coincidentally, rather likely to be the background from which influential commentators and policymakers are drawn. Perhaps the solution to this myth is for our national conversation to listen to slightly fewer people from Westminster and Woking, and slightly more to people from Wigan, Wolverhampton and Wakefield. Now that some of the basic data has been presented, we can move on to other misconceptions. The next is another widely prevalent one and deals more specifically with the graduate labour market.

'There aren't enough jobs for graduates'

When the argument is made that 'too many people go to university' it is often really a commentary on the perceived challenging state of the graduate labour

Table 5.2 Proportion of the English and Welsh population with a degree or equivalent qualification at the end of 2016, by urban area. Data comes from the APS

Urban area	Proportion of age group 30–39 with a degree or equivalent qualification	Proportion of workforce with a degree or equivalent qualification
Bath	68	61.5
Birmingham	36.6	38.3
Blackburn	32.6	37.2
Blackpool	32.8	31.6
Bolton	42.2	42.2
Bournemouth	53.5	41
Bradford	18.4	25.6
Brighton and Hove	60.2	59.4
Bristol	62.7	52.7
Cambridge	54.8	71.4
Cardiff	61.2	54.8
Chelmsford	47.7	48.2
Cheltenham	67.1	55.6
Chester	41	49.9
Colchester	51	48.2
Coventry	47.3	36.5
Derby	40.1	38.7
Exeter	61.2	54.5
Gloucester	34.8	26.1
Grimsby	29.5	25
Guildford	59.3	58.1
Huddersfield	45.5	38.9
Ipswich	38.9	35.8
Kingston upon Hull	41.1	34.7
Leeds	47.1	40
Leicester	29	31.3
Lincoln	35.1	36.3
Liverpool	46.8	38.8
London	64.6	59.7
Luton	36.5	36.6
Manchester	59.2	53.6
Middlesbrough	34.2	32.9

(*Continued*)

62 Charlie Ball

Table 5.2 (Continued)

Urban area	Proportion of age group 30–39 with a degree or equivalent qualification	Proportion of workforce with a degree or equivalent qualification
Milton Keynes	49.7	40.8
Newcastle upon Tyne	52.6	47.6
Newport	36.4	34.3
Northampton	38.8	38.2
Norwich	35	38.2
Nottingham	45.9	41.3
Oxford	75.9	65.1
Peterborough	35.4	32.5
Plymouth	45.6	37.6
Portsmouth	42.6	37.9
Preston	40.3	33.8
Reading	65.2	54
Salford	45.7	45.7
Sheffield	45	46.5
Southampton	49.3	40.7
Southend-on-Sea	32.1	32.1
St Albans	76.6	63.7
Stoke-on-Trent	31	25.2
Sunderland	35.5	26.4
Swansea	45	39.3
Wakefield	36.4	34.6
Wigan	36.3	30.7
Woking	53.7	52.6
Wolverhampton	27.2	32.4
Worcester	50.4	48.1
York	56.3	44.3

market. It seems unlikely that one of the crucial issues in the UK is that young people are continuing to be educated after the age of 18. What is usually meant is that there is not sufficient labour market demand for the number of graduates we produce.

The first thing to stress is this is not the same as denying the existence of underutilised graduates. Graduate underemployment certainly does exist and a great deal of very high quality research has been done on the phenomenon. Elias and Purcell's (2014) work on the effects of mass higher education on graduate

Graduate labour market myths 63

labour market outcomes and Green and Henseke's (2016) series of examinations of underemployment amongst graduates in the OECD countries make the point firmly that underemployment amongst graduates is a real phenomenon and readers wishing to learn more are strongly recommended to read these two papers. But the existence of graduate underemployment does not automatically mean that the UK has too many graduates. Underemployment is not always straightforward to measure, not every graduate measured as 'underemployed' considers their qualification to lack value in the role that they are in, not every graduate who is underemployed now will be underemployed in the future, and occupational change is rapid and accelerating, meaning that roles that might not be considered 'graduate level' or utilising appropriate skills at one point might evolve into such roles in the future. In a recent example from 2017, the College of Policing put forward proposals that represent such an evolution in roles in UK law enforcement.

Most importantly, the existence of underemployed graduates does not mean that there cannot be occupational shortages elsewhere in the economy and indeed that is exactly what the UK currently experiences. There are widely publicised shortages of nurses and of graduates in technical disciplines across the country. Most recently the Bank of England (2017) warned that 'Recruitment difficulties remained elevated. Conditions were becoming tight for many skills' and cited engineering, finance, healthcare and construction – all sectors with known graduate shortages – as industries of particular concern. So what is the picture? Are there jobs for graduates?

The first thing that we can do is to examine DLHE data. 128,170 UK graduates from 2016 were known to be in professional level jobs in the UK six months after graduating – 71.3 per cent of all UK-domiciled graduates from 2016 who were working in the UK. The debate over what, exactly, constitutes a 'graduate job' is a difficult, complex and long-standing one with no clear conclusion. Using 'professional level' – jobs classed under the Standard Occupational Classification (SOC) system of occupational coding under major groups 1, 2 and 3 – managerial, professional and associate professional jobs[2] – is not a perfect measure, but it is not so imperfect that it does not provide an acceptable guide. SOC will be revised in 2020 and the 'professional level' classification is likely to more closely reflect what is considered to be a 'graduate job' after that point. In addition, 66 per cent of graduates questioned said that their qualification was a requirement or gave them advantage in getting their job. It is clear that there are many jobs for graduates every year. A more detailed examination can be found in the annual publication, *What Do Graduates Do?* (HECSU/AGCAS, 2017).

As the Annual Population Survey has shown, the proportion of graduates in the workforce has steadily and systematically increased year-on-year. This could, of course, involve a mass movement of graduates into jobs that do not need degrees and thus a significant erosion of the direct economic value of a degree. There is some evidence of a marginal reduction in the lifetime earnings premium for a higher education qualification, but it is difficult to quantify and the academic literature is divided. But we can examine the Annual Population Survey in more detail.

In the 10 years from 2006, data from the Annual Population Survey shows that the UK economy added over 2.475 million new jobs in managerial, professional and associate professional occupations. It comes to over 247,500 new jobs at 'professional' level, year on year for the last decade – which includes the entirety of the last recession and the slow recovery from that recession. And it only measures jobs added to the economy, and not replacement demand, the job vacancies opened up by people leaving the jobs market due to retirement and so on. Indeed, if you look deeper into the data, every single sub-category of graduate employment saw an increase in the total number of jobs in the UK over that period. By the end of 2016, 14,169,000 people were employed in professional level roles in the UK.

By contrast, the rest of the economy in SOC categories 4 to 9 created a net of 45,100 jobs in those 10 years. Many occupational areas shrank, including relatively well-paid and secure jobs in skilled trades and in office jobs. They were replaced mainly by roles in care work and at the very elementary level, often in insecure, poorly paid jobs with long hours. It is unsurprising that those who do not go to university have a rather different view of the recession, recovery and general UK economy than those who do. The loss of office roles may also have a detrimental knock-on effect on graduates as traditionally these positions have been an important way for new graduates with little work experience to enter the labour force and subsequently to move into professional positions. Figure 5.2 shows the net changes in the number of people working in the UK in each major SOC category.

Taking a look at 2016 in isolation reinforces this impression. The UK economy added just under 441,000 new jobs at professional level through 2016. Graduate destination data from DLHE showed that 291,000 new graduates, at all levels from HNC to PhD, and of all nationalities were known to have entered the workforce. This is not a set of figures that speak of an economy that is obviously oversupplied with graduates, but rather one that has an ever-increasing demand for higher levels of education.

With obvious areas of graduate underemployment, and similarly obvious issues of graduate supply, it is clear that we could benefit from having a much clearer, systematic and granular view of occupational demand. The Working Futures series of publications (Warwick Institute for Employment Research, 2016) make it clear that this trend towards higher skilled work is only set to continue and that it may not be long before more than half the jobs in the economy will need a degree or equivalent, and the series makes an excellent attempt at this very difficult job of forecasting future occupational demand.

There are also unresolved questions about the earnings premium for graduates – although it's possible for graduate earnings to fall and for that to potentially be good for the national graduate economy, such as if many more graduates got jobs outside London – but that will be examined in the next myth.

The data does not suggest that we have too many graduates as such – but it is fair to say that there are mismatches between graduate supply and demand that ought to be examined and for which solutions ought to be sought in order to

Graduate labour market myths 65

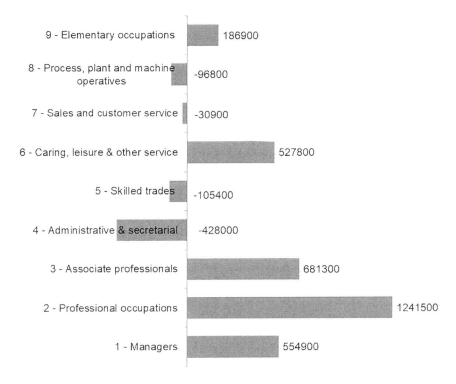

Figure 5.2 Net changes in UK occupational structure 2006–2016

ensure that the country in general and graduates in particular can gain maximum value from our higher education system.

As we have seen, graduate opportunities are not evenly spread around the country. But the view appears to persist that they are especially concentrated in one area. So our next myth examines that particular question.

'All the graduate jobs are in London'

There is no doubt that London dominates the national conversation. The UK's political and media establishment are largely based in London, live in and around the city, and are preoccupied with the concerns of the capital. This is not the venue to rehash the very clear centralisation of political, social and economic power in London; it can be taken as read.

One of the effects of this has been the long-standing assumption that London is the centre of the UK graduate labour market, that graduates – or at least ambitious graduates – will naturally move there if they can, and that as a consequence, all other parts of the UK are constantly losing their best young minds to the capital in a 'brain drain'. The respected think tank Centre for Cities produced one of

66   Charlie Ball

the most recent substantial studies of this phenomenon (Swinney and Williams, 2016) but many of the conclusions of 'brain drain' examined how large civic institutions take graduates from outside their host cities in large numbers – many of whom then leave for elsewhere on graduation. It is not obvious that the export of skilled workers to the rest of the economy by large universities represents a clear issue – many would argue that is a core purpose of those institutions. But how far does London dominate the graduate labour market? And does it really take the lion's share of graduate jobs?

As the Centre for Cities reported in their 2017 Cities Outlook report (Swinney, 2017) 15.2 per cent of the UK population lives in London and 19.4 per cent of UK graduates live in London. They further report that 23 per cent of the country's businesses are in London. Data from DLHE shows that 21.1 per cent of 2016 graduates started their career in London. Many of those jobs were confined to a relatively small area of London – over half of all new graduates employed in London were in one of six boroughs: Westminster; City of London; Camden; Tower Hamlets; Southwark; or Islington. Nevertheless, London is comfortably the most common employment location for new UK graduates. 11.7 per cent of graduates go to work in the south-east, in areas on the periphery of the capital. But 10.7 per cent of graduates go to work in the north-west, and Manchester is a rapidly growing, diverse centre of skilled employment in which DLHE data tells us that 3,790 graduates are known to have started their careers in 2016. Birmingham is even larger, employing 4,080 graduates from 2016.

Indeed, when we examine the data in detail, the story seems to be less 'graduates all move to London' and more that 'graduates tend to move to cities'. And as London is much the largest of the cities, it can often appear that graduate employment is dominated by the capital. But the true situation is that although London is the largest jobs market for graduates, most UK graduates do not work in London – and never will.

This is an important message for UK students and those who support them. Higher education and the policy environment around the sector can find the idea that graduates will consult data on earnings and outcomes and opt to maximise their salaries seductive. If graduates were concerned principally by getting the highest salaries available, then this would advantage sector metrics on earnings and help to alleviate Government concerns about the repayment of student loan debt – as graduates would be more motivated to earn more and presumably pay more of their loans off more quickly. And naturally, in most cases, the highest salaries available are in London. At the end of 2016, average weekly earnings in London were £697, compared to £525 nationally – a significant difference. But students and graduates are also mindful that the cost of living in the capital has ramped up dramatically. As the Cities Outlook shows (Swinney, 2017), the average house price in London had reached £561,400 by the end of 2016, a multiple of 16.7 times average salary. Only the overheated housing market in Oxford is as unaffordable in the UK. Compare with university cities such as Glasgow (houses 5.6 times average salary), Liverpool (5.4 times) or Hull (4.9 times), and the attractiveness of those large London salaries starts to wane. It is possible that this

Graduate labour market myths 67

may prompt some graduates to make a rational decision that London is not an attractive destination for them to seek work.

So, where do graduates go to get jobs? A previous Higher Education Careers Service Unit (HECSU) report on graduate migration (Ball, 2015) examined graduate migration using four groups: Loyals, who were domiciled and studied in the same region and then remain there to work; Stayers, who move away from their home region to study and then remain in that region to work; Returners, who move away to study but then return home to work; and Incomers, who go to one region to study and another to work.

Although much of the popular discourse about student choice and graduate employment seem to suggest that Incomers – who travel to wherever in the country has the 'best' course for them and then travel for the 'best' employment, representing an idealised graduate experience – they actually made up only 18 per cent of the 2016 employed graduate cohort. But they make up the largest part – 34 per cent – of the London labour market, and 42 per cent of all Incomers work in London. For those who live and work in London, Incomers _are_ the most commonly occurring. But 45 per cent of graduates are actually Loyals, who do not move from their home region. Twenty-four per cent are Returners, who come home after study to get their job. And the remainder, 13 per cent, are Stayers, who remain near to their institution to find work. There are differences between outcomes – Returners are the most likely to be in non-graduate employment, and Incomers and Stayers are much more likely to be in high salary, professional jobs. But, in all, 58 per cent of 2016 graduates went to work in the region in which they took their degree, and 69 per cent in the UK region in which they had grown up. The data we have suggests that mobility may even be falling, although this data needs to be monitored for longer to be sure if a trend is apparent. Many of these graduates hail from and/or study in London, but even for graduates, employment in London and particularly leaving another part of the country and going to work in London is not the typical experience, and it is best that we recognise it. The final myth is less often stated outright, and most people in the sector actually know it to be broadly untrue. But it is one that is at least unconsciously often believed by students and by graduates, and it is worth examining the figures. It is also a little more straightforward to examine.

'Graduates all work for big business'

Go to any group of prospective university students and ask them what they think a graduate job is. They will almost always speak in terms of the classic, iconic graduate training schemes at brand name employers with large graduate intakes. Indeed, the perception persists through university, and there are influential sector publications that view and portray the most desirable graduate employment options through this lens.

And large graduate training schemes are a vital part of the graduate employment landscape. The Institute of Student Employers (ISE, formerly the Association of Graduate Recruiters) has for some time been the de facto voice of this group and produce research and surveys of the employers on their schemes. Their most recent report (2017) covers 200 employers who hired 31,630 students in 2017 and who collectively employ over 2.8 million staff. The importance of this option should not be understated, but as we established earlier, nearly 130,000 graduates are known to have entered professional level employment last year, and so the employers covered by the ISE report recruit only a minority of graduates entering professional occupations.

In fact, most – but not all – graduates *do* work for large employers, as shown in Figure 5.3.

Most graduates actually work at very large employers. Part of this is because much the most common industry of graduate employment is the hospital sector, and nearly all hospitals employing graduates comfortably exceed 1000 employees. But even setting that aside, larger employers dominate. So this is one myth that has more of a grain of truth. Nevertheless, last year, 34 per cent of graduates went to work for companies with fewer than 250 employees, and one in six were with companies with fewer than 50 employees. The small and medium sized employment (SME) sector is also a very important part of the graduate employment milieu and cannot and should not be underestimated. It is especially important to graduate employment in certain industries – the arts; design; architecture;

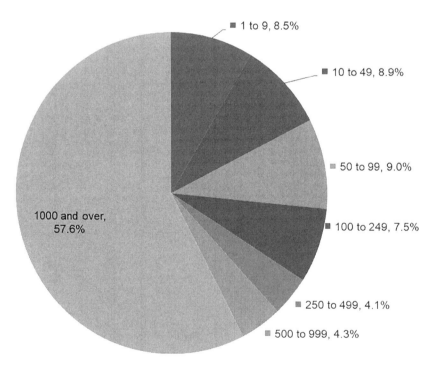

Figure 5.3 Proportion of UK-domiciled graduates from 2016 working in the UK after six months, who were employed at businesses of different sizes

marketing, PR and advertising; sports and fitness; law; and web design to name some of the most significant. And it is also particularly important in London and the south-east. The relative difficulty of engagement between universities and SMEs can make them less visible to students and graduates, as can simple lack of brand recognition. But this is a misconception that, although not without some grounding in fact, is relatively easily addressed and which can be confronted with valuable results.

Conclusion

Like all the best stories, there is a grain of truth at the heart of some of these tales. Most people in the UK do not have degrees. But if you are from a middle-class background with parents in the professions, it is likely that almost everyone *you* know is a graduate. So although it is a myth that 'everyone has a degree nowadays', to our opinion-formers and policy-makers it will nevertheless often appear as if a university education is a norm.

The UK graduate labour market is large, robust and growing. But with relatively rapid expansion of higher education has come an increasing focus on the issue of graduate underutilisation. With media and policy examining those graduates who have yet to realise an obvious benefit from their higher education, it can sometimes seem as if those individuals are typical of the whole cohort rather than a small but significant minority. At the same time, the well-known issue of graduate occupational shortages is recognised but receives much less focus. It is a myth to say that 'there are no jobs for graduates', but it is clear that supply and demand are not as well matched, or even understood, as they could be.

The economic, social and political dominance of London, and the relative lack of visibility of the rest of the country, means that it sometimes appears that London monopolises the supply of good quality jobs. London is and will remain the most popular location of graduate employment, but the majority of graduates do not work there. The myth that 'all the jobs are in London' may, however, conceal a related truth – that graduate employment may be concentrated in the larger cities and that this concentration may be increasing, to the potential detriment of the supply of skilled labour to the rest of the country.

Myths and misconceptions about graduate employment are long-lived and will persist. There are others which can be addressed – it is not uncommon, for example, to hear that 'there are so many people with degrees that you need a Masters to stand out' (this is another relatively easily debunked myth), and doing so can help us all to better understand the graduate labour market and the evidence base upon which guidance and labour market information stands and so better serve our communities and the students and graduates who look to us for guidance.

Notes

1 At www.nomisweb.co.uk/
2 Details on SOC 2010 can be found here: www.ons.gov.uk/methodology/
  classificationsandstandards/standardoccupationalclassificationsoc/soc2010

Bibliography

Amis, K. (1960). "Lone voices", *Encounter*, July, 6–11.

Ball, C. (2015). *Loyals, Stayers, Returners, Incomers – Graduate Migration Patterns*. Manchester: HECSU.

Bank of England (2017). *Agent's Summary of Business Conditions Q3*. (online) available from: www.bankofengland.co.uk/agents-summary/2017/2017-q3.

Elias, P., and Purcell, K. (2014). *Is Mass Higher Education Working? Evidence from the Labour Market Experiences of Recent Graduates*. London: National Institute Economic Review.

Green, F., and Henseke, G. (2016). "Should governments of OECD countries worry about graduate underemployment?" *Oxford Review of Economic Policy*, *32*(4): 514–537.

HECSU/AGCAS (2017). "What do graduates do? Graduate prospects". (online) available from: www.hecsu.ac.uk/current_projects_what_do_graduates_do.htm.

Institute of Student Employers (2017). *The ISE 2017 Annual Survey*. London: Institute of Student Employers.

Swinney, P. (2017). *Cities Outlook*. London: Centre for Cities.

Swinney, P., and Williams, M. (2016). *The Great British Brain Drain*. London: Centre for Cities.

University Grants Committee (1966). *First Employment of University Graduates 1965–66*. London: HMSO.

Warwick Institute for Employment Research (2016). *Working Futures 2014–2024*. UK Commission for Employment and Skills.

6 Graduate gap years

Narratives of postponement in graduate employment transitions in England

Katy Vigurs, Steven Jones, Diane Harris and Julia Everitt

Introduction

For UK higher education students, the 'gap year' or 'year out' is historically conceptualised as an amassing of wider life experience, often overseas, during a twelve-month period between the completion of A-level studies and the first year of a university degree. However, in a recent comparative study, which saw interviews conducted in both 2014 and 2015 with final year undergraduate students (n74) from different social backgrounds, across two English universities (one Russell Group university and one Post-1992 university), the term 'gap year' was being re-appropriated to capture something different. The term was being used to describe a period following graduation in which graduands planned to take low-paid work or 'ordinary' jobs, take stock of their financial situation, and attempt to save money and/or repay urgent debt. A high proportion of students in the 2015 stage of the study (16/37) spoke of taking a graduate gap year, compared with 9/37 in 2014. It may be that the increasing costs of debt-based forms of higher education payment coinciding with growing precarious employment has contributed to this situation. By borrowing the term gap year to describe a new and different phenomenon, some of the student interviewees may be legitimising the predicament in which they find themselves. This chapter explores the experiences of students who spoke of taking a graduate gap year. It examines the different roles of a graduate gap year and discusses wider implications for unequal graduate outcomes.

The archetypal gap year and gap year taker

The term 'gap year' is largely conceived as a pre-university experience in the literature (Birch and Miller, 2007; Stehlik, 2010). It is useful to begin by briefly exploring definitions of traditional gap years and gap year takers. The Jones (2003) review of Gap Year Provision, for the Department for Education and Skills, described a gap year as a particular period of time, usually 12 consecutive months, when students take a year out between finishing college and starting university.

72 *Katy Vigurs, Steven Jones, Diane Harris, Julia Everitt*

Traditional gap year takers have been found to come from more advantaged socio-economic backgrounds and better performing schools (Birch and Miller, 2007; Crawford and Cribb, 2012). These students have usually deliberately planned to take a gap year and are also more likely to have applied and accepted a place at university before their gap year begins. Indeed, a profitable industry has grown up around the traditional notion of the gap year. It is important to note, however, that Crawford and Cribb's (2012) analysis revealed another type of gap year taker. These are students that did not intend to take a year out. They often have either not applied for or not achieved the grades to be offered a place at university. Their gap year usually comprises low wage employment or returning to full-time education to retake examinations. These gap year takers are usually from lower socio-economic backgrounds and are less likely to go to straight on to university after their year out.

Additionally, Holmlund et al. (2008) identified four types of pre-university gap year, which can be mapped to the two main types of gap year taker in Crawford and Cribb's study:

1 Those where individuals develop specific skills
2 Those where individuals are waiting for better educational opportunities (such as needing to retake qualifications to achieve passes or get higher grades or avoiding going through the university clearing process)
3 Those where individuals learn about their broader preferences and/or abilities
4 Those where individuals take an extended break or holiday

The findings in the literature suggest that the traditional pre-university gap year is not a homogeneous experience for young people and is likely to be a classed experience (Nieman, 2010; Stehlik, 2010; O'Shea, 2011; Crawford and Cribb, 2012). Before considering how this might this relate to the phenomenon of a graduate gap year, the chapter now reflects upon transitions to adulthood and graduate transitions more generally.

Troubling transitions

As Arundel and Ronald (2015: 2–3) point out, transitions to adulthood in general represent:

> a key period for individual development but also contribute to processes of social stratification. Growing evidence has pointed to increased complexity, postponement and individualisation in transition dynamics . . . Transition into adulthood represents a key stage in the life-course where decisions and events can have long-lasting effects for individual development.

They explain that pathways to adulthood have diversified with increasingly non-linear pathways through education and employment, which is characterised by growing employment instability, often leading to 'boomerang' transitions for young adults (Arundel and Lennartz, 2015). Holdsworth (2015: 1) notes that as a response to this context of uncertain futures related to precarious and casualised employment or unemployment:

> young people are increasingly encouraged to invest in practices of distinction that enable them to stand out from the crowd in the pursuit of employability. These practices include the acquisition of experiences, such as work experience, internships, volunteering, travel and membership of organisations, which are assumed to give young people an edge over their peers in a crowded and increasingly globalised youth labour market.

She is concerned that the practice of gaining experience is an attempt by young people to protect themselves against a changeable graduate labour market but that ultimately the 'distinctions that matter and where new cleavages of domination will be formed . . . in an era of austerity is between those who can master unpredictability and be creative and those who cannot' (p. 4).

Howie and Campbell (2016: 906) suggest that nowadays young people in general are expected to 'become rational, autonomous, choice making, risk aware, prudential, responsible and enterprising' in response to neo-liberal hardships. However, as Abrahams (2016) reminds us, writing specifically about inequality in graduate employment, there is not an equal chance of securing graduate employment. Graduates from non-traditional higher education backgrounds are less likely to study at the more elite universities, and this may impact on these individuals' future employability. Indeed she points out that mass expansion in the UK higher education sector may have led to an increasingly diversified student body, but going to university alone is not the key to equality.

Bradley and Waller (2018) found that initial transition phases for graduates into adulthood, the labour market and a career revealed classed and gendered differences in the pace and direction of graduate trajectories. Some of their participants deferred starting graduate employment by travelling. This was seen as a way to recover from the pressures of academic achievement. The authors observed some graduates wanting to spend time as a 'free spirit' before adulthood ties them down. They conclude by commenting that their graduate participants did not seem too daunted as they moved towards adult independence, although it may be significant that their participants started university in 2010 under the lower university fees regime in England and therefore would have graduated with less student debt. This chapter seeks to extend their findings by presenting the views of students graduating in 2014 and 2015, with the latter leaving university with higher levels of student debt and with a noticeably more apprehensive and less hopeful outlook.

Research methods

There is currently little in the literature that explores the emergence of the concept of a graduate gap year in England and the role that the phenomenon plays

74   Katy Vigurs, Steven Jones, Diane Harris, Julia Everitt

in constructing graduate transitions, particularly in a climate of higher university fees and higher levels of student debt. This chapter starts to address this under-researched area by drawing on a qualitative study (Vigurs et al., 2016) that comprised interviews about graduate transitions with final year undergraduate students (n74) in two universities in central England (46 studied at a Russell Group university and 28 studied at a Post-1992 university). Half of the students graduated in 2014 (lower fees, approximately £3000 per year) and the other half graduated in 2015 (higher fees, approximately £9000 per year). The students interviewed in 2014 (n37) were selected by socio-economic background, gender, degree subject/discipline and secondary school type. The 2014 sample was matched in 2015 to ensure that another 37 final year students were selected from the same university, socio-economic background, gender, degree subject/ discipline and secondary school type. In order to ensure anonymity pseudonyms have been allocated.

Table 6.1 shows that the sample of students was additionally classified using widening participation categories (WP status/Non-WP status). It is important to note that students did not necessarily self-identify as having WP status (this was not directly asked), but rather they met certain indicators – such as low parental income, being first in their family to attend HE, coming from a low HE participation area, etc. – which meant that they had access to university bursaries and larger maintenance grants. This information is significant as access to different levels of capital (financial, cultural, social) is likely to influence graduate decision-making (Vigurs et al., 2018).

A significant theme that emerged was the phenomenon of taking a graduate 'year out' or 'gap year' (see Table 6.1). In 2014, 9 out of a sample of 37 (24%) reported an intention to take a graduate gap year, whereas in 2015, 16 (43%) out of a matched sample were planning to take a graduate gap year. The chapter will now explore reasons identified for taking a graduate gap year and how these differed between the graduates of 2014 (lower fees) and the graduates of 2015 (higher fees).

Table 6.1 Number of students in the sample (n74) planning a graduate gap year

Students planning a graduate gap year by institution & widening participation (WP) status	*Students graduating in 2014*	*Students graduating in 2015*
Post-1992 University, WP status	1 / 4	5 / 5
Post-1992 University, Non-WP	3 / 10	4 / 9
Russell Group University, WP status	3 / 14	5 / 14
Russell Group University, Non-WP status	2 / 9	2 / 9
Total	9 / 37 (24%)	16 / 37 (43%)

Typology of graduate gap years

Four types of graduate gap year emerged from the data analysis of the 25 interview transcripts where students communicated their intention to take a year out immediately after graduating:

1 A year out to build up work experience
2 A year out to work out next steps
3 A year out to take a break
4 A year out to get 'ordinary work' to earn money

Interestingly, only one of these categories was experienced by graduates of both 2014 and 2015 (taking a year out to build up work experience). Taking a graduate gap year to work out next steps was only experienced by those graduating in 2014, and the final two categories were only experienced by those graduating in 2015 (to take a break, and to get an ordinary job to save money). Table 6.2 demonstrates the types of graduate gap year taken by different students.

A year out to build up work experience

In 2014, three male students without WP status (RG: Peter; Post-1992: David, Olly) described the purpose of their 'year out' to be about taking up opportunities that would build valuable professional work experience in the same discipline as their degree. They felt this would make them more attractive to the graduate labour market in their field:

> I've actually got an [advertising] internship in London so I'm going straight down to do that . . . I'm lucky because my parents are able to support me.
> (David, Post-1992, Non-WP, BA)

All three acknowledged that familial financial support would need to be drawn upon to cover the costs of a year out to build professional experience often in a voluntary capacity.

In 2015, only one student without WP status (RG: Annabel) felt she needed a year out to build employability experience in relation to a chosen career: 'I feel there's got to be . . . more stages before I can get to any job that I'd actually want to do' (Annabel, RG, Non-WP, BMus). However, three students from WP backgrounds (Post-1992: Annie; RG: Francesca, Vazir) also reported an intention to take a graduate gap year to build up experience. Annie and Francesca both planned to combine travel with building up work experience in a broader sense through temporary jobs:

> I haven't had a year out yet so I'm thinking of doing work experience this summer to try to build the CV up and then I want to travel a bit as well but

76 *Katy Vigurs, Steven Jones, Diane Harris, Julia Everitt*

Table 6.2 Type of graduate gap year by participant

Type of graduate gap year	Year of graduation	Type of HEI	Socio-economic background	Graduate gap year takers
A year out to build up experiences	2014	Russell Group	Non-WP	Peter
		Post-1992	Non-WP	David Olly
	2015	Russell Group	Non-WP WP	Annabel Francesca Vazir
		Post-1992	WP	Annie
A year out to work out next steps	2014	Russell Group	Non-WP WP	Nia Munnas Abdul Lydia
		Post-1992	Non-WP WP	Gemma Ellie
A year out to take a break	2015	Russell Group	Non-WP WP	Olivia Shaila
A year out to get 'ordinary work' to earn money	2015	Russell Group	WP	Max Helen
		Post-1992	WP	Claudia Joanne Sophie Veronika
			Non-WP	Jamie Adelle Mark Dan

not extreme like some people; just around Europe just to see a few countries before I get too old and get stuck in a job.

(Annie, Post-1992, WP, BA)

Vazir was clear about what career he wanted to enter, but felt he was currently lacking experience in that particular field, which was preventing him from getting the job he wants when he graduates:

I want to start working within the [Finance] sector. I've applied to many graduate schemes but I'm now settling on [temping] agencies after I graduate, just to get experience, because I was faltering [on the graduate scheme applications] through experience mainly, rather than grades, so a year of experience could help me.

(Vazir, RG, WP, BA)

A key distinction in this category is between those who take a graduate gap year because they do not feel they have developed the skills for graduate employment and those who take a year out to complete an internship. One is reactive and one is proactive. Perhaps surprisingly, those taking up an internship all referred to it as a year out, although less surprisingly they were all from more advantaged backgrounds.

A year out to work out next steps

Only those in the sample who graduated in 2014 experienced this category of graduate gap year. Two male and four female students reported the reason for taking a year out was to create thinking space to help them work out their next steps in relation to work, adulthood and independence. These students were unsure what they should do with their future. Two were planning to gain this thinking space by travelling. Lydia (RG, WP, BA) had saved money whilst being at university and felt she did not need to 'rush into a job', and Gemma (Post-1992, Non-WP, BA) said she would 'probably travel because I've got nothing else to do', which would be funded by her mother. The other four students were planning to create thinking space by either turning their current part-time job into full-time hours or taking on low paid work. Munnas (RG, WP, BA), Abdul (RG, WP, BSc) and Nia (RG, Non-WP, BSc) described already having part-time 'good', 'proper' jobs in retail, which they would be taking on in a full-time capacity after university, whilst they work out what to do next. It transpired that Munnas and Abdul had been focusing solely on their studies to try to achieve as good a degree classification as possible rather than planning their future. Though both were aware that graduate transitions were unlikely to be smooth. Munnas said, 'I think it is going to be hard because when you're applying for a job there's probably thousands of others so it's trying to stand out.' Nia claimed she was indecisive. Ellie (Post-1992, WP, BA) was unsure about how to get a job in her field of choice (disability sport), suspecting it might involve needing to study a postgraduate course and therefore needed 'time out' to look into this.

A year out to take a break

Only two female students in the sample experienced this category. Both graduated in 2015 and studied at the Russell Group University. Olivia was from a non-WP background and was educated at an independent school. She was planning to take a postgraduate course but first wanted a 'year off' to be able to unwind from the strains of studying:

> I'm thinking about doing a masters but I want to take a year off to decide . . . I'm just going to . . . relax basically and pursue hobbies and things like that, just take some time to do things that I haven't had time to do for the last few years . . . [I don't want] to take a job that I don't enjoy or just to pay the bills. I don't want to get sucked into something that I don't like.
>
> (Olivia, RG, Non-WP, BA)

Shaila was from a widening participation background and also desired to discontinue academic study. However, she was clear that this would not be a temporary break. She did not enjoy studying at university and was not sure what her future would now hold. For Shaila, her planned year out in America sounded more like a means of distraction and escape:

> I don't know exactly what I want to do after I graduate . . . I don't want to carry on studying. I'm done with uni now, I'm definitely finished. I don't like studying, I don't want to do research or anything . . . hopefully I'm moving to America [for a year], that's the plan.
>
> (Shaila, RG, WP, BA)

A year out to get 'ordinary work' to earn money

This category of gap year was only reported by those who graduated in 2015. Taking a graduate gap year in a low paid job aligned with one of three specific goals. The first goal was taking 'ordinary work' in order to save money to fund postgraduate study in the future. All three of these students were from WP backgrounds (Post-1992: Claudia, Joanne; RG: Max).

Max had already been offered a place on a master's programme at the RG University, but he was waiting to see if he had won a bursary to fund the costs of postgraduate study. If this did not happen, his next option was to defer the place for one year and to find paid work to build up savings. For Max, building up financial reserves was crucial, but doing this via 'ordinary work' would be a last resort as a result of the financial support potentially provided by his University:

> If it turns out that I don't get funding [for postgraduate study] this year, I will take a gap year, and look for work and possibly with the [University] Internship Programme . . . I think finance is the number one thing in deciding what I'm going to do, it's just whether I can afford it or I can't. It absolutely decides what I'm doing next year.
>
> (Max, RG, WP, BA)

Building up savings was also essential for Claudia and Joanne if they were to take up postgraduate study (it is worth noting that the students interviewed were not aware of the imminent introduction of postgraduate loans). However, Claudia was not sure what postgraduate course to apply for:

> The priority is to get a few years just with ordinary work while I decide what postgraduate degree to take. I'm going to have to take one to follow a career path . . . but only after I manage to build up my savings . . . I'm already in my overdraft for this semester as a result for having to pay out for a new laptop and it's had a knock-on effect . . . I'm from a family that doesn't have much to support me financially so I've got to try to find a job as soon as possible and build up finance as soon as possible.
>
> (Claudia, Post-1992, WP, BA)

Joanne could have gone to university a year earlier, but had to do an extra year at college to re-take some of her examinations, so she ended up starting university the year that higher fees were introduced. This means that she ended up having two (unintended) years out:

> I need to do a counselling diploma when I graduate . . . if I take a year out to save, I can afford it. I'll get a temporary job for 12 months, hopefully one that is psychology related . . . but I'm not sure how likely this is . . . I feel confident about getting a temporary job, because I've worked since I was 15 . . . so I've had quite a lot of experience in those sorts of jobs.
>
> (Joanne, Post-1992, WP, BSc)

Joanne had a clearer idea of the postgraduate course she wanted to study. She knew she needed to save up money to fund this, but she also knew that getting employment in the field related to her future course would support her application. However, Joanne demonstrated that she felt more confident about getting an 'ordinary' low paid job during her year out.

The second goal identified in this category of graduate gap year was to save money for travelling purposes, although only one student in the sample fitted this type and she was from a WP background and graduated in 2015 from the Post-1992 University:

> I'm not thinking of starting my career for another two years. I just want to take a few years out and travel. I've been looking at internships in America, like doing receptionist jobs, hotel work, things like that. I'm not sure I'm confident enough to start my career yet so I'm hoping that travelling might spark something off in my brain . . . I've got to work in a retail or low paid job for a few months, maybe a year so I've got money saved up.
>
> (Sophie, Post-1992, WP, BA)

Sophie had the aspiration to travel to North America to try to gain confidence and career inspiration whilst working temporary contracts in the service industry over there, but she also needed to take another year out prior to travelling in order to build up financial savings.

The third goal identified in this category of graduate gap year was students wanting to increase the level of their bank balance. One of these students was graduating from the RG University and was from a WP background (Helen); the other five were graduating from the Post-1992 University. One was from a WP background (Veronika) and the others were from non-WP backgrounds (Jamie, Adelle, Mark, Dan).

Helen was keen to get full-time employment in the short term as a stopgap in order to earn a regular wage and was not discerning about what sort of job this might be. She explained that she was more confident applying for low paid retail jobs as this was where her current work experience lay:

> I've no idea what I want to do when I graduate . . . I've worked for a supermarket for four years now so I think that provides quite a good work

experience . . . I mean I could stay in my current job [for a year] if I didn't find anything after uni.

(Helen, RG, WP, BSc)

Veronika's priority was to take a year out to earn money in a low paid job, whilst gaining events management experience in her spare time. She was unable to gain this sector specific experience during her degree due to needing to earn money in her spare time to cover her university costs:

> I've got a part-time job at the minute [working in a restaurant] and I've just got to go full-time for a year when I graduate and look for opportunities to do events management roles as like my side job.
>
> (Veronika, Post-1992, WP, BA)

Jamie wanted a year out because he spent his final year focused on completing his coursework for his degree so he had not started to apply for jobs related to his degree and was under immediate financial pressure to find paid employment:

> I haven't actually applied for jobs because I've been focussing on finishing my [university] work . . . I feel confident about my skills and stuff . . . I've had jobs but it's not been like what I want to do for the rest of my life . . . I need to get earning money as soon as possible because I come from quite a poor family so, without the student loan, I'm going to be needing something immediately.
>
> (Jamie, Post-1992, Non-WP, BSc)

Mark had also not yet applied for graduate jobs in his field of study. He was planning to become an hourly paid care worker to ensure that he was earning money as soon as he graduates. He also expressed concern that his degree would not give him an advantage in the labour market and he communicated financial anxiety about the future in relation to living costs, housing and postgraduate study.

> I'm not [applying for graduate jobs] at the moment . . . I'm really just looking for, you know, care jobs maybe, just to get something coming in . . . I just fancy a year off from education . . . I don't feel like I've got as much of an advantage on those who don't go to university, as much as say ten years ago . . . I just don't think there's an availability of jobs. When I start looking at the costs of living away somewhere or paying for a house or paying for a Masters, then I start panicking.
>
> (Mark, Post-1992, Non-WP, BA)

Dan and Adelle were both focused on finding a way to save money in order to build up deposits to buy houses as soon as they graduated. In their interviews it felt like the initial graduate gap year was likely to extend into the future, particularly if a regular non-graduate wage provided the means to get onto the housing ladder. Dan craved security and planned to move back to the family home and get 'the first normal job' he could:

> Being realistic I see myself working in the first normal job that I can get my hands on . . . I haven't had a fixed job for the three years that I've been studying . . . now I'd like a fixed reliable wage . . . I need to keep my bank level up . . . The plan is to move back home to live with parents and find my first full-time job to save up for the deposit on a house . . . I just need to be secure at the moment rather than being a freelance creative kid.
>
> (Dan, Post-1992, Non-WP, BSc)

Adelle lived at home whilst studying so she wanted her graduate gap year to give her more independence from her family. She also communicated scepticism about the graduate job market. It is clear that her goal was to get into a financial position where she could buy a house:

> 'I'd like to work for a charity for a year . . . I need to start looking . . . I just want to start working now and live away from home and have a change . . . I feel like graduate jobs aren't all they're made out to be or they're not as common as they make out. So I'm like, where do I go from here, will it get me anywhere towards the deposit for a house?
>
> (Adelle, Post-1992, Non-WP, BSc)

Reflection on graduate gap years

It turns out that Holmlund et al.'s (2008) typology of pre-university gap years is a useful starting point when thinking about the nature and purpose of the phenomenon of graduate gap years. Indeed, three of their categories map neatly to those of graduate gap year takers (see Table 6.3).

However, the fourth graduate gap year category, as presented in this chapter, is quite different in nature and purpose to those described by Holmlund et al. and

Table 6.3 A comparison of pre-university and graduate gap year types

Pre-university gap year type (Holmlund et al. 2008)	*Graduate gap year type*
Those where individuals develop specific skills.	Those where individuals build up work experience.
Those where individuals learn about their broader preferences and/or abilities	Those where individuals work out their next steps.
Those where individuals take an extended break or holiday	Those where individuals take a break.
	Those where individuals get 'ordinary work' to earn money.

also Bradley and Waller (2018). It was only experienced by the graduates of 2015 (higher fees) and involved taking a graduate gap year in order to generate financial capital urgently, which prompts them to make compromises about the type of work they will pursue after graduation. This may suggest that graduate transitions in a climate of higher university fees and student debt are being marked by both austerity and precarity. It was notable that students from non-WP backgrounds at the RG institution did not experience this final category. Thus the feeling of financial stress was only an issue for students from WP backgrounds and for some of those at the Post-1992 institution from non-WP backgrounds, perhaps speaking to the anxieties they felt concerning the lower institutional status of their university.

As with pre-university gap years, this chapter demonstrates that the graduate gap year is not a homogeneous experience for young people and that it is also likely to be a classed experience. The issues raised by many of the graduate gap year takers in our 2015 sample appear compounded and more financially motivated than for those graduating in 2014. It is plausible that this may be an impact of higher education finance reform in England.

As noted earlier, Bradley and Waller (2018) have conducted complementary work in this area by investigating graduate transitions to work in a climate of lower university fees and student debt. They found that some of their graduate research participants were deferring their career straight after graduation (taking a break from education and competitive employment) and some were 'drifting', having left university (working out what to do with their lives). In particular, they highlight how those found to be 'drifting' – because of a lack of insider knowledge of the professional world and its cultural and social parameters – were more likely to be working-class women. In contrast our study with students across two HE finance systems found that both male and female graduates from widening participation (RG & Post-1992) and non-widening participation backgrounds (Post-1992 only) were sharing narratives of postponement in relation to transitions to the graduate labour market.

However, the fine-grained qualitative data analysis further suggested that the emergent concept of the graduate gap year might extend, rather than lessen, social advantage for some. For example, Peter, David and Olly all look to be benefitting from having pro-actively secured graduate gap years that will involve them undertaking graduate work experience in the same field as their degree. But this opportunity is only possible because they can draw on the financial support of their families. For others like Annie, Vazir and Veronika their narratives of postponement come across as riskier, harder and less certain to lead to a graduate job in the medium term. There is a concern that such decisions and events might have long-lasting, disadvantaging effects for the individual development and progress of some graduates. Furthermore, data from our sample suggested that some students were preparing themselves to have not just one year out after graduation, with some expecting 2–3 years of postponement and uncertainty (e.g., Mark, Shaila, Claudia and Joanne). Elias et al. (1999) found that the graduates of earlier HE systems in England took about three years to settle into a

Graduate gap years 83

chosen graduate direction. However, a concern raised by our study is that some groups of students are extending this time to 'settle' by taking a graduate gap year/s. Further longitudinal research is now needed to investigate whether some graduates end up being disadvantaged taking different types of graduate gap year.

Atkins and Tummons (2017) argue that policymakers are resistant to the idea that transitions are not ladder-like and unproblematic, but the findings presented in this chapter about different types of graduate gap years add further weight to the argument that not all graduates are experiencing smooth transitions out of university. The likelihood is that some of these transitions characterised by uncertainty and postponement immediately after graduation will lead to longer-term inequality, which threatens to increase social stratification. Universities and policy-makers must be vigilant when it comes to the phenomenon of graduate gap years and consider interventions that could decrease precarity in graduate transition pathways.

References

Abrahams, J. (2016). "Honourable mobility or shameless entitlement? Habitus and graduate employment", *British Journal of Sociology of Education*, *38*(5): 625–640.

Arundel, R., and Lennartz, C. (2015). *Returning to the Parental Home: Boomerang Moves of Younger Adults and the Welfare Regime Context*. Working Paper, Centre for Urban Studies, University of Amsterdam, pp. 1–36.

Arundel, R., and Ronald, R. (2015). "Parental co-residence, shared living and emerging adulthood in Europe: Semi-dependent housing across welfare regime and housing system contexts", *Journal of Youth Studies*, *19*(7): 885–905.

Atkins, L., and Tummons, J. (2017). *Precarious Youth Transitions to the Labour Market: What Difference Does a Degree Make?* Paper presented at the British Educational Research Association Annual Conference, University of Sussex, Brighton, 5–7 September 2017.

Birch, E., and Miller, P. (2007). "The characteristics of 'Gap-Year' students and their tertiary academic outcomes", *The Economic Record*, *83*(262): 329–344.

Bradley, H., and Waller, R. (2018). "Gendered and classed graduate transitions to work: how the unequal playing field is constructed, maintained and experienced", In: Waller, R., Ingram, N., and Ward, M.R.M (Eds.), *Higher Education and Social Inequalities: University Admissions, Experiences and Outcomes*, Abingdon, OX: Routledge.

Crawford, C., and Cribb, J. (2012). *Gap Year Takers: Uptake, Trends and Long Term Outcomes*, London: Department for Education, Research Report DFE-RR252.

Elias, P., McKnight, A., Pitcher, J., Purcell, K., and Simm, C. (1999). *Moving On: Graduate Careers Three Years After Graduation*. Manchester: HECSU.

Holdsworth, C. (2015). "The cult of experience: Standing out from the crowd in an era of austerity", *Area*, *49*(3): 296–302.

Holmlund, B., Liu, Q., and Nordstrom Skans, O. (2008). "Mind the gap? Estimating the effects of postponing higher education", *Oxford Economic Papers*, *60*(4): 683–710.

Howie, L., and Campbell, P. (2016). "Guerrilla selfhood: Imagining young people's entrepreneurial futures", *Journal of Youth Studies*, *19*(7): 906–920.

Jones, A. (2003). *Review of Gap Year Provision, London: Department for Education and Skills*, Research Report RR555.

Nieman, M. (2010). "The perception of higher education students of the influence of their gap year on their personal development", *Tydskrif vir Geesteswetenskappe*, *50*(1).

O'Shea, J. (2011). "Delaying the academy: A gap year education", *Teaching in Higher Education*, *16*(5): 565–577.

Stehlik, T. (2010). "Mind the gap: School leaver aspirations and delayed pathways to further and higher education", *Journal of Education and Work*, *23*(4): 363–376.

Vigurs, K., Jones, S., and Harris, D. (2016). *Higher Fees, Higher Debts: Greater Expectations of Graduate Futures?* Research Report. London: SRHE. http://bit.ly/SRHEgradfutures.

Vigurs, K., Jones, S., Everitt, J., and Harris, D. (forthcoming). "Higher fees, higher debts: Unequal graduate transitions in England?", In: Riddell, S., Weedon, E., and Whittaker, S. (Eds), *Higher Education, Funding and Access*. Bingley: Emerald.

7 Geography, mobility and graduate career development

Rosie Alexander

Introduction

The issue of geographical space is often overlooked in discussions of graduate employment and the graduate labour market. In practice, graduates are either assumed to be a highly mobile population with equal access to employment opportunities or there is an ideological imperative that graduates *should* be mobile in order to gain access to national and international labour markets. Using a case study of graduates from two specific communities in the UK (the Orkney and Shetland Islands), this chapter identifies how the career, migration and employment decisions of graduates can have a complex interrelation. As a result, it is proposed that careers and employability provision in UK higher education needs to much more fully engage with issues of geography and mobility. Two potential positions for higher education staff to adopt are sketched out: 'mobiliser' or 'integrator'. These positions are marked by different ideological stand-points in terms of how far mobility for the sake of career advancement is promoted to students.

Higher education and mobility

Education has long been associated with social mobility and geographical mobility. The idea that education and social mobility are interrelated has been widely discussed (see, for example, Burke, 2016). Although geographical mobility and education have been less widely discussed, in a particularly important piece of work in Atlantic Canada, Corbett (2007) has suggested that through engagement in, and success in, the schooling system students from rural and remote communities 'learn to leave'. Mobility for the pursuit of higher education has also resulted in concerns of many smaller communities in the UK and internationally about youth depopulation as young people leave to pursue further study (see, for example, Highlands and Islands Enterprise, 2015a and 2015b).

The association of mobility and higher education has been explored by Finn (2017), who discusses the historical tradition within the UK of participation in higher education being based on residential mobility. Finn's focus is particularly on how the association of mobility and higher education impacts on (largely working-class) students who choose to study from home, noting how they are positioned unfavourably on the wrong side of the binary of mobile/immobile, and local/non-local students. The association of class and mobility draws together issues of geographical and social mobility, identifying how higher education narratives are predominantly both middle class and mobile.

Following Finn's work an interesting question is raised about the way that students from working-class or less mobile backgrounds experience higher education environments. Considering class, it has been widely discussed how working-class students are expected to 'adapt' to their environments, and how simply through engaging with higher education they are expected to experience social mobility into the middle classes. As Burke (2016) has identified, this has led to a tradition whereby there has been a significant focus on helping disadvantaged students *access* higher education, but very limited focus on how to support students while at university. It could be argued that there is a similar tradition in terms of geographical mobility, with some focus on increasing recruitment from disadvantaged post-code areas, for example, but with little focus on geographical mobility beyond entry to higher education (with students simply expected to 'become' more mobile through engagement with higher education).

With graduate mobility positioned as the 'norm', mobility becomes almost a moral imperative, something graduates *should* possess in order to access the full range of graduate jobs. Pennington et al. (2013) state: 'Graduates need to consider where their best long-term interests lie and plan accordingly; this might entail considering jobs some distance from home or even moving closer to where more graduate jobs exist'. However, despite the mobile narratives of higher education, research has shown that graduate migration pathways are actually 'complex, non-linear and precarious' in the five years after graduation, and with the parental home remaining a 'crucial safety net' (Sage et al., 2012: 1). Further, research from Ball (2015) has also shown how only 18% of graduates are in regional locations different from their home or university regions at six months after graduation.

With evidence showing that graduate mobility is complex, and with evidence that graduate labour markets are geographically distributed, it is perhaps unsurprising that employment outcomes also differ for graduates displaying different migration trajectories (Ball, 2015). Therefore although higher education narratives may be based on an assumption of student and graduate mobility, it is apparent that geography and mobility are complex issues that impact on graduate employment. With graduate employment and employability being of such significance within the current UK Higher Education landscape (see Artess et al., 2017), this raises a question about whether universities and their careers services need to take greater consideration of issues of geography and migration.

How careers services and professionals can work with issues of geography and migration has not received a great amount of attention in terms of higher education (partly perhaps because of the assumed association of higher education and mobility). However, in terms of school careers provision, research conducted in schools in coastal Kent specifically addressed geographical considerations, and identified how teachers and careers advisers tended to adopt one of two positions: mobiliser or community activist (Shepherd and Hooley, 2016). Where mobilisers encouraged students to look beyond their communities for opportunities for progression, community activists were keen to find and 'promote opportunities that are available locally and develop the local economy' (*ibid:* 17). The difference between the two roles is predominantly between mobilisers with a 'strong commitment to the individuals that they are working with' and activists who have a 'strong attachment to the local community' (*ibid*: 17). The position of community activists in this research is particularly interesting, because this position questions the ideological assumption that mobility and individual pursuit of higher status/higher paid work is necessarily a good thing (Alexander, 2017). Instead community activists recognize that there may be valid reasons for remaining in a community, both potentially in terms of supporting the community, and in terms of making a positive choice around the lifestyle benefits that may come from prioritizing living in a certain location (Alexander and Hooley, 2018).

For universities and their careers services beginning to question the role of geography and migration in graduate career paths may be necessary in order to work more effectively and ethically with individual students. However, equally it may be important for Higher Education institutions themselves (particularly those based in more remote or marginal areas) who are measured according to the 'employability' of their students. This is clear from the research of Savage et al. (2015), who, when analysing the percentage of 'elite' graduates from different universities, found a distinct weighting towards universities based in and around London. This was mirrored by analysis of the levels of economic and cultural capital graduates possessed which was also weighted towards graduates from London based institutions. On the other side with low cultural and economic capital are 'a group of new universities mainly in the English provinces, where graduates are low in both economic and cultural capital' (Savage et al., 2015: 253). What this suggests is that when considering employability, alongside divisions of universities into different mission groups, there may also be an important geographical axis of division between universities. Just as where graduates are presumed to be mobile in Higher Education rhetoric, so institutions are understood to exist somehow out of space and place. This does not recognize, for example, that opportunities for work experience, placements and paid work for students are dependent on the local and regional economies of the areas in which their universities are based.

Case study: Orkney and Shetland

To explore the relationship of geography, migration, higher education and graduate career paths further the next section of this chapter will consider a case study: the experience of graduates from two specific communities in the UK – the Orkney and Shetland Islands. These islands have been the field for two research projects, one looking at the experience of graduates living in the islands (Alexander, 2013), and one longitudinal research project looking at the experiences of higher education graduates originally domiciled in the islands and their education and employment pathways (Alexander, 2016). The first of these projects involved focus groups and interviews with a total of fourteen recent graduates who were living in Orkney. The second of these projects is an ongoing piece of PhD research which has involved interviewing 23 students who were domiciled in Orkney or Shetland prior to entering higher education at the point of graduation and then again one year later. Alongside the qualitative data collected from the interviews, the project has also involved analyzing existing data for all full-time first degree graduates from Orkney and Shetland from the Destinations of Leavers from Higher Education (DLHE) survey for the period 2008/9–2012/13 (Alexander, 2015). The researcher in these projects (and author of this chapter) does herself live in Orkney, and work as a careers adviser, but although she was born in Shetland, she grew up in Cornwall and therefore maintains something of both insider and outsider perspective.

As archipelagos Orkney and Shetland both contain approximately 16–20 inhabited islands and populations of approximately 21–25,000. Orkney and Shetland provide a valuable case study because as island communities 16km and 475km north-east of mainland Scotland (respectively) issues of geographical location are highlighted. Importantly, although there are of course pockets of deprivation, the islands are relatively prosperous with very low unemployment rates in both island groups (Highlands and Islands Enterprise, 2014a, 2014b). And although salaries in Orkney are slightly below Scottish averages (Highlands and Islands Enterprise, 2011a), salaries in Shetland are higher, largely due to the 'high share of employment in relatively high paying (if occasionally erratic) sectors notably the oil industry and fishing' (Highlands and Islands Enterprise, 2011b). This means that in this particular community issues of remote location do not correspond with issues of deprivation as research in some other geographically isolated communities has found, for example in coastal Kent (Shepherd and Hooley, 2016; Reid and Westergaard, 2017).

Within the island groups there is significant concern about the migration of young people away from the islands for the purposes of education or employment (Highlands and Islands Enterprise, 2015a, 2015b). And indeed although both Orkney and Shetland have a campus of the University of the Highlands and Islands, the research projects show that for most students leaving for higher education is something that is assumed, something that is 'common sense' (Alexander, 2016). As a result many students refer to 'going south' and 'going to university' interchangeably (Alexander, 2013). The association of mobility and academic success in the first research project was so strong, that one student reported that staying at home would be a mark of 'failure' (*ibid*: 39). In the second research project, students who had stayed at home to study did not offer such an extreme critical perspective, but both presented clear practical justifications for staying at home (in terms of work and family reasons), which suggested a feeling that they needed to justify their choices.

Considering the destinations of Orkney and Shetland students progressing to higher education, it is clear that students from the islands are not selecting equally from all Scottish Higher Education institutions, with Aberdeen being a popular destination (Alexander, 2015). Exploring students' preferences, the appeal of Aberdeen was often that it allowed students to leave home but not to go too far. In addition their familiarity of the city was often identified as important – as the city is a major port for ferries to both islands, most students had spent time in the city. In addition because of the ferry links, historical patterns of migration, and the importance of the oil and gas industry in all three locations, students often had friends and family based in the city. Even when students chose to go elsewhere 'familiarity' remained an important factor, with some students choosing different locations depending on their personal histories (Alexander, 2016).

Considering migration choices at the point of graduation, students commonly report a confidence in their ability to move anywhere. This suggests that their experience in higher education has indeed led them to develop a mobile sense of themselves and their futures. However, analysis of the actual destinations of students in the research project show quite a different picture – being broadly consistent with statistics which show that six months after graduation almost 40% of graduates have returned to (or remain in) Orkney or Shetland (Alexander, 2015). In addition it is clear that those who are elsewhere are not distributed around the country (or internationally) but Aberdeen and Aberdeenshire remain a popular location with 14% of Orkney and Shetland graduates based in the region (*ibid*). Therefore although students 'feel' more mobile, they are not necessarily (all) enacting this mobility.

Considering the employment outcomes of graduates in terms of their locations, the statistics show that although the professional level employment of graduates from the islands is comparable with national graduate rates, those back in the islands have a rate a few percentage points lower (*ibid*). It is notable that a high proportion of graduates working in nursing or midwifery, or education (approximately half) had returned or stayed in the islands six months after graduation (*ibid*). There is some evidence statistically therefore that the labour market in the islands is impacting on the kinds of work that graduates undertake (*ibid*). Turning to the qualitative research findings to understand the movements of graduates, graduates described a range of factors being important for their decision about where to live – with employment certainly one of the factors, but with being at least 'close enough' to their island homes also very important. Home was mentioned as important primarily for family considerations, but issues of identity, social and cultural context and physical characteristics were also mentioned (Alexander, 2016). The positive attachments to their home islands seems replicated in attitudes of young people generally to the islands, with recent research conducted with young people in the islands finding that there were 'very strong and positive feelings amongst young people from [the islands] about the place in which they live'(Highlands and Islands Enterprise, 2015a: 32; 2015b: 32).

Alongside these early decisions after graduation, location remained a consideration for graduates when considering their future career paths. Indeed in many cases it became more important, with graduates commonly visualizing a return to home for raising children, or, if necessary, to be closer to ageing relatives.

90 Rosie Alexander

This was a difficult topic for graduates to consider, being aware that this would depend on a number of factors including how their career progressed, what their priorities were at the time, the health of ageing relatives, whether they had a partner who was willing to relocate, and indeed (in the case of returning to raise children) whether they could have children at all (Alexander, 2016). What this demonstrates is that the decision to stay, leave or return is not made at one point (the point of going to university) but is revisited often. This perspective offers a significant counterpoint to the narrative of 'youth depopulation' that characterizes much of the regional development literature of the islands. Young people are not simply leaving for education or employment never to return again, but in most cases retain an attachment to the community and are open to the possibility of returning.

The potential challenge of a later return to the islands depending on how a graduate's career had progressed demonstrates the challenge of the specific labour market of the islands. It is possible both that over time graduates may find themselves in forms of work that are simply not available in the islands, but equally it is also possible that they will not have developed the specific skills needed to thrive in their island communities. So, graduates who have made their career in Orkney reported different skills may be valued in Orkney than in larger urban centres – things like enterprise skills, problem solving and creative thinking and so on (Alexander, 2013). This finding is consistent with Crew's findings (reported in chapter four of this book) on the importance of localized forms of career skills or career capital in terms of language skills in the North Wales labour market.

Responding to issues of geography and mobility in higher education

The case study of graduates from Orkney and Shetland highlights some of the complexities of graduate migration and employment. Despite a prevailing assumption of graduate mobility, students from these island groups are not free from the constraints of space, choosing freely where to live to pursue their careers; instead, familiar locations remain significant destinations. It is striking that graduates themselves seem to internalize a narrative of mobility, describing themselves as potentially highly mobile, at the same time as explaining their personal choice to remain in familiar locations. This finding is reminiscent of findings from Burke (2016) and Holton and Finn (2017) whereby students adopt and articulate neoliberal narratives of personal choice and responsibility, even where their outcomes are heavily influenced by structural factors (e.g., class). This creates a social justice issue where social and structural problems are individualized, so that the individual becomes responsible for their own success or otherwise (Sultana, 2014; Hooley and Sultana, 2016). In terms of migration, if location becomes viewed as an entirely personal choice by students, then it potentially blinds them to structural issues and structural inequalities caused by geographical differences in the labour market. Within universities, if we exist in a context which emphasises

Geography, mobility and graduate career development   91

graduate mobility, and see immobility as a result of personal graduate *choice*, then we may become drawn into neglecting to consider geographical issues in terms of strategies and services designed to support students.

In terms of potential responses to issues of geography and migration for higher education students and graduates, I would suggest that there are two possible positions that institutions, careers services and staff can take. These are adapted from Shepherd and Hooley's (2016) mobiliser and community activist positions, but with the position of community activist adapted to suit a university context. The adaptation recognizes that for universities, students may be drawn both from a local community and communities some distance from the university, so a role which recognizes the importance of place will not just recognize the importance of the immediate locality. In addition, the key difference between a mobiliser or integrator position is not between their commitment to individuals *or* their communities, but rather how they feel an individual's best interests may be served.

> **Mobilisers**: believe that students' best interests lie in breaking ties with their local communities and freely pursuing the best career opportunities. They recognize the challenge of mobility but believe in building confidence and skills to enable students to become more mobile.
>
> **Integrators**: believe in a holistic notion of career, understanding that paid work is only part of the picture, and that factors such as family life, community and geographical location are important. Integrators challenge the notion that career success can be measured by pay or status; they encourage students to integrate their career decisions within their wider life choices.

These are ideological positions, and fundamental to the difference between mobilisers and integrators is how far they challenge neo-liberal and higher education norms about mobility and individualism. Mobilisers fundamentally believe in the importance of 'raising aspiration'; for them, attachment to place can hold an individual back, and in order to help individuals to 'reach their potential' mobilisers have an almost moral duty to challenge an individual's spatial restrictions. In contrast integrators question the primacy given to the individual, and career status and income in neo-liberal norms. Integrators recognize the importance of quality of life, family and community, and may adopt a fully inclusive definition of 'career' that encompasses all parts of life, not just paid work. There is a recognition that students, exposed to dominant notions of highly mobile individualized career paths, may internalize these notions, finding it difficult to conceptualise 'successful' careers in any other light, and integrators may feel an ethical or moral duty to question these dominant neo-liberal norms. The fear of integrators is that students may follow pathways that they think will lead them to career satisfaction and yet not find this satisfaction, having compromised too much along the way.

Integrator and mobiliser positions are largely ideological, and, I would argue, the potential of either position, as yet, has not been fully explored by careers and employability services and staff in the majority of cases (because of a general lack of focus on issues of geography and mobility in the sector). In terms of practical implications, a mobilising position would recognize the challenges of mobility but seek to address these by, for example, assisting with practical support for mobility, and building confidence and networks to enable mobility. Alongside one to one advice services that incorporate support for mobility, mobilising approaches from a service and institution level may mean instituting opportunities for students to build up mobility experience (e.g., exchange programmes, study trips, etc.) and for building up social connections in other parts of the country, which may support later mobility (e.g., mentoring schemes, networking through social media, etc). Although schemes like this are relatively common for increasing international mobility (Artess et al., 2017; Diamond et al., 2011), the use of similar approaches to increase *domestic* mobility have been less widely discussed.

A wider scope still is important for services and staff taking on an integrator position. Integrators consider career choices alongside other lifestyle choices which are perceived as equally, and potentially more, important. Issues of purpose or meaning not just in career terms but in wider life-path terms may need to be addressed. This brings careers services into much closer relationship to other student development and student support functions and services, such as counselling. Careers information, education and guidance are likely to have a much wider scope in terms of supporting holistic student development. In addition there would be a role for careers education in terms of facilitating students to critique dominant neo-liberal notions of careers and employability and to develop a critical and reflexive stance to their own career progression (Alexander, 2017; Irving and Malik, 2005).

There are practical challenges for adopting either the mobiliser or integrator position, as both involve an expanded remit for careers and employability services. This raises a question about how far services and individual advisers are supported to increase the scope of their work. What resources are available, for example, for supporting students to build confidence and experience with domestic mobility? Do advisers feel able, within their professional boundaries, to explore an individual's personal life and their desires beyond immediate career and employment? How far do the resources we use overlook geographical considerations in career choice?

There are also significant ethical considerations in adopting either position. In many ways the difference between mobilisers and integrators is mirrored in the orientations of advisers to other forms of diversity – for example, class and gender. With class, questions have been raised about whether when we encourage students to become part of middle-class university life, do we risk creating a double loss, a 'risk of being caught between the "old" and the "new," no longer feeling they belong to one, but not (yet) accepted in the other' (Lehmann, 2013: 12)? Or can students find ways to hold on to their working-class identities, becoming 'fugitives' in higher education (Loveday, 2015). In terms of gender there have long been questions of whether we should be encouraging more girls into male dominated careers and to follow career 'norms' which are implicitly male or whether we should be developing new models and theories appropriate for women (Bimrose, 2001). The difference between mobilisers and integrators could be seen as adopting different orientations to whether we should be encouraging achievement in terms of the 'norm', or whether it is more ethical to be seeking alternative models of career development and careers practice.

Although the two positions represent fundamentally different ideological positions, in practice it is likely that careers and employability services and staff may switch between positions depending on the students they are working with. Indeed, as career development and geography are inextricably intertwined it is highly likely that staff are already engaging explicitly or implicitly in issues around geography and mobility, and find themselves adopting a version of either the mobiliser or the integrator position. Most advisers, for example, may have spoken to students about opportunities in distant places, only for a student to then volunteer their fear of moving, or their wish to remain closer to romantic partners, family or friends. Given the association of mobility with life course in this research (young people move, older adults 'settle down') it is perhaps particularly likely that staff may use a life-course frame for their work, adopting a mobiliser approach with younger adults and an integrator approach with older adults. However, given the lack of focus on geography and mobility in the current higher education landscape it is quite possible that staff and services are engaging in these conversations without having the resources, support or, in some cases, the knowledge to support them. Indeed an even greater risk is that without support, resources and training staff and services may not recognize geographical issues, and that students, given their internalization of 'mobile', individualized graduate career narratives, may not volunteer them either, meaning that they may not be addressed at all.

Conclusions

This chapter has explored the role of geography and mobility in terms of graduate transition to the workplace. Two potential positions that institutions, services and advisers may adopt in working with geographical issues have been sketched out. Although these represent positions that may already be being adopted to some extent, especially by individual advisers when faced with clear issues of geography and mobility, the full implications of each position involve an extension of the scope and remit of most higher education careers and employability services as they currently exist. Some indication of what these positions would look like if they were fully realised has been sketched out. However, before the full potential of either position is fully explored, and before the ethical issues implicit in these positions can be explored, we must start by increasing our geographical awareness and our understanding. Policy makers, universities, services and staff need to start treating geography and mobility as important issues in terms of graduate transition, and further work is needed to enhance our understandings of this under-researched area.

Bibliography

Alexander, R. (2013). "'Here You Have to be a Bit More Fluid and Willing to do Different Things': Graduate career development in rural communities", *Journal of the National Institute for Career Education and Counselling*, *31*: 36–42.

Alexander, R. (2015). "A case study of higher education pathways of rural students", *Graduate Market Trends Autumn*, *2015*, (online) available from: www.hecsu.ac.uk/current_projects_graduate_market_trends.htm (accessed 15 January 2014).

Alexander, R. (2016). "Migration, education and employment: Socio-cultural factors in shaping individual decisions and economic outcomes in Orkney and Shetland", *Island Studies Journal*, *11*(1): 177–192.

Alexander, R. (2017). "Social justice and geographical location in careers guidance", In: Hooley, T., Sultana, R., and Thomsen, R. (Eds.), *Career Guidance for Social Justice: Contesting Neoliberalism*. London: Routledge.

Alexander, R., and Hooley, T. (2018). "*The Place(s) of Careers: The Role of Geography in Career Development*", In: Cohen-Scali, V., Rossier, J., and Nota, L. (Eds.), *New Perspectives on Career Counseling and Guidance in Europe: Building Careers in Changing and Diverse Societies*. Cham: Springer International Publishing.

Artess, J., Hooley, T., and Mellors-Bourne, R. (2017). *Employability: A Review of the Literature 2012–2016, A Report for the Higher Education Academy*. York: Higher Education Academy. (online) available from: www.heacademy.ac.uk/knowledge-hub/employability-review-literature-2012-2016.

Ball, C. (2015). *Loyals, Stayers, Returners and Incomers: Graduate Migration Patterns*. Manchester. HECSU.

Bimrose, J. (2001). "Girls and women: Challenges for careers guidance practice", *British Journal of Guidance and Counselling*, *29*(1): 79–94.

Burke, C. (2016). *Culture, Capitals and Graduate Futures: Degrees of Class*. London: Routledge.

Corbett, M. (2007). *Learning to Leave: The Irony of Schooling in a Coastal Community*. Halifax: Fernwood Publishing.

Diamond, A., Walkley, L., Forbes, P., Hughes, T., and Sheen, J. (2011). "Global graduates: Global graduates into global leaders", *CIHE/AGR/CFE*. (online) available from: www.ncub.co.uk/reports/global-graduates-into-global-leaders.html.

Finn, K. (2017). "Multiple, relational and emotional mobilities: Understanding student mobilities in higher education as more than 'Staying Local' and 'Going Away'", *British Educational Research Journal*, *43*(4): 743–758.

Highlands and Islands Enterprise (2011a). 'Area profile for Orkney', *Highlands and Islands Enterprise*.

Highlands and Islands Enterprise (2011b). 'Area profile for Shetland', *Highlands and Islands Enterprise*.

Highlands and Islands Enterprise (2014a). 'Orkney area profile', *Highlands and Islands Enterprise*. (online) available from: www.hie.co.uk/regional-information/economic-reports-and-research/archive/area-and-settlement-profiles-2014.html (accessed August 2017).

Highlands and Islands Enterprise (2014b). 'Shetland area profile', *Highlands and Islands Enterprise*. (online) available from: www.hie.co.uk/regional-information/economic-reports-and-research/archive/area-and-settlement-profiles-2014.html (accessed August 2017).

Highlands and Islands Enterprise (2015a). *Our Next Generation: Young People in Shetland Attitudes and Aspirations*. (online) available from: www.hie.co.uk/

regional-information/economic-reports-and-research/archive/young-people-and-the-highlands-and-islands – attitudes-and-aspirations-research.html.

Highlands and Islands Enterprise (2015b). *Our Next Generation: Young People in Orkney Attitudes and Aspirations.* (online) available from: www.hie.co.uk/regional-information/economic-reports-and-research/archive/young-people-and-the-highlands-and-islands – attitudes-and-aspirations-research.html.

Holton, M., and Finn, K. (2017). "Being-in-motion: The everyday (gendered and classed) embodied mobilities for UK university students who commute", *Mobilities.* (online early view) available from: www.tandfonline.com/doi/full/10.1080/17450101.2017.1331018?src=recsys.

Hooley, T., and Sultana, R. (2016). "Career guidance for social justice", *Journal of the National Institute for Career Education and Counselling*, 36: 2–11.

Irving, B.A., and Malik, B. (2005). "Introduction", In: Irving, B.A., and Malik, B. (Eds.), *Critical Reflections on Career Education and Guidance: Promoting Social Justice Within a Global Economy.* London: Routledge.

Lehmann, W. (2013). "Habitus transformation and hidden injuries: Successful working-class university students", *Sociology of Education*, 87(1): 1–15.

Loveday, V. (2015). "Working-class participation, middle-class aspiration? Value, upward mobility and symbolic indebtedness in higher education", *The Sociological Review*, 63: 570–588.

Pennington, M., Mosley, E., and Sinclair, R. (2013). "AGCAS/AGR graduate success project: An investigation of graduate transitions, social mobility and the HEAR", *AGCAS.* (online) available from: www.agcas.org.uk/articles/694-Graduate-Success-Project-AGCAS-findings-launched.

Reid, H., and Westergaard, J. (2017). "'Oh I do Like to be Beside the Seaside': Opportunity structures for four un/underemployed young people living in English Coastal Towns", *British Journal of Guidance and Counselling*, 45(3): 341–355.

Sage, J., Evandrou, M., and Falkingham, J. (2012). The complex migration pathways of UK graduates: CPC briefing paper 9. ESRC Centre for Population Change, UK. (online) available from: http://www.cpc.ac.uk/publications/cpc_briefing_papers.php.

Savage, M., Cunningham, N., Devine, F., Friedman, S., Laurison, D., McKenzie, L., Miles, A., Snee, H., and Wakeling, P. (2015). *Social Class in the 21st Century: A Pelican Introduction* UK: Pelican.

Shepherd, C., and Hooley, T. (2016). *'They've Got their Backs to the Sea': Careers Work in Kent's Coastal Schools.* Derby: International Centre for Guidance Studies, University of Derby. (online) available from: http://derby.openrepository.com/derby/handle/10545/620945.

Sultana, R. (2014). "Pessimism of the intellect, optimism of the will? Troubling the relationship between career guidance and social justice", *International Journal for Educational and Vocational Guidance*, 14(1): 5–19.

8 Learning to be employable

Jane Artess

Introduction

Futuretrack was a six-year longitudinal study tracking the progression of the 2006 cohort of UCAS (Universities and Colleges Admissions Service) applicants through higher education (HE) and into the labour market conducted by the Institute for Employment Research at the University of Warwick on behalf of Higher Education Careers Services Unit (HECSU). Data was collected at four stages, the first as prospective students made applications to HE in 2006, the second approximately eighteen months later, a third in 2009 and 2010 as most were approaching their final examinations and the fourth in 2012 between eighteen and thirty months post-graduation, when most of the cohort had either entered the labour market or were undertaking postgraduate study/training (Purcell et al., 2012).

This chapter presents findings about the relationship between Futuretrack respondents' participation in employability-related activities and indicators of their subsequent job satisfaction, optimism about their long term career prospects and skills development. Findings are contextualised via a commentary on the rationale for employability-related activities in HE, including the potential impact of the Teaching Excellence and Student Outcomes Framework (TEF) on policy and practice in this area.

Relationship between higher education and employment

Enhancing future employment prospects is one of the main reasons to enter higher education; learning to become employable has become a primary focus of participation in HE. In the Futuretrack study Purcell et al. (2008) found that accepted applicants' top three reasons for applying to HE were 'to enable me to get a good job', ' it is part of my longer-term career plans' and because 'I want to study the particular subject or course'. Within popular discourse, a major value of HE is often framed as the capacity of graduates to secure employment that is compatible with their higher level skills and knowledge; this leads some commentators to see graduate employment outcomes as the primary benefit of participation in HE and universities' purpose to 'build a bridge of skills across which every student, rich or poor, can walk towards a better life' (Farrell, 2011). Higher education providers (HEPs) have a vested interest in their graduates becoming employable as employment outcomes are a key metric in judgements on their success.

The relationship between higher education and employment has been consolidated over many years by public policy imperatives that determine HEPs' performance on a range of key indicators including graduate employment. Graduate employment was measured by data reported to the Higher Education Statistics Agency (HESA) via the Destinations of Leavers from Higher Education (DLHE) surveys (HESA, 2017a). The DLHE is comprised of two self-reported graduate surveys: the first is a census of HE qualifiers at approximately six months following graduation undertaken by each HEP, and the second is a sample survey at approximately three years following graduation (Longitudinal DLHE) undertaken by an independent survey contractor. Data collected via the DLHE survey have been widely used, for example, by the media to rank institutions, by HEPs to compare graduate employment outcomes by subject, by other stakeholders to provide overview of the graduate labour market landscape (HECSU, 2016), and DLHE data is used in online information to prospective students such as the Unistats website. All this is about to change.

Following an extensive review, from 2018 the DLHE is to be replaced with a survey of Graduate Outcomes (GO) to be undertaken by an independent survey contractor fifteen months following graduation. The GO survey will capture occupational and further education and training activity as the DLHE but importantly will also aim to capture the 'graduate voice' as exemplified by questions aimed to tease out: how meaningful or important graduates feel their activity to be, whether they are using the skills they gained from their qualification in their current activity, and how they are progressing towards their future goals (HESA, 2017b). The GO survey will provide a more nuanced understanding of what counts as graduate success than its predecessor and will sow the seeds of a better understanding of graduates' satisfaction with their employment and training outcomes.

As the result of enabling legislation (DBIS, 2015a) government departments are now able to link data on prior educational achievement and HESA data on leavers and continuing students with taxation and benefits data to produce Longitudinal Education Outcomes (LEO) which will show graduates' employment and training activity at one, three and five years following graduation (DfE, 2017). Whilst LEO data are currently considered 'experimental' and LEO is not (yet) a key performance indicator of HE, by using existing administrative data and obviating the need for additional surveys of graduates, it is likely that a future version of LEO will provide the earnings assessment of Graduate Outcomes.

Teaching excellence and student outcomes framework

These recent developments in the capture of graduate employment outcomes data are important for HEPs as the TEF assessment uses DLHE data as a key metric within a process to confer Gold, Silver or Bronze awards on HE providers. Whilst much controversy surrounds the TEF as a measure of teaching excellence, the progress of graduates into the labour market remains a key priority for policy-makers, institutions and graduates to such extent that the inclusion of employ-ment metrics in an approach to the evaluation of teaching appears to have gone largely unchallenged.

Currently participation in the TEF is voluntary and almost all universities sub-mitted evidence for the first publicly-reported TEF assessment in 2017. The TEF was introduced (DBIS, 2015b) to evaluate and recognise excellent teaching over and above existing quality assurance mechanisms and alongside a proposal that providers that scored highly would be able to vary the level of tuition fees upwards in line with inflation. Recently the Government announced a freeze on the level of tuition fees, thus removing the financial incentive for HEPs to participate in the TEF whilst at the same time reinforcing the relationship between HE and employment and acknowledging that graduates make substantial financial invest-ment in their future earnings by their participation in HE (Theresa May, 2017).

Arguably the most controversial feature of the TEF is that it does not measure teaching excellence at all, and the proposal to re-name it the Teaching Excellence and Student Outcomes Framework (whilst retaining the acronym TEF) better reflects its use of proxy measures of excellence such as student satisfaction, reten-tion, learning gain and employment outcomes. Commentators have suggested that naming TEF the student experience framework might have been more apt; argued that TEF is part of a long-term process of marketisation of HE which under-emphasises the relationship between teaching and research; and warns that TEF could risk unintended consequences for the recruitment of international students (Bagshaw, 2017, Neary, 2016, Bothwell, 2017, Porter, 2017).

Consideration of a range of metrics forms the first stage of the TEF assess-ment process; HEPs also submit narrative evidence which is used by the assess-ment panel to revise the initial score of Gold, Silver or Bronze. Such contextual information takes account of a broad spread of factors such as the geographic location, student characteristics, extra-curricular activities, student support, etc. Early evaluation of the TEF assessment process (Beech, 2017) has identified that institutions that were successful in getting their initial score revised upwards were those who provided persuasive narratives including evidence of a strategic and continuing focus on employability programmes and careers support.

As it is likely that employability provision will be further developed in order to maximise TEF outcomes it would not be unreasonable to infer that the process of evaluating teaching excellence through the TEF is set to have continuing and increasing influence on the way HEPs plan for and deliver employability support.

Employment-related activities in higher education

Higher education providers have responded vigorously to the need to support students' transition into working life. This is despite HEPs being unable to control the operation of graduate labour market, the vagaries of which impact directly on the assessment of their performance. As well as the pressure of performance measurement, HEPs have been described as having a moral duty to ensure that graduates are able to become employed (secure a job or self-employment), are employable (in specific ways in relation to the labour market aimed for), and have employ-abilities (skills, attributes and knowledge) that will equip them for work, life and citizenship across the lifespan (Artess et al., 2017). This moral duty arguably stems from before the 1960s when HEPs were 'in loco parentis' and has now become firmly embedded in the culture of HE.

An extensive literature on employability supports innovation in pedagogic practice in HE, and there is a growing consensus that employability provision needs to be multi-dimensional, experiential and embedded in the curriculum and other institutional processes and provision (Artess et al., 2017: 5). In practice, learning to become employable entails the offer and take-up of a wide range of employment-related activities both within and alongside higher education study.

Artess et al. (2017) found that employability in HE is a widely used concept but remains difficult to define as each HEP responds to the needs of its students in different ways. One definition of employability persists perhaps because it captures the notion that employability is both a personal and a public good. This suggests that employability should not be considered simply as an outcome metric of HE but as a process engaged with across working life.

> A set of achievements – skills, understandings and personal attributes – that make individuals more likely to gain employment and be successful in their chosen occupations, which benefits themselves, the workforce, the community and the economy.
>
> (Yorke and Knight, 2006: 8)

The Higher Education Academy (HEA) offers a framework for the development of employability in HE comprising a four-step model: defining employability, auditing and mapping, prioritising actions and measuring impact. HEPs are invited to embed employability practice via broad curricular goals for learning. Employable graduates should have been enabled to develop the following capabilities: confidence, resilience and adaptability; experience and networks; attributes and capabilities; specialist technical and transferable skills; knowledge and application; behaviours, qualities and values; enterprise and entrepreneurship; career guidance and management; self, social and cultural awareness; and reflection and articulation (HEA, 2015).

The development of career management skills (CMS) such as career planning, occupational awareness and career decision-making in graduates is sometimes positioned as the outcome of effective employability learning in HE. There is a view that graduates who have developed CMS are more 'work ready' and more able to optimise their potential and achieve social mobility. Yet there is some evidence that CMS are not evenly distributed in the graduate population (Jackson and Wilton, 2016) and that personal and social factors may be of greater importance in graduates' transitions into work (Chin and Shen, 2015). Social class also

100 *Jane Artess*

appears to affect graduate employability. Gordon (2013) found that middle-class graduates were generally more successful in the graduate labour market than their working-class peers, and Christie (2016) noted how careers information and advice can be adapted in order to more actively reach traditionally disadvantaged students approaching the labour market. Purcell et al. (2012) discovered a 'cumulative pattern of advantage' resulting from the socio-economic background of graduates as they made their transitions to work.

Futuretrack study

The insights into graduate career progression offered by the Futuretrack study are unparalleled. By tracking a cohort of applicants into and through higher education until approximately two years following graduation the research team was able to not only capture the views of respondents at each stage of the study, but also use data longitudinally to observe whether aspirations and plans expressed at the outset were realised. The study was of sufficient size to enable statistical analyses to be carried out on the basis of variables such as gender, ethnicity, socio-economic status, subject of study,[1] type of institution, geographical location, whether studying while living at home, student debt, employment and study goals, earnings, etc. During the study, new classification systems were developed to distinguish HEPs on the basis of UCAS tariff points required for entry (Purcell et al., 2009a) and graduate occupations (Elias and Purcell, 2013).

What follows is brief summary of some Futuretrack findings which relate to students learning to become employable, together with some new analyses aimed to contribute to debate about what is provided by HEPs to support them. A major caveat is that the Futuretrack study was carried out between 2005 and 2012. During that time the global economy experienced a deep recession and most Futuretrack respondents graduated in 2009 and 2010 into an uncertain labour market. It is likely that knowledge of this may have affected their responses to survey questions and their employment and further study outcomes.

Clear ideas, careers information and guidance

As Futuretrack respondents applied for higher education (stage 1) they were asked a range of questions about how they had made their choice of subject and institution, what if any were their plans for the future and what careers information and advice had been offered to them. One question sought to identify how clear respondents were about their future plans: respondents were asked to position themselves on a scale of 1–7 where 1 means 'I have a clear idea about the occupation I eventually want to enter and the qualifications required to do so' and 7 means 'I have no idea what I will do after I complete the course I have applied for'. This question is used here as proxy for judging the extent of career clarity and to embody the extent of career planning and decidedness about the future.

Learning to be employable 101

Generally applicants reported they did have a clear idea about the occupation they eventually want to enter and the qualifications required to do so as they applied to HE, but greater clarity was associated with being female, being older (21+ years at the time of application), belonging to Black ethnic groups, having higher entry qualifications, applying for courses in Medicine, Dentistry and Education, and not being from a Higher Professional or Managerial category of social background. Conversely those who were less clear were male, young (19 years or less on application), White or Asian, having lower entry qualifications, applying for Languages, History and Philosophical courses, attending a private school at the time of application and being from a Higher Professional or Managerial background (Purcell et al., 2008).

The Futuretrack research team also found systematically gendered responses in respondents' self-assessment of skills. Women rated themselves more highly than men on written and spoken communication, and men rated themselves more highly on numerical skills, computer literacy and, importantly, self-confidence. Access to careers education and guidance activities likely to assist in career planning, decision-making and having a clear view of the future was found to be adequate for more than half of all respondents, although this was affected by socio-economic background – with those from Professional and Managerial backgrounds more likely to indicate that they had 'had what they needed' than those from Routine and Manual backgrounds, and more respondents from Intermediate or Routine and Manual backgrounds likely to report they had 'not had enough' or 'no' careers information and guidance information at all. Responses suggested that there was also differential access to careers information on the basis of type of school attended with those having attended selective, single sex and fee-paying schools less likely to report having had inadequate careers information and guidance. More than two thirds felt they had had adequate information on HE courses, and although overall more than half felt information about the relationship between courses and employment options had been sufficient, those applying for non-vocational courses were more likely to feel they had not had enough information on this topic.

Nearly one third of applicants wanted more help in choosing their course – particularly those who were older, from minority ethnic groups and those applying for Social Studies courses. Those who did not feel they had needed more help in choosing their course were more likely to be second generation HE applicants, younger, White and give a positive response to questions about access to careers education and guidance activities. Over 60 per cent of Futuretrack respondents reported that teachers at school/college had been helpful to them, and around one third felt that careers advice had been helpful in making application to HE.

In reviewing these findings, a new research question emerged: to what extent is participation in careers education and guidance activities associated with greater clarity of ideas about what to do after the course? Figure 8.1 shows a selection of careers education and guidance activities prior to HE alongside respondents' self-rating of career clarity, where 1 means 'I have a clear idea about the occupation

I eventually want to enter and the qualifications required to do so' and 7 means 'I have no idea what I will do after I complete the course I have applied for'.

Figure 8.1 suggests that those who had experienced these activities and felt they had had what they needed are more likely to have clear ideas about their future than those who felt they had not had enough. Whilst this finding is striking and may have implications for pre-HE careers education and guidance in schools and colleges, what is even more striking is that Futuretrack respondents who reported having had no access to these career education and guidance activities were only slightly less clear about their future than those who did. This probably indicates that career planning is taking place without formal inputs such as classroom based teaching on career or life planning, individual guidance or consideration of the relationship between courses and employment options. At the policy level this finding suggests that career education and guidance activities prior to HE may have utility in helping students to clarify their career goals but ensuring widespread access to such activities remains a challenge.

Futuretrack respondents were asked to agree or disagree with the statements 'careers guidance at my school or college was very helpful to me' and 'I have had excellent careers guidance'. Again, there is a correspondence between thinking that careers guidance was helpful or excellent and clarity of career ideas, with 78

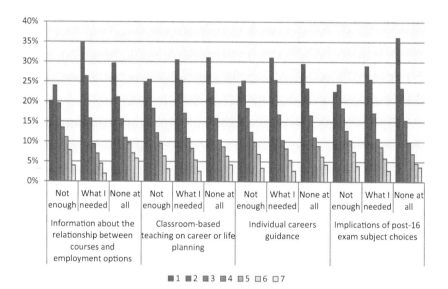

Figure 8.1 Selected career education and guidance activities prior to HE by self-rating on clarity of career ideas

Source: *Futuretrack composite file (unweighted)*.

Key: *I have a clear idea about the occupation I eventually want to enter and the qualifications required to do so, where 1 = I have a clear idea and 7 = I have no idea.* Note: Chi-square tests of independence indicate a significant association between clarity of ideas and each of the activities displayed in Figures 1, 2, 3 and 4.

per cent and 80 per cent respectively of those who agreed strongly with the statements rating themselves positively for clarity of career ideas – that is, 1, 2 or 3 on the 7 point scale.

A year of becoming employable

Respondents' view of their career clarity was again captured as Futuretrack respondents neared the end of their first year of study (stage 2). Purcell et al. (2009b) found that the most frequently used forms of careers information and guidance were careers events organised for first year students, advice from family and friends, visits to the careers service website and careers events for students studying on the same type of course.

Career clarity overall was found to have reduced with more respondents indicating a lack of certainty – perhaps as a result of the career implications of their subject becoming better known. For example, being very clear about studying Medicine upon application to HE is likely to give rise to some uncertainty about whether one's future career lies in gynaecology, orthopaedics, research, etc., as the course develops.

Factors associated with a change of career idea over the first year of HE were found to be: being mature (21 years or older on application), female and of Black ethnicity, undertaking specialist vocational subjects and studying at specialist vocational institutions, self-reporting excellent or very good self-confidence, having completed a compulsory module to develop employment-related skills and having obtained careers advice from an employer or work organisation representative. Conversely factors associated with no change of career ideas were: being younger (under 21 years), male and White, studying discipline-based subjects at highest entry-tariff institutions, self-reporting good, adequate or not very good levels of self-confidence, and having visited the careers service's website. These factors imply that some students are more engaged in career planning and the acquisition of CMS than others. It may be difficult to know which students are engaged without a diagnostic mechanism such as the careers registration initiative being developed through the Higher Education Funding Council's Learning Gain project outlined in chapter thirteen.

Analysis of respondents' report of career clarity alongside a selection of careers education and guidance activities taken advantage of during the first year of study (Figure 8.2) suggests that having a clear idea is likely to be enhanced by participation in these activities. Having completed a compulsory module to develop employment-related skills and having talked to a careers service consultant about one's course or career options appear to have had the most benefit in helping students to clarify their career ideas.

Moving towards the labour market

As Futuretrack respondents approached graduation they were again asked to position themselves on the scale of 1–7. It might be expected that as students approached the end of their courses that their ideas would have clarified;

104 Jane Artess

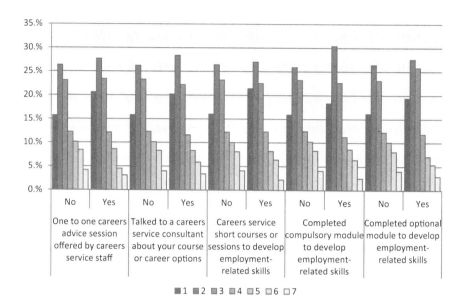

Figure 8.2 Selected career education and guidance activities during the first year of HE by self-rating on clarity of career ideas

Source: *Futuretrack composite file (unweighted)*.

Key: *I have a clear idea about the occupation I eventually want to enter and the qualifications required to do so, where 1 = I have a clear idea and 7 = I have no idea.*

Figure 8.3 tends to support this assumption. The careers education and guidance activities that appear to have impacted positively on career clarity are having advice on CV writing and attending a careers event for students on the same type of course. Interestingly those who had not visited the careers service website reported the highest career clarity (=1 on the 7 point scale) and those who had not attended a university-wide careers event for final year students reported a similar score; this might suggest that by the final year students have already developed their plans and are not looking to HEP resources to help achieve them.

One interpretation of the findings expressed in Figures 8.1, 8.2 and 8.3 is that career education and guidance activities provided pre-HE and during years one and two (of a typical undergraduate degree programme) might be more impactful in supporting career development and clarity of career ideas than activities provided during the final year.

Students' career plans affect their job-seeking behaviours and ultimately their employment outcomes. Purcell and Atfield (2010a) confirm that the majority of finalists had started looking for work at the time of the Futuretrack survey (stage 3) and around half of those were looking for a job related to their long-term career plans, and most hoped to achieve a job related to the subject they had studied.

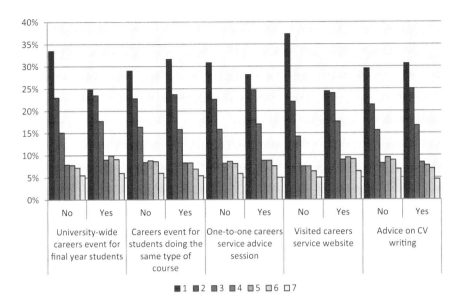

Figure 8.3 Selected career education and guidance activities reported by final year students by self-rating on clarity of career ideas

Source: *Futuretrack composite file (unweighted)*

Key: *I have a clear idea about the occupation I eventually want to enter and the qualifications required to do so, where 1 = I have a clear idea and 7 = I have no idea.*

Students' belief about the development of generic employability skills (e.g., numeracy, self-confidence, leadership, computer literacy) was found to vary by gender, ethnicity, subject and type of institution attended, and overall 80 per cent of respondents felt they had developed the skills employers would be looking for when recruiting for the kinds of job they wanted to apply for (Purcell and Atfield, 2010b). Students of vocationally oriented courses were the most likely to agree the subject they had studied would be an advantage in looking for employment, and students of arts subjects (e.g., Creative Arts & Design and Linguistics and Classics) were the least likely to agree that 'the skills I have developed on my course have made me more employable'. These findings reinforce the notion that learning to become employable comprises acquisition of subject-specific knowledge and skills as well as more generic attributes.

Learning to use employ-abilities

Following graduation Futuretrack respondents' labour market and further education history was tracked for between 18 and 30 months. Findings reveal the complexity of transition into the graduate employment landscape. Respondents were asked whether skills developed in HE were being used in the workplace.

Spoken communication and the ability to work in teams were thought to be used extensively at work but were not extensively developed in HE; conversely research and critical evaluation skills were developed extensively in HE and were not used a great deal at work. Entrepreneurial skills were not well developed in HE nor used widely in the workplace. This kind of discrepancy may be of interest to curriculum planners devising ways to facilitate employability learning.

Three quarters of graduates thought they possessed the skills employers were looking for but just over three fifths were using these skills in their current job. The appropriateness of the current job for people with high level skills and qualifications was found to be strongest for those working in large organisations. Job appropriateness was differentiated by subject studied, as was access to 'expert' (which is the category of job most likely to be done only by graduates), 'strategist', 'communicator' and 'non graduate' graduate jobs. Of all respondents, 29 per cent felt their current job was 'exactly the type of work I wanted' and this too was found to be associated with subject of study. General satisfaction with respondents' current job was found to be linked to promotion and career prospects, opportunity to use initiative, the job role itself, job security, pay and hours of work.

Those respondents who had hoped to work in a job related to their degree as they neared graduation 'were indeed more likely to use their skills and knowledge in their jobs.' (Purcell et al., 2012: 93) albeit this was found to be associated with greater levels of self-confidence. Of those graduates who had wanted to obtain work related to longer term career plans during their final year, nine out of ten reported that they were now in employment that used the skills they learned in HE and three quarters were using knowledge acquired through their studies. However, these positive findings are counter-balanced by a finding that respondents' assessment of whether the skills learned had made them more employable had fallen slightly between their final year and experiencing the labour market. That this is due to the recession or employers placing greater emphasis on skills than qualifications cannot be known, but it does suggest that experience of the labour market exerts an influence on graduates' perception of their own employability.

Figure 8.4 shows that respondents who felt that they have the skills employers are looking for, are optimistic about their long-term prospects, and are satisfied with their present job tend to be those who have agreed they 'have a clear idea about the occupation I hope to have in five years' time and the qualifications required to do so'; and conversely those who tend to disagree that they have a clear idea of what they hope to do in 5 years' time report they do not have the skills employers look for, are less optimistic about their futures, and less satisfied with their current job. This finding suggests graduates' relationship with their own employability is complex, and clarity of idea about their futures may be bound up with their understandings of how they fit into the graduate labour market. It would appear some graduates are content with their employment outcomes, but a sizeable minority may be feeling rather miserable.

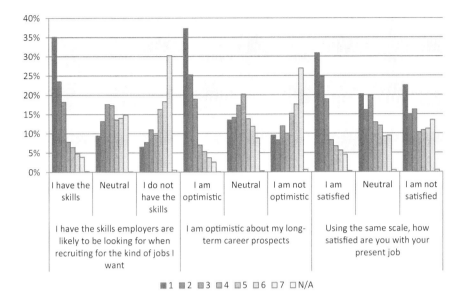

Figure 8.4 Selected employment-related outcomes by agreement with the statement 'I have a clear idea of the occupation I hope to have in 5 years' time and the qualifications required to do so'

Source: *Futuretrack composite file (unweighted)*

Key: *I have a clear idea about the occupation I eventually want to enter and the qualifications required to do so, where 1 = I have a clear idea and 7 = I have no idea.*

Conclusion

The evidence offered here suggests there is a likelihood that provision of effective forms of careers education and guidance interventions, particularly prior to HE and during the early years of HE study, could promote a sense of clarity about career intentions which in turn may lead to better satisfaction with working life, greater optimism about longer term career prospects, and a stronger sense of possessing the kinds of skills employers look for. Participation in career education and guidance activities appears to support employability learning in students and graduates. These findings suggest that investment by HEPs in careers education and guidance interventions can be justified, not only in terms of gaming the TEF or other performance measures, but also in terms of increasing the likelihood of graduates making a satisfactory transition into the labour market.

The whole notion of graduate employability is fundamentally employer-centric and assumes deficit in students that HEPs are well-positioned to remedy. Analysis of the Futuretrack data would suggest that a more learner-centred conception of career development and progression might be valuable in shaping curricula to support graduates facing an increasingly uncertain labour market. More research

108 *Jane Artess*

into graduates' views of their employability development within employment (Higgins, 2017) could only deepen understanding.

Note

1 Subject categories used in the Futuretrack study were based on the Higher Education Statistics Agency, JACS Principal Subject Codes. See www.hesa.ac.uk/support/documentation/jacs/jacs3-principal

References

Artess, J., Hooley, T., and Mellors-Bourne, R. (2017). *Employability: A Review of the Literature 2012–2016*, York: Higher Education Academy.

Bagshaw, A. (2017). *A Beginner's Guide to the Teaching Excellence Framework.* (online) available from: http://wonkhe.com/blogs/a-beginners-guide-to-the-teaching-excellence-framework/.

Beech, D. (2017). Going *for Gold: Lessons from the TEF Provider Submissions.* London: Higher Education Policy Institute.

Bothwell, E. (2017). "TEF ratings set to shape international student choice – survey", *Times Higher Education.* (online) available from: www.timeshighereducation.com/news/englands-tef-could-be-big-factor-in-international-student-choice.

Chin, W.S., and Shen, Q.L. (2015). "Factors affecting individual career management among undergraduates in higher education institutions", *International Journal of Academic Research in Business and Social Sciences*, 5(10): 56–68.

Christie, F. (2016). "Careers guidance and social mobility in UK higher education: practitioner perspectives", *British Journal of Guidance and Counselling*, 44(1): 72–85.

Department for Business and Skills (BIS) (2015a). *Small Business, Enterprise and Employment Act.* London: Department for Business, Innovation and Skills.

Department for Business and Skills (BIS) (2015b). *Fulfilling Our Potential: Teaching Excellence, Social Mobility and Student Choice.* London: Department for Business, Innovation and Skills.

Department for Education (DfE) (2017). *Employment and Earnings Outcomes of Higher Education Graduates by Subject and Institution: Experimental Statistics Using the Longitudinal Educational Outcomes data. Statistical First Release 18/2017.* London: HMSO.

Elias, P., and Purcell, K. (2013). *Working Paper 5: Classifying Graduate Occupations for the Knowledge Society.* Manchester: Higher Education Careers Service Unit.

Farrell, R., (2011). *What Should the Purpose of a University Be? Classbase Website.* (online) available from:www.classbase.com/News/What-Should-the-Purpose-of-a-University-Be-157 (accessed 19 August 2017).

Gordon, D.A. (2013). *Employability and Social Class in the Graduate Labour Market.* PhD Thesis. Cardiff, Cardiff University.

HEA (2015). *Framework for Embedding Employability in Higher Education.* York: Higher Education Academy.

HECSU (2016). *What Do Graduates Do?* Manchester: Higher Education Careers Service Unit.

HESA (2017a). *Employment of Leavers – Introduction.* Cheltenham: Higher Education Statistics Agency. (online) available from: www.hesa.ac.uk/data-and-analysis/performance-indicators/employment.

HESA (2017b). *Graduate Outcomes Project: The Data- the Student Voice.* Cheltenham: Higher Education Statistics Agency. (online) available from: www.hesa.ac.uk/innovation/outcomes/data.

Higgins, H. (2017). *Meeting the Demands of Graduates' Work: From a Higher Education for Employment to a Higher Education for Performance.* PhD Thesis, Cardiff, Cardiff University.

Jackson, D., and Wilton, N. (2016). "Developing career management competencies among undergraduates and the role of work-integrated learning", *Teaching in Higher Education, 21*(3): 266–286.

May, T. (2017). *Theresa May's Speech to Conservative Party Conference.* (online) available from: www.conservatives.com/sharethefacts/2017/10/theresa-mays-conference-speech.

Neary, M. (2016). "Teaching excellence framework: A critical response and alternative future", *Journal of Contemporary European Research, 12*(3): 690–695.

Porter, A. (2017). "Is the teaching excellence framework shaping international students' choice?", *Guardian Newspaper,* 16 October 2017. (online) available from: www.theguardian.com/higher-education-network/2017/oct/16/is-the-teaching-excellence-framework-shaping-international-student-choice (accessed 17 October 2017).

Purcell, K., and Atfield, G. (2010a). *Working Paper 2: Job Search Strategies and Employment Preferences of Higher Education Students.* Manchester: Higher Education Careers Service Unit.

Purcell, K., and Atfield, G. (2010b). *Working Paper 4: The Fit Between Graduate Labour Market Supply and Demand: 3rd Year Undergraduate Degree Final Year Students' Perceptions of the Skills they Have to Offer and the Skills Employers Seek.* Manchester: Higher Education Careers Service Unit.

Purcell, K., Elias, P., and Atfield, G. (2009a). *Working Paper 1: Analysing the Relationship Between Higher Education Participation and Educational and Career Development Patterns and Outcomes: A New Classification System.* Manchester: Higher Education Careers Service Unit.

Purcell, K., Elias, P., Atfield, G., Behle, H., Ellison, R., Hughes, C., Livanos, I., and Tzanakou, C. (2009b). *Plans, Aspirations and Realities: Taking Stock of Higher Education and Career Choices One Year On: Findings From the Second Futuretrack Survey of 2006 Applicants for UK Higher Education.* Manchester: Higher Education Careers Service Unit.

Purcell, K., Elias, P., Atfield, G., Behle, H., Ellison, R., Luchinskaya, D., Snape, J., Conaghan, L., and Tzanakou, C. (2012). *Futuretrack Stage 4: Transitions into Employment, Further Study and Other Outcomes.* Manchester: Higher Education Careers Service Unit.

Purcell, K., Elias, P., Ellison, R., Atfield, G., Adam, D., and Livanos, I. (2008). *Applying for Higher Education – The Diversity of Choices, Plans and Expectations: Findings From the First Futuretrack Survey of the Class of 2006 Applicants to Higher Education.* Manchester: Higher Education Careers Service Unit.

Yorke, M., and Knight, P. (2006). *Embedding Employability Into the Curriculum. (Learning and Employability Series 1).* York: Higher Education Academy.

9 Life in the graduate graveyards

Making sense of underemployment in graduate careers

Tracy Scurry and John Blenkinsopp

Introduction

For over eighty years the interaction of waves of university expansion and the economic cycle has ensured concern about the ability of the UK economy to absorb increased numbers of graduates, and the calibre of jobs they obtain has been a perennial debate (Brown and Hesketh, 2004; Wolf, 2004). As early as 1937 the National Union of Students (NUS) observed that university graduates could 'look forward only with uncertainty to employment of a kind appropriate to their academic achievements' with many in the end having to content themselves with work 'in which their capacities were not fully used' (NUS, 1937: 8). Recent analysis suggests that between 2001 and 2012 the UK economy managed to absorb the increased supply of graduates from Higher Education, through the upskilling of existing occupations and creation of new ones, but a significant proportion found employment in non-graduate occupations (Green and Henseke, 2016). There remains a dearth of research which examines the experience of underemployed graduates, and how they make sense of the experience in career terms. In this chapter we report on an in-depth, qualitative study of underemployed graduates to explore how they made sense of and responded to their underemployment.

Graduate underemployment

The most recent figures from the Office for National Statistics (ONS) indicate 46.4% of recent graduates[1] in the UK are in non-graduate jobs. This is defined on the basis that the 'tasks associated with post holders in these jobs do not normally require knowledge and skills developed through Higher Education to enable them to perform these tasks in a competent manner' (Elias and Purcell, 2013: 8; Behle, 2016). This is up from 37% in 2001 (ONS, 2013; ONS, 2017). In the latest Destinations of Leavers from Higher Education Longitudinal survey, which examines the activities and perspectives of graduates three and a half years after graduation, 11.8% of respondents were not satisfied with their career to date, 16.8% were in non-professional employment and 3% were on zero hours contracts in non-graduate employment such as retail, waiting and bar work and the care industry (HESA, 2017).

Life in the graduate graveyards 111

Underemployment is generally defined in terms of a discrepancy between educational attainment and occupational level, and measured in terms of wage differentials, human capital or education levels and underutilisation of skill (Livingstone, 1998). These markers of 'objective underemployment' (Khan and Morrow, 1991) draw upon 'accepted standards' in gauging whether an individual is underemployed. There has been considerable debate in the literature about what constitutes a graduate job or a non-graduate job and how this can be measured (Scurry and Blenkinsopp, 2011; Behle, 2016). However, whilst these discussions and classifications are valuable in establishing macro level trends, it would also be valuable to further examine the subjective side of underemployment (Burris, 1983; Jones-Johnson and Johnson, 1992), taking into account how individuals feel about their employment in light of their educational attainment and future career aspirations. Such an approach would align with the recent reforms to collecting graduate outcomes data in the UK which now asks students to evaluate their employment related to the meaningfulness of it and relationship to future plans.[2] Whilst a graduate may be objectively underemployed they may not perceive themselves as being so (Maynard et al., 2006). This self-evaluation of success can further our understanding of the extent to which individuals perceive themselves to be underemployed and place their employment in the context of their wider career and life plans. Furthermore, recent work has questioned the assumption that individuals seek employment that makes full use of their education and skill, highlighting that some individuals may *choose* to be underemployed either to facilitate early career explorations or opt out of 'typical' career paths (Thompson et al., 2013; Steffy, 2017).

Graduate underemployment is often positioned as a period of exploration and transition while graduates find their feet in the labour market, before the 'real career' begins. However, some find themselves in situations of persistent underemployment, and it becomes untenable to frame their situation as a temporary state before a transition to employment 'appropriate' for their skills and education (Wilkins and Wooden, 2011). This increased persistence of graduate underemployment has great societal implications (Green and Henseke, 2016), especially since certain groups may experience disproportionate disadvantage. Recent research from Steffy (2017) found US college graduates from working-class backgrounds were more likely to experience 'woeful' underemployment (being in a position of involuntary overqualification) and greater negative impact than middle-class groups.

Research has highlighted the effect underemployment may have on individuals' attitudes toward their present and future employment. Feelings of frustration, disappointment and low levels of job satisfaction occur as individuals who perceive themselves to be underemployed feel they deserve better employment with 'higher pay, prestige, autonomy and challenge' in light of their education and qualifications (Jones-Johnson and Johnson, 1995: 75). Individuals who desire and feel entitled to 'better jobs' compare their personal employment situation to a referent standard (McKee-Ryan et al., 2009) which is neither objective nor temporally static (Feldman et al., 2002). The sense of satisfaction or dissatisfaction an individual experiences is thus dependent largely on comparisons with others – a sense of relative deprivation (Johnson et al., 2002). For research on underemployment the lack of a standard referent is generally problematic, both theoretically and methodologically, in terms of developing more nomothetic explanations (Mckee-Ryan and Harvey, 2011). However, this is less problematic for research into underemployment among recent graduates. Having limited work experience they are largely defined in terms of their graduate status, so they are a group for whom there can be some generally accepted referent points, e.g., a generic referent linked to prevailing perceptions of graduate employment (investment in human capital) or a more specific referent linked to the relative progress of others with whom one graduated. This aligns with work in the area of career success (e.g., Heslin, 2005) which emphasises that individuals evaluate their employment situation by comparison with a referent standard – typically a referent other. These theoretical perspectives are useful to explore the ways in which individual graduates frame their underemployment and the implication this has for their reactions to it.

Reactions to underemployment

Most prior research on underemployment has focused on the negative consequences for the individual, organisation and society. Underemployment has negative implications on work-related (individual's job attitudes, commitment and performance) and wellbeing outcomes (mental health and physical wellbeing) (Allan et al., 2017; Bolino and Feldman, 2000; Feldman, 1996; Jones-Johnson and Johnson, 1992) with knock-on effects on family functioning and relationships (Scurry and Blenkinsopp, 2011). Underemployment is a source of frustration and discontent for individuals (Burris 1983) with the underemployed faced with challenges to their self-identity, interpersonal relationships and a sense of meaning in life (Borgen et al., 1988: 157). Furthermore, there have been long-standing concerns that the failure of society to 'make good' on the implicit promise that investment in educational attainment will 'pay off' economically will lead to social, political and economic problems as underemployed individuals become increasingly disillusioned and frustrated (Livingstone, 1998; Mills, 1953). A recent report highlighted underemployment as a key contributing factor to disillusionment in Europe's young people that may undermine future political, economic and social stability (PACE, 2012).

Another area of concern relates to the long-term effects of periods of underemployment on graduates' career prospects. Underemployment may be entered as a means to avoid unemployment (Borgen et al., 1988; Feldman, 1996; Leana and Feldman, 1995), reflecting the assumption that any job (even if underemployed) is better than no job (unemployment) in terms of future career trajectory. This premise is supported by evidence that once graduates are unemployed there is a decline in their ability to move into graduate jobs (Green and Henseke, 2016). However, 'unsatisfactory employment' experiences can have the same psychological effects for young people as unemployment (Winefield et al., 1991). Nunley et al. (2017) raise questions about the value of periods of underemployment on employment prospects. Creating a set of randomised fictitious CVs for college graduates with differing periods of unemployment and underemployment, they submitted these to 2300 online recruitment advertisements (making a total of 9396 applications). They found that periods of underemployment appeared to be perceived more negatively by employers than periods of unemployment. Applicants who were underemployed were 30% less likely than those who were unemployed to be selected by employers for interview (Nunley et al., 2017). Such findings reflect a sense that employers may perceive that the attributes developed through Higher Education have a 'use by' date. This helps to explain the finding from the same study that gaining internship experience whilst studying reduced the negative impact of the period of underemployment.

Whilst research suggests underemployed individuals reassess their career goals and engage in job search activity to obtain 'better' employment (Borgen et al., 1988; Feldman and Turnley, 1995), we know little about how and when they do this – for example, what career planning and management occurs and how sustained it is. There has been very little research on if or how individuals attempt to shape or craft the role in which they are underemployed. Lin et al. (2017) argue the focus on the negative implications of and reactions to underemployment reflect an assumption that the content of a job is fixed. There is a need to challenge this understanding and explore the extent to which underemployment may lead to individuals proactively crafting their roles as a means to align their employment with a positive self-image – as a coping mechanism in response to their underemployment. Those in positions of underemployment may bring creativity and high levels of organisational citizenship behaviours to the organisations, and managers should seek to support individuals in this crafting (Lin et al., 2017). This echoes the argument of Thompson et al. (2013) that organisations may 'harness' the potential of underemployed individuals through providing opportunities for them to contribute beyond their roles. They frame this as job enrichment, but it must be acknowledged that it may simply result in job enlargement, and thus exploit an already vulnerable group.

In the remainder of this chapter we present a narrative analysis of underemployed graduates to explore how graduates frame and respond to their experience of underemployment.

The study

This aim of this study was to explore graduates' experiences of underemployment. All participants were employed as call centre operatives, in roles that had little discretion, low levels of skill variety and very little control. This was a specific group, selected to gain insight into the phenomenon of graduate underemployment. There were few opportunities for career progression and those available often required further study specifically related to the sector. This would not be seen as a graduate job, either in the 'traditional sense' or within the new classifications of graduate work (Purcell et al., 1999; Scurry and Blenkinsopp, 2011).

114 *Tracy Scurry, John Blenkinsopp*

Over a period of 18–24 months we gathered data from 17 individuals, 12 of whom worked for the same employer. There were 5 women and 12 men, and the ages of the individuals ranged between 21 and 27. All had bachelor degrees in social sciences or humanities.

Findings

Three main themes emerged from the data. Firstly the graduates framed their initial experiences as something that they had voluntarily entered and expected. Secondly, that this then framed the way in which they responded to and accounted for their situation. Thirdly, that time played a significant role in shaping graduates' experiences to underemployment. We shall now go on to explore these in more detail.

Expectation of voluntary underemployment

All of our participants framed their situation as 'something that they had expected' reflecting a lack of urgency to concern themselves about their employment opportunities and prospects upon graduation. They expected there to be 'a period of time' (a phrase they all used) in which they planned to 'sort themselves out'.

> I just thought well when I leave university I have probably got about a year to sort myself out. I had just envisaged maybe doing any old job for a year until I had sorted myself out and got a job that I was supposed to be getting.
>
> (Ollie, Male, 23)

None of the individuals pinpointed why they expected there to be this 'period of time', exactly how long they had expected it to last, or how they intended to bring this phase to an end. There was little mention of job search activity. Individuals were reluctant to take any job which might require a commitment they felt they could not give. They seemed in some ways to take a moral stance towards taking on 'proper' jobs, feeling it would not be right to do so when they expected soon to quit to go travelling or similar (though this could equally be a rationalisation of their failure to act):

> I don't like doing something if I'm not gonna do it properly. So I didn't wanna go and get a graduate job do it for six months, like it, think I had prospects of going somewhere and then have to pack it in.
>
> (Brian, Male, 22)

All had envisaged subsidising this period through temporary employment, similar to the jobs they'd held at university, believing (rightly) they would be able to get 'something' (through employment agencies or ads in the local paper) to tide them over. Try (2004) observed a similar pattern of continuing after graduation

Life in the graduate graveyards 115

with the kind of jobs they'd held as students, and suggested this could serve as a 'stepping stone' from education to employment. Our participants viewed their jobs solely as a means to support a continuation of the student lifestyle; they did not view the jobs as part of their 'career'. The positive aspects of their work were identified as wages, hours worked and the people they worked with, plus the fact these three elements enabled them to have a certain lifestyle.

Initial responses to underemployment

Participants talked about the 'proper job' they would get in the future, which had the characteristics traditionally associated with high level managerial roles – a 'typical graduate job' (Elias et al., 1999). Although aware of the general expectations regarding graduate employment, their current situation was interpreted and 'justified' through relating it to their future plans at that point, albeit that these plans were very hazy. This didn't seem to concern them, as their underemployment and lack of specific plans for the future was consistent with many other graduates they knew:

> I was surprised at how many of us [graduates] there are, one of the managers always laughs about it and says [these places are] like graduate graveyards.
> (Jack, Male, 26)

Collin (2000) suggested we make sense of our career situation by taking 'readings' against widely shared norms and expectations and, more personally, against our lives as a whole and in interaction with significant others (Jenkins, 1996). The participants certainly did this, but often in a very selective fashion. They perceived others as having negative views of their employment, yet in general spoke of these views in an almost nonchalant manner, as if they were of little importance and rather secondary to their own perceptions of their employment, which they justified in terms of the benefits and its temporary nature. They noted that when talking about their job to others they remained vague about the details, although some said they emphasised the money they earned, which was one of the positives – their peers in ostensibly better jobs were often surprised to discover how well they were paid.

When speaking of those who did have a 'graduate job' they were keen to stress how hard these individuals had worked to gain the role, the effort and hours they were required to put into the job and the limited financial reward they received for doing so. They did not view these individuals' jobs in terms of the long-term career benefits, reflecting what Hesketh (2000) terms career immaturity, where immediate gratification is sought as opposed to long-term gains. In the graduates' case the immediate gratification came from their ability to support and maintain their 'student' lifestyle. This attitude also played a part in the formation of their 'reading' of where they were in terms of their employment, relative to their life as a whole.

The accounts did highlight negative aspects of their work. The jobs were described as routine, monotonous and highly controlled with little opportunity for discretion. Many referred to themselves as 'phone monkeys', a derogatory term reflecting the lack of skill required in their role:

> I say the same crap to the same people. You get a small sense of satisfaction if you sell it, but I still know that a trained monkey could do my job.
>
> (Jack, Male, 26)

One individual joked about the possibility of a friend becoming a 'senior phone monkey':

> He says 'well I could stay in the position that I am in or leave, but then any one could look at my CV and see that I've been a phone monkey for a year, or I can be a senior phone monkey and I can boss the other phone monkeys around', but I mean, I think that like a manager phone monkey is worse, because it looks like you're taking it seriously.
>
> (Ollie, Male, 23)

It was interesting that the graduates were keen to distinguish themselves from what they saw as 'real' phone monkeys, individuals who were not graduates and were working in the call centres for the long term.

Despite their disdain for their jobs, participants did recognise the opportunity for skill use and development, if they chose to 'make the most of it':

> If I wanted to go on and do a team manager's position that would develop a lot more skills. But I am not going to. I can see people who are doing it and they are developing a lot more skills by doing it but I don't see the point.
>
> (Fran, Female, 27)

They saw little point pursuing opportunities in a job and an organisation in which they didn't plan to stay for the long term.

Previous research has suggested that the transition between graduation and work can be a tumultuous one, with individuals' expectations not being met and a sense of disillusionment occurring (Arnold and MacKenzie Davey, 1992; King, 2003). Similarly, after the initial novelty and excitement of entering employment and earning a wage, individuals who are underemployed will become disillusioned (Borgen et al., 1988). Neither response was visible among our participants, for at least the first 12 months. The majority of participants claimed the job still met the expectations they had held when they entered it; that the work would not be a meaningful experience but a means to an end, albeit a somewhat ambiguous 'end' for most. This absence of unmet expectations may explain why the individuals' experience of underemployment did not result in the expected levels of job searching for alternative employment (Burris, 1983).

Making sense over time

Time serves as an indicator by which individuals can compare their experiences with others, and 'timetable norms' may exist that help individuals to structure their experience, utilising 'signposts', drawn from consensus of expectation, as reference points (Roth, 1963). In the initial interviews the graduates felt the period of time they had been in their current employment was consistent with the notion of it being a temporary stop-gap, but they recognised the longer they remained in this situation, the more difficult it would be to 'justify' it to future employers and to significant others, and there was consensus on the need to 'move on' in the near future in order to make the 'stop-gap' status of their situation credible to both themselves and others. Although they had constructed a 'reality' that their situation was acceptable and comparable to many other graduates, this could not be sustained in the long term as they were aware of societal expectations of what a graduate should be doing and when a graduate should be doing it.

As time passed and they did not move on to the 'proper jobs' they had previously talked about, they began to get exasperated at the limited scope for adding to their roles, and made increased references to not using their degree:

> It was alright at first, you know the money, the hours and all that but it's not something I want to be doing forever and it seems like I have been. I am getting more stupid by the day, repeating myself all day long. And at the end of the day what am I doing? I'm not doing anything just reading off a script and that's it.
>
> (Emma, Female, 22)

The positive elements of money and hours were still mentioned but it became apparent this was no longer enough and they were beginning to look for 'something more' from their employment. References to what they thought they 'should be doing' were made on an increasingly frequent basis. It was at this point the majority of the participants, about two thirds of the initial sample, now started to make and pursue specific plans. This planning was often talked about with reference to the length of time they had been in their situation and how they thought others, particularly future employers, would view this.

> they are going to look at my CV and be like 'that's interesting two years as a Phone Monkey, did you do any training at the company?' No. 'Did you get any skills that you can use here?' No. 'Can you shed some light on why you were there so long?' No. It just looks bad, it's definitely time for me to get off my backside now, I've had a good time and enjoyed myself but it's, well I mean two years is a bloody long time for nothing to happen.
>
> (Dan, Male, 23)

The plans developed took three forms – to go travelling, to obtain more 'appropriate' employment, or to consider seeking promotion within the call centre.

All had started to take some actions to achieve their plans. The would-be travellers planned itineraries, booked tickets and saved money, the individuals looking for more 'appropriate' employment started to search and apply for jobs, while those looking for promotion took on extra responsibilities, put in more effort and took up development opportunities as a way of working towards promotion.

As they took steps that served to reconfirm their situation as a temporary stopgap, they once again focused on the positive elements. Although they still experienced boredom and frustration this was tempered by the focus they now had on achieving their future plans.

> I still think this is a crappy job, but I am really focussed now [and so] I don't see the point of leaving this for another crappy job that might not be as good. It wouldn't be worth it as I'm only here for a little bit longer now.
>
> (Ollie, Male, 23)

Although some had previously spoken of the possibility of pursuing promotion within the call centre, this had been as a way to gain something extra from their time in the call centre, not as a possible career. As time passed, however, several seemed to be changing their views and expectations of their employment, and were beginning to speak more positively about their roles, the call centre and the company itself.

> There is a real possibility of moving further up now, and they've also offered to pay for like umm Chartered Institute of Insurance . . . which you know I could use to get into insurance as a career.
>
> (Dan, Male, 23)

They started to see potential for a 'career' to be developed from this employment. This was not an option previously considered as part of their long-term plans and although they now saw it as an option it still did not seem to sit comfortably with them.

> One week I think yeah this is an alright thing to do and it could go somewhere but then the next week I think I could probably do a little bit better, and its time I moved on.
>
> (Dan, Male, 23).

Those individuals planning to pursue promotion now talked much more positively of their situation, apparently reluctant to say anything that did not gel with their notion of it being an appropriate career path. Those who had 'moved on', or were taking steps to do so, had begun a 'process of renewal' (Borgen et al., 1988). The extent to which they experienced the situation as underemployment had lessened as a result of the activities they were undertaking in order to end their situation. For those who remained, but now had a fixed end-point in sight, it was as if they were back to where they had been in the initial interviews.

The jobs could again be seen as a 'means to an end', as this view of the situation reflected their new 'reading' of their position.

Conclusion

Our findings suggest some graduates remain in non-graduate jobs for much longer than previous survey data has captured, and this 'persistent underemployment' may be more of a formative period for their careers than previously thought. The findings show how the phenomenon of graduate underemployment has become sufficiently common to provide an alternative reference point for graduates taking 'readings' of their career position. For an extended period our participants could compare themselves to large numbers of graduates whose position was similar to their own. The comparison was made in objective career terms – they were looking at graduates who they saw as similar to themselves (in background and academic performance) and who had been in a non-graduate job for a similar period after having left university. For at least a year after graduating they found it relatively easy to justify their situation as comparable with significant numbers of their peers. Only gradually did the number of comparators dwindle to a point where their narrative became less credible.

Had they made comparisons in terms of the subjective career, they may have found much greater differences. Though there appears to be a general trend for young people to delay the launch of their careers (Feldman and Whitcomb, 2005), what they do during this delay and how they frame it may be very different. Even where two individuals appear to have a very similar pattern of employment, one may perceive the situation as a series of dead-end jobs while the other may frame it as 'browsing' the labour market and available career options, and gaining useful experience, as a prelude to a delayed career launch. Our participants had very similar objective careers, but their subjective careers – the way in which they framed their situation and engaged with work – became progressively more varied over time. The subjective career perspective is thus vital in helping us understand how and why a period of underemployment may have lasting effects on attitudes to work and career.

These findings raise questions about 'what happens next' for underemployed graduates and if it has an impact on an individual's subsequent career. There are three key areas to explore in this regard. First, the graduates' underemployment triggered a great deal of sensemaking, which produced a working career script (Barley, 1989) which seemed fragile yet enduring. Whilst events can overturn such interpretations and alter our career narratives (Glanz, 2003), we speculate these early career scripts may have long-term implications for the careers of these individual and also for how they are perceived by future employers (Blenkinsopp and Scurry, 2007). Second, we might also examine what kind of disruptions (e.g., parental prompting, friends who move on) are most likely to trigger fresh sensemaking and the writing of a new career script, and whether different triggers produce different outcomes. A final issue is that our study suggests underemployment led some of the graduates to lower their career expectations, most obviously by taking a post within the call centre that they could have obtained without ever having gone to university. Caution must be exercised here – Elias and Purcell (2004) found the graduate premium in earnings develops over a 10–15 year period after graduating, and it is possible these individuals will gain benefit from their graduate status eventually. For example, although a graduate obtaining a Team Leader post aged 24 might observe s/he is in the same position as a colleague who left school at 16 and had worked for eight years, in the long run the graduate may be in a better position to apply for further promotions. This highlights a potentially important issue for underemployed graduates, which is that opportunities to progress and realise their potential may require them to commit to, and engage with, employment which they would not have imagined to be their lot. The response of our participants was to keep work at arm's length, consciously resisting commitment. The tension between the graduates' view that their jobs were dull and routine and their acknowledgement that they nevertheless could be vehicles for career development was an ongoing feature of their talk. None of them maintained a constant position towards this, even in the initial interviews, and it was fascinating to see how an individual's account of their work varied as they were making sense of their employment for the researcher and themselves.

There is clearly a need for longitudinal research exploring the consequences of early career underemployment on both objective and subjective career. University education is a significant investment for the individual and society, and the careers of graduates are in many ways the most obvious product of that investment. Our study has highlighted a number of ways in which that investment can fail to pay dividends, leading to negative consequences for individuals, organisation and society. Developing a greater understanding of the career implications of graduate underemployment will provide a basis for career guidance interventions that help to prepare graduates for managing and making sense of periods of underemployment. There is clearly scope for future research in this space, in particular work that examines the interactions of wider structures, such as social class (Burke et al., 2017), and the impact on who experiences underemployment and how they experience and respond to underemployment.

Notes

1 Defined as those who left full time education within 5 years of the survey date.
2 Details of the review and the revised survey can be found here: www.hesa.ac.uk/innovation/records/reviews/newdlhe/model/survey/all

References

Allan, B.A., Tay, L., and Sterling, H.M. (2017). "Construction and validation of the subjective underemployment scales (SUS)", *Journal of Vocational Behavior, 99*: 93–106.

Arnold, J., and Mackenzie Davey, K. (1992). "Beyond unmet expectations: A detailed analysis of graduate experiences at work during the first three years of their careers", *Personnel Review*, 21(2): 45–68.

Barley, S.R. (1989). "Careers, identities, and institutions: The legacy of the Chicago School of Sociology", In: Arthur, M.B., Hall, D.T., & Lawrence, B.S. (Eds.), *Handbook of Career Theory*. Cambridge: Cambridge University Press, pp. 41–65.

Behle, H. (2016). *Graduates in Non-graduate Occupations*. Report to HEFCE and SRHE by Warwick Institute for Employment Research, October 2016. (online) available from: http://dera.ioe.ac.uk/27628/1/2016_gradoccup.pdf (accessed 16 November 2017).

Blenkinsopp, J., and Scurry, T. (2007). "GRINGO stars: The challenge of managing graduates in non-graduate employment", *Personnel Review*, 36(4): 623–637.

Bolino, M.C., and Feldman, D.C. (2000). "The antecedents and consequences of underemployment among expatriates", *Journal of Organisational Behaviour*, 21(10): 889–911.

Borgen, W.A., Amundson, N.E., and Harder, H.G. (1988). "The experience of underemployment", *Journal of Employment Counselling*, 25(4): 149–159.

Brown, P., and Hesketh, A. 2004. *The Mismanagement of Talent – Employability and Jobs in the Knowledge Economy*. Oxford: Oxford University Press.

Burke, C., Scurry, T., Blenkinsopp, J., and Graley, K. (2017). "Critical perspectives on graduate employability", In: Tomlinson, M., & Holmes, L. (Eds.), *Graduate Employability in Context: Theory, Research and Debate*. London: Palgrave Macmillan, pp. 87–107.

Burris, B.H. (1983). *No Room at the Top – Underemployment and Alienation in the Corporation*. New York: Praeger.

Collin, A. (2000). "Dancing to the music of time", In: Collin, A., & Young, R. (Eds.), *The Future of Career*. Cambridge: Cambridge University Press, pp. 83–97.

Elias, P., McKnight, A., Pitcher, J., Purcell, K., and Simm, C. (1999). *Moving on: Graduates Careers Three Years After Graduation*. Manchester: CSU/DfEE.

Elias, P., and Purcell, K. (2004). "Is mass higher education working? Evidence from the graduate labour market experiences of recent graduates", *National Institute Economic Review*, 190: 60–74.

Elias, P., and Purcell, K. (2013). *Classifying Graduate Occupations for the Knowledge Society*. Futuretrack Working Paper No. 5. Warwick Institute for Employment Research. (online) available from: https://warwick.ac.uk/fac/soc/ier/futuretrack/findings/stage4/ft4_wp5_classifying_graduate_occupations_for_the_knowledge_society.pdf.

Feldman, D.C. (1996). "The nature, antecedents and consequences of underemployment", *Journal of Management*, 22(3): 385–407.

Feldman, D.C., Leana, C.R., & Bolino, M.C. (2002). "Underemployment and relative deprivation among re-employed executives", *Journal of Occupational and Organizational Psychology*, 75(4): 453–471.

Feldman, D.C., and Turnley, W.H. (1995). "Underemployment among recent business college graduates", *Journal of Organizational Behaviour*, 16(6): 691–706.

Feldman, D.C., and Whitcomb, K.M. (2005). "The effects of framing vocational choices on young adults' sets of career options", *Career Development International*, 10(1): 7–25.

Glanz, L. (2003). "Expatriate stories: a vehicle of professional development abroad?", *Journal of Managerial Psychology*, 18(3): 259–274.

Green, F., and Henseke, G. (2016). "The changing graduate labour market: Analysis using a new indicator of graduate jobs", *IZA Journal of Labor Policy, 5*(1): 14.

Hesketh, B. (2000). "Time perspective in career-related choices: Applications of time-discounting principles", *Journal of Vocational Behaviour, 57*(1): 62–84.

Heslin, P.A. (2005). "Conceptualizing and evaluating career success", *Journal of Organizational Behavior, 26*(2): 113–136.

Higher Education Statistics Agency (HESA) (2017). (online) available from: www.hesa.ac.uk/data-and-analysis/publications/long-destinations-2012-13/views.

Jenkins, R. (1996). *Social Identity*. London: Routledge.

Johnson, W.R., Morrow, P.C., & Johnson, G.J. (2002). "An evaluation of a perceived over qualification scale across work settings", *Journal of Psychology, 136*: 425–441.

Jones-Johnson, G., and Johnson, W.R. (1992). "Subjective underemployment and psychosocial stress: The role of perceived social and supervisor support", *The Journal of Social Psychology, 132*(1): 11–21.

Jones-Johnson, G., and Johnson, W.R. (1995). "Subjective underemployment and job satisfaction", *International Review of Modern Sociology, 25* (Spring): 73–84.

Khan, L.J., and Morrow, P.C. (1991). "Objective and subjective underemployment relationships to job satisfaction", *Journal of Business Research, 22*(3): 211–218.

King, Z. (2003). "New or traditional careers? A study of UK graduates' preferences", *Human Resource Management Journal, 13*(1): 5–26.

Leana, C.R., and Feldman, D.C. (1995). "Finding new jobs after a plant closing: Antecedents and outcomes of the occurrence and quality of reemployment", *Human Relations, 48*(12): 1381–1401.

Lin, B., Law, K.S., & Zhou, J. (2017). "Why is underemployment related to creativity and OCB? A task-crafting explanation of the curvilinear moderated relations", *Academy of Management Journal, 60*(1), 156–177.

Livingstone, D.W. (1998). *The Education-Jobs Gap – Underemployment of Economic Democracy*. Boulder, CO: West View Press.

Maynard, D.C., Joseph, T.A., and Maynard, A.M. (2006). "Underemployment, job attitudes and turnover intentions", *Journal of Organizational Behaviour, 27*(4): 509–536.

McKee-Ryan, F.M., and Harvey, J. (2011). " 'I have a job, but . . .': A review of underemployment", *Journal of Management, 37*(4): 962–996.

McKee-Ryan, F., Virick, M., Prussia, G.E., Harvey, J., & Lilly, J.D. (2009). "Life after the layoff: Getting a job worth keeping", *Journal of Organizational Behavior, 30*: 561–580.

Mills, C.W. (1953). *The White Collar Worker*. New York: Oxford University Press.

NUS (National Union of Students) (1937). *Graduate Employment*. A report of the 1937 Congress of the National Union of Students of England and Wales, London.

Nunley, J.M., Pugh, A., Romero, N., and Seals, R.A. (2017). "The effects of unemployment and underemployment on employment opportunities: Results from a correspondence audit of the labor market for college graduates", *ILR Review, 70*(3): 642–669.

ONS (2013). *Full Report – Graduates in the UK Labour Market 2013*. November 2013, Office for National Statistics. (online) available from: www.ons.gov.uk/ons/dcp171776_337841.pdf.

ONS (2017). *Graduates in the UK Labour Market 2017.* November 2017, 2013, Office for National Statistics. (online) available from: www.ons.gov.uk/employmentandlabourmarket/peopleinwork/employmentandemployeetypes/articles/graduatesintheuklabourmarket/2017.

PACE (Parliamentary Assembly of the Council of Europe) (2012). *The Young Generation Sacrificed: Social, Economic and Political Implications of the Financial Crisis.* Strasbourg: Committee on Social Affairs, Health and Sustainable Development.

Purcell, K., Pitcher, J., & Simm, C. (1999). *Working Out?: Graduates' Early Experiences of the Labour Market.* CSU (Publications) Limited.

Roth, J. (1963). *Timetables: Structuring the Passage of Time in Hospital Treatment and Other Careers.* New York: Bobbs-Merrill.

Scurry, T., and Blenkinsopp, J. (2011). "Under-employment among recent graduates: a review of the literature", *Personnel Review*, 40(5): 643–659.

Steffy, K. (2017). "Willful versus woeful underemployment: Perceived volition and social class background among overqualified college graduates", *Work and Occupations*, 44(4): 467–511.

Thompson, K.W., Shea, T.H., Sikora, D.M., Perrewé, P.L., and Ferris, G.R. (2013). "Rethinking underemployment and overqualification in organizations: The not so ugly truth", *Business Horizons*, 56(1): 113–121.

Try, S. (2004). "The role of flexible work in the transition from higher education into the labour market", *Journal of Education and Work*, 17(1): 27–45.

Wilkins, R., & Wooden, M. (2011). "Economic approaches to studying underemployment", In: Maynard, D.C., & Feldman, D.C. (Eds.), *Underemployment: Psychological, Economic, and Social Challenges.* New York, NY: Springer, pp. 13–34.

Winefield, A.H., Winefield, H.R., Tiggemann, M., and Goldney, R.D. (1991). "A longitudinal study of the psychological effects of unemployment and unsatisfactory employment on young adults", *Journal of Applied Psychology*, 76(3): 424–431.

Wolf, A. (2004). "Education and economic performance: Simplistic theories and their policy consequences", *Oxford Review of Economic Policy*, 20(2): 315–333.

Part 3

Professional and organisational issues relating to employability

10 Organisational responses to the employability agenda in English universities

Bob Gilworth

This chapter is informed by a study which I completed in 2012 and by observations of developments in UK Higher Education subsequently. It seeks to use these sources to construct an overview of the ways in which English Universities have configured their resources to deal with strategic imperatives relating to student and graduate careers and employability. It is of particular relevance to anyone who requires a greater understanding of the scale and scope of modern higher education careers and employability services and the strategic forces which shape their organisation.

Background

The original study sought to answer the question 'How is the employability offer conceptualised, constructed, managed and measured and what choices about organisational configuration and capability are being made and acted upon?'

The study was based on five in-depth case studies. It was an abductive enquiry in the sense that Hammersley (2005) describes abduction as 'the development of an explanatory or theoretical idea, this often resulting from close examination of particular cases.' The study required the development of a deep understanding of the 'story' of employability within a manageable number of institutions from which themes and patterns of organisational response could be derived.

The need for depth, the establishment of narrative and an essentially abductive enquiry lent itself to a case study approach. The nature of the study was to describe, compare and contrast the approaches being adopted and to understand how and why they are playing out as they are. 'Case study research generally answers one or more questions which begin with "how" or "why".' (Soy, 1997). The approach borrowed from the realist methodology championed by Pawson (1996) and echoed by Kazi (2003) which asks the question 'what works for whom and under what circumstances?' Pawson and Kazi both look at the evaluation of 'human service programmes' (usually in the areas of health and social care) and take the view that these are open systems with many intervening and context-specific factors likely to mean that programmes which are similar or even identical in purpose will play out differently in different contexts.

Key themes

I will use the key themes from the original work, whilst taking the opportunity to provide updated commentary in the light of subsequent events over the last five years.

The key themes to emerge from the original study were as follows:

- The constant challenge of balancing Environment, Values and Resources (E,V, R).
- The underlying constant of positional/status competition between institutions.
- The importance of co-production between student and institution.
- The notion of Issue Awareness – the importance of the distinction between careers and employability being 'important' and being 'an issue' in driving change.
- The ways in which the external environment (E) is translated into the internal operating environment through the medium of institutional identity.
- The why, the what and the who of institutional strategy.
- Starting points, directions of travel and strategic fit for the configuration of professional services in this area.
- The emergence of new forms of HE careers service organisation and leadership roles.

Environment, Values and Resources (E, V, R)

A feature of strategic management is the constant attempt to balance Environment (the external forces at work and the context in which we must operate) Values (what we are about and how we do things around here) and Resources (those assets which we can deploy in pursuit of our strategy), **E,V, R** (Thompson and Martin, 2005).

Higher education careers and employability services are departments of their institutions. For the leader of the service and his/her colleagues, the external 'E' is always translated through the medium of institutional interpretation and the operating environment *within* the institution. They may have to manage the V at both institutional and service levels. A particular risk in managing the balance between E, V and R is that of drifting into 'conscious incompetence.' This is the situation in which the dominant values drag scarce resources away from responding to the real and current needs generated by the environment. In a Venn diagram, V and R overlap, whilst E is detached. This phenomenon has played out in relation to the institutional careers service in several institutions in the past. The 'back story' in three of the institutions in my original five case studies included situations in which a previous approach to managing the relevant professional service was deemed to be no longer fit for purpose because they were seen by the institution as being driven by dominant (service) values which were misaligned with institutional ambitions and priorities, and significant change followed.

Environment: the policy environment

This section summarises the main issues and drivers in the policy environment as key components of the external 'E' to be considered by those responsible for configuring the careers and employability offer in English universities.

The numerous policy initiatives are well-documented elsewhere and space precludes going into detail here. However, it is clear that the position that we find in 2017/18 reflects a direction of travel which was already in train in 2012. The publication of the 'Browne Review' report 'Securing a Sustainable Future for Higher Education' (Browne, 2010) and the subsequent government decision to lift of the cap on tuition fees in England to a maximum of £9000 per annum from 2012, moved English higher education into an era in which the individual undergraduate student is expected to make a far higher contribution to the cost of their education than ever before on the basis that it is a private (as well as a public) good – 'we took higher education out of the public sector' (Willetts, 2017).

League tables including scores for graduate employment outcomes had been in existence for some time, but the Browne review kick-started a policy drive to link employment outcomes to student choice (of institutions/courses) which has continued and gathered pace to the present day. A clear line can be seen running from Browne, through the introduction of 'consumer data' such as the Key Information sets (KIS) and 'Unistats', the Wilson Review of university-business collaboration in 2012, the introduction of the Teaching Excellence Framework (TEF) and the first release of Longitudinal Employment Outcomes (LEO) data and the Higher Education and Research Act in 2017 to the creation of The Office for Students and the launch of the Graduate Outcomes (as the successor to the current DLHE survey), in 2018.

The Wilson review combined notions of student consumer choice with the 'Knowledge Economy' context:

> Better informed students are more likely to choose a university and a course that provides them with the right learning experiences, and best prepares them for work in their desired career. Universities will need to respond to the demands of informed students and improve their practices in order to compete for students, and businesses will profit from being able to recruit energised and innovative graduates.
>
> (Wilson, 2012: 29)

The Knowledge Economy and regional engagement expectations in relation to graduate talent continue now and are articulated through the government's Industrial Strategy and its links to Higher Education funding through the Catalyst Fund, for example (HEFCE, 2017).

The Office for Students could be seen as the ultimate expression of the existence of a consumer market through the introduction of a market regulator. Its Chair, Sir Michael Barber, seemed clear that employability and graduate outcomes are key components of the mission of the regulator when commenting on the appointment of Nicola Dandridge as chief executive of the new organisation:

> Nicola will be instrumental in ensuring that the Office for Students enables the sector to improve outcomes for students. I look forward to working with her to shape the brand new regulatory framework, putting student participation, academic success, and employability at its heart.
>
> (DfE 2018).

The reform of the DLHE survey and the move to Graduate Outcomes has been partly driven by the sector itself. However, one of the policy drivers has been to make the survey more independent by moving away from collection of data by institutions themselves. TEF is another mechanism for rating HE institutions in a visible way in which graduate employment outcomes again feature prominently.

All of the above should be seen in the context of sustained policy to marketise the sector and increase competition, not least by opening the market to more alternative providers. This was a key element of the Higher Education Act 2017. This follows on from the effective deregulation of undergraduate student recruitment through the abolition of the numbers cap for 2015/16.

The policy element of the environment in which those with institutional responsibility for careers and employability must lead/manage could be summarised as follows:

- Employability is publicly aligned with perceived institutional quality, student (consumer) choice, value for money and public accountability to an unprecedented degree.
- Institutions are judged on metrics-based exercises and league tables and employability features strongly in all of them.
- The expectation that HE institutions will be key providers of skills for the Knowledge Economy of and drivers of regional economic development continues.
- A new regulatory organisation (OfS) is being established with the interests of the student as the (paying) consumer of higher education at the heart of its mission.
- Widening Participation is more overtly concerned with social mobility. It is increasingly seen as being about 'getting on, not just getting in' (Gilworth, 2017) and the role of careers services is being highlighted (Bridge Group, 2017). Access missions and employability missions are more strongly connected than ever and the OfS has a regulatory role in this.
- Metrics used to judge the performance of institutions in employability terms will be derived from sources which are independent of the institutions – Graduate Outcomes and salary data via the Longitudinal Educational Outcomes (LEO) data.
- All of this takes place in a marketised sector in which a combination of policy and demographics have increased competition for home undergraduate

students and in which examples of winners and losers are already starting to emerge.
- Many measures are overtly designed for institutional comparison and/or used by the media for that purpose.

Co-Production

Although aspects of the policy environment seek to position the student as a consumer and seek to protect their interests as such, this does not necessarily accord with the way that students see their involvement in higher education. Rather, there is evidence to suggest that students still understand, value and expect co-production. The recent UUK report 'Education, consumer rights and maintaining trust: what students want from their university' (UUK, 2017) showed that students value the special 'co-production' relationship that they have with their universities. Employability is a classic example of co-production between student and institution. This must continue to influence the ways in which institutions configure and manage their careers and employability strategies and offers.

What might be the primary product of co-production in employability terms? I would argue that the available evidence tends to point in the direction of the definition of employability that I have been using for some time now, which is: 'the capability to make well-informed realistic plans for the future, and to be able to execute these in a changing world'. The HE environment can create opportunities to build skills and other 'employability' but it must also support the informed choice, career planning and development of career management skills which will enable students to turn these assets into fulfilling futures. As we will see below, co-production is a long-standing feature of status competition between institutions.

Environment: positional/status competition

Competition between higher education institutions is hardly new. As Marginson (2004) points out, these institutions play a central role in the production/allocation of social status (social advantage, social position). Universities both convey and acquire the social good of status and accompanying economic, political and cultural advantages, notably career success of alumni. Producing graduates who obtain high level jobs also conveys status to the institution. Success is co-produced between student and institution, creating a circular, win/win situation.

Marginson argues that competition between higher education institutions has always been based on status, rather than say, revenues for their own sake as might be the case in genuine economic competition. Status competition persists within the increased marketisation of higher education in many societies and systems in recent years. He goes on to argue that the impact of status competition is heightened in societies in which neo-liberal assumptions underpin the public policy which governs the operating environment. This would seem to be a fair description of what has occurred in this country.

Marginson suggests that students want the status goods with the highest possible (labour market) value and that they identify these by making educated guesses based on an understanding of status derived from what he calls 'common sense' or 'common gossip' (Marginson, 2004: 185). There are many who would argue that this understanding of institutional status is 'common gossip' in some socio-economic circles and not others, meaning that some guesses are more educated than others. The proponents of a greater volume of more visible and more standardised consumer information might argue that not only does this help to take out the guesswork to some degree, it does so in a way which creates more equality of information upon which to base informed choices. Recent policy creating very patchy provision of careers guidance in schools is arguably at odds with this, as access to professional and/or parental mediation of the huge volume of new data is not equally distributed across society.

Pre-existing positional competition continues in an atmosphere in which the public are being encouraged more strongly than ever before to test claims and assumptions about the positional/status benefits of attending institution x as compared to institution y. This can apply just as much to institutions whose claims to delivering good employability outcomes are based on a perception of being 'vocational' as it might to those whose claims are more strongly connected to traditional status.

Issue awareness

One of the implications of positional competition between institutions in an era of greater scrutiny and transparency in which employability features so strongly is that fundamental questions about the institutional approach to employability may be/should be raised. These questions are much more likely to be asked if employability, however defined, is seen as an issue at the most senior levels of the institution.

Issue awareness (Johnson and Scholes, 1993) refers to that element of strategy-making which asks the question 'is there something amiss?' or 'is there a problem which must be fixed?' in order for the organisation's strategy to be successfully pursued. A strategic consideration such as employability can be important without necessarily being 'an issue.' For example, amongst the examples of major players in the provision of sandwich placements cited in the Wilson Review, there are some very successful institutions, which regularly occupy places in the upper reaches of league tables. They are former Colleges of Advanced Technology (CATs) which became universities in the 1960s. In the sense of founding ethos employability is undoubtedly important to them, but it is not an issue, because the available measures suggest that this is all going rather well. As part of my previous study (but not as one of the case studies), I discussed this with a Pro Vice Chancellor of one of those institutions, who made it clear that the importance of employability to the 'DNA' of the institution was such that if it ever became an issue, it would be seen as a major one requiring swift and decisive action.

HE Careers Service colleagues have sometimes been bemused by the fact that signals that employability matters in their institution have not translated into increased traction or resources for their services. The notion of issue awareness helps to make it clear that action and resource allocation at the institutional level is often driven by the identification of issues, not simply by what is seen as important. This is particularly the case when there are multiple competing priorities. Many things are 'important' but it is the issues which receive attention and drive change. In a tight resource environment, there will be winners and losers in allocating scarce resources. One of the institutions in my original study declared its intention to 'disinvest' in areas which did not directly serve institutional strategy. In that particular case, employability was seen as an issue and as directly related to institutional strategy. As such, it attracted significant investment and executive determination to drive change and development in this area.

Institutional approaches and responses to the employability aspects of TEF have been very interesting in this regard. In the institutions with which I have regular interaction, I have seen little or no ambivalence about the employability aspect. Instead, employability has tended to be seen as a strength which must be protected or enhanced or a weakness which must be addressed. This may be because the internal processes leading up to TEF submissions and the internal debate afterwards has highlighted the impact of employability offer and outcomes to senior institutional stakeholders in the context of sharpened positional competition. Those stakeholders have been directly involved in the process in a way in which many of them have not been previously involved in the DLHE. In cases where employability is seen as a problem to be fixed or a position of advantage to be defended, TEF seems to have either led to or accelerated pre-existing consideration of fundamental institutional approaches to employability and/or related resource deployment. My research case studies pre-dated TEF by several years, but in two of them at least, issue awareness based on positional competition was high as was executive determination to solve the problem, and significant change followed. Issue awareness creates change in the relationships between E, V and R. The demands of the environment (E) are perceived to have changed (though the underlying theme of positional competition is constant), 'the way we do things around here' (V) – in this case the structure of the employability offer – is challenged and more resources (R) are deployed. The challenge to V means that the increased resources are rarely deployed to do 'more of the same.' My observation is that TEF seems to have increased issue awareness around employability. It seems to be both important and an issue in more places now than it was before. The policy and market environment and issue awareness, together, tend to drive the Why (strategic purpose) of the organisational response to the employability agenda.

Institutional ethos and identity

As autonomous institutions, universities build up dominant cultures over time, and these tend to exert significant influence over institutional strategy, priorities and decision-making. Approaches to employability are not exempt from this. Despite the nuanced diversity of the institutions in question, my previous work in this area (Gilworth, 2013) boiled down institutional 'employability identity' to just two types. These were 'Employability Intrinsic' and 'Employability Added.' The first of these relates to those institutions in which professional and/or vocational education is fundamental to the foundation and ongoing character of the institution. This is often reflected in the significant offer and take-up of sandwich degrees with industrial placements, with placement units in the academic departments, seen as integral to the educational offer and infrastructure. This is by no means a simple pre-'92/post-'92 divide. The Wilson report showed that 'a small number of universities in the UK provide the majority of sandwich placements' (Wilson, 2012). The examples quoted were: Loughborough, Bath, Aston, Surrey, Brunel, Ulster and Bournemouth. Five of these are pre-'92 universities and two are former Polytechnics. The pre-'92 universities are all former Colleges of Advanced Technology (CATs).

The number of multi-faculty institutions which are genuinely employability intrinsic is (perhaps surprisingly) small. The rest tend to be employability added, where the institutional foundation and dominant academic culture has not traditionally paid attention to employability; sandwich degrees are relatively rare and there is little or no employability infrastructure built into the fabric of the majority of academic departments (with notable exceptions in medicine, health and teacher training). In these cases, elements of employability have been added into and around the curriculum and the broader student experience. Institutional employability identity was an emergent category from cross-case analysis in my earlier study. Of the five in-depth case studies, four of them were identified as employability added.

Leaders of institutional careers and employability organisations need to understand the employability identity of their institutions. Issue awareness and executive determination drive change per se, but institutional employability identity can be key to shaping the nature of that change. Crucially, for some institutions, there may be a difference between perceived and actual identity. Identities may change over time and perception may or may not have caught up with reality. When issue awareness kicks in and 'something must be done' the organisational response is likely to be effective if it is rooted in an understanding of current reality and future direction.

Most mainstream institutions are mixed economies. Some of the institutions which may be perceived as the most purely academic in general terms actually contain what might be seen as the most vocational programmes of all, in areas such as medicine and dentistry, to name just two. Equally, some institutions which may be perceived as being strongly vocational have large programmes in arts, humanities and social sciences. Most careers and employability leaders must work with these mixed economies, but in some cases, there will be a prevailing institutional sense of identity which is historically rooted. This can dominate the internal employability discourse and may need to be challenged in order for the institution to move forward.

Organisational responses to the employability agenda   135

The following are generalised examples. They are not offered as case studies of specific institutions, but they are based on direct observation and offer illustrations of type.

One example might be an institution which has a particular history and is known for a certain subject area with famous alumni in that area, but which has grown and diversified over the years since those famous people graduated. An institution known in the popular imagination as say, an art college may actually graduate significantly more students in other subjects these days. If the internal sense of identity is dominated by an outdated public perception and self-image, this could create problems in framing a careers and employability strategy, offer and organisation which works for the whole institution as it is now.

Another might be a former polytechnic, which may have been highly vocational with a very high proportion of sandwich degree programmes at its inception and for a large part of its history. It may be in a city in which it is 'paired' with a research-intensive pre-92 university and is routinely viewed by students, staff and public as the more 'vocational' of the two. Meanwhile, over time, the actual student take-up of sandwich placements has dramatically declined, three year arts, humanities and social science programmes have proved much more popular (than technical, industry-linked sandwich degrees) with potential students and have grown in both absolute and proportional terms and the academic staff profile has changed to become more engaged with research and less engaged with the nuts and bolts of placement learning. In short, the real employability identity is now closer to employability added than employability intrinsic. Any strategic approach to employability should take this into account.

Institutional identity tends to shape the How and the Who (the configuration of delivery organisations) of institutional responses to the employability agenda.

The patterns emerging from the original case studies suggested that in employability added institutions, the internal organisations developed to lead, coordinate and deliver the strategy for careers and employability tend to be based on and built around/built out from the central professional careers service. This was the case in all four of my employability added case studies. Observation of developments in the sector suggest that this pattern has continued since then. Some consideration of starting points and evolution of structural delivery models may help to illustrate this.

The report 'Break-Out or Break-Up?' (Watts and Butcher, 2008) introduced the useful concept of extended and non-extended careers services. In the extended services, the remit of the services was broadened beyond the traditional core of Information Advice and Guidance (IAG) and the provision of opportunities for students to meet employers. The process of extension has continued in many institutions since the Watts and Butcher report. Extended services have drawn in resources and responsibilities for related activities, such as enterprise, volunteering and/or the design and delivery of relevant modules in formal curricula. Significantly, the extended services in the Watts and Butcher study, and in many cases since, have played a central role in the establishment and coordination of work placements and internships, an area of activity which had historically

136 *Bob Gilworth*

lacked impetus and infrastructure in employability added institutions and was (and remains) school/faculty-based in employability intrinsic institutions. Now, over three-quarters of university careers services are directly involved in managing placements and internships (Zhu, 2017).

New forms of HE careers service organisation and leadership roles

The organisational responses to the employability agenda have produced variations which have extended beyond the two dimensions of non-extended/extended, and I offer a typology below.

- **Non-extended central services.** Though primarily focused on the central provision of IAG and employer engagement, these services are now more extended than that original concept as it is now quite rare to have a central service which does not manage one or more placement/internship programmes. Once the norm across the sector and the basis of many external perceptions, these services are few in number now. Non-extended should not be interpreted in a pejorative sense. In many cases, the existence/continuation of a relatively non-extended service relates to institutional fit. Such services may be well aligned in institutions with very able and highly motivated students, with strong employer support and many co-curricular opportunities, where the students voluntarily engage with the service in large numbers. Such services may also be found in those employability intrinsic institutions which have stuck most closely to their missions and structures, with strong faculty-based placement units, high levels of placement expectation, offer and take-up and a self-perpetuating cycle of attracting students who have consciously chosen this style of higher education. Where all stakeholders are comfortable with this institutional fit, E, V and R can be seen to be aligned. However, there will be cases in which it is incumbent on the leader of the central service to establish the value-adding role of the service in the institutional employability ecosystem with their teams and with institutional stakeholders, so that E, V and R are aligned.
- **Extended central services.** Probably the most common form of Careers and Employability organization in the sector at the moment. They are often comprehensive in covering most if not all (co-curricular) activities which could be construed as contributing to employability. The range of activities means that the staffing profile is less homogeneous than in non-extended services. In some cases, this form has grown organically (sometimes over many years) out of an original non-extended set-up. In other cases, this form is the outcome of change instigated through issue awareness and perceived misalignment of E, V and R in a non-extended service. In some cases, the change took place a decade or more ago and astute leaders who came into position at that time have been able to develop on to other forms outlined below. There are cases in which the reform was undertaken primarily to

'fix' the problem of the alignment of a central service and not as part of a broader strategic evaluation of the whole institution approach to careers and employability. In some of these cases, the extended central service has no control over uncoordinated development of employability activity elsewhere in the institution and the E, V, R alignment issues can re-surface across the institution.

- **Extended and institutionally embedded.** These tend to be mature examples of extended services in which the leader (or successive leaders) and his/her team have developed the services' connectivity with all the other relevant parts of the institution to the point that interaction with, respect for and reference to the service is natural and ubiquitous. Examples of this in action would include more or less universal reference to the service in the employability sections of all programme information, the service being positioned as the natural coordinator of whole institution co-curricular skills development efforts and the 'go- to' organisation in relation to the consideration of careers and employability by the institutional learning and teaching community. One of my original case studies was a very good example of this and a recent visit showed that it continues to be so. E, V and R are generally well aligned.
- **Integrated-whole institution.** These are the services which have been consciously developed as 'hub and spoke' models, usually through a process which was based on high levels of issue awareness and executive determination. These are whole institution careers and employability organisations, with both central and distributed provision. They have physical space and staff teams in a central location and in each of the major academic units (the academic home of the students), but they are a single, coherent entity under one senior leader. One of the original case studies was the first large-scale example of the hub and spoke model. It has since been followed by one other genuine, whole-institution example. Both have been very successful in relation to public measures of institutional performance. Other institutions are developing this approach. Some have this in a partial sense, where particularly interested academic departments have funded dedicated teams, physically located in the department, but organisationally part of and managed by the central professional service. In many cases, the professional service staff will be organisationally aligned with the academic units in a 'business partner' model, even though there is not a formal hub and spoke structure. This happens to varying degrees in all the other service models described above. It is one of the reasons why the job title of 'Careers Adviser' has been changed to 'Careers Consultant' in numerous institutions. A strong business partner approach in an extended and institutionally embedded organisation may well be seen as delivering the same benefits as a fully developed hub and spoke model.
- **The role of the leader.** The importance of the employability agenda and the organisational responses to it have driven a significant change in the role of the careers and employability professional service leader. It is increasingly

common for this to be a dual role combining management of the central professional service unit with the role of principal strategic adviser to the institution on all matters relating to careers and employability. With a few exceptional cases of very high levels of voluntary involvement, the issue of student engagement with careers and employability provision is a challenge across the sector. Institutions seek ways to make engagement structurally unavoidable, and the hub and spoke model is a particularly visible manifestation of this. Careers and Employability leaders in any model of service need to ensure that the provision not only engages large numbers of students, but that scarce resources are particularly directed to where they will make the most difference. This is an evidence-based task increasingly informed by large data sets, particularly (though not exclusively) Careers Registration (Gilworth and Thambar, 2013). In some cases, the job title of the leader suggests an institutional role which is not restricted to the management of the central service, e.g., Director of Student Employability or Director of Careers and Employability (not 'service'). These are demanding roles. They are effectively responsible for aligning E, V and R in employability terms, for the whole institution. This may involve using data and evidence to challenge some entrenched views and perceptions. Institutional backing is crucial to success and this can vary. Theoretical hub and spoke approaches, without line management authority and a clear mandate from the top, can be challenging. It is very difficult for an individual to meet tacit expectations of a hub and spoke model if 'no-one told the spokes.'

Conclusion

In conclusion, two major observations can be made in relation to organisational responses to employability. Firstly, a recognition of the shift in how careers and employability leadership is enacted. The shift to the dual role (strategic leader and service manager) may not be universal but it is a significant trend and it is gathering pace. It should be firmly on the radar of those who occupy the roles, aspire to them, work in their teams, recruit and manage them, train and develop the current leaders and their successors and partner with them within and outside their institutions (not least employers). Secondly, outdated and evidence-light views of the role, scope and scale of modern HE careers and employability organisations are quite common and frequently expressed. It would be a pleasing result if this chapter went some way to updating some of those views. More important is the fact that those in and close to the HE sector who need to be concerned with careers and employability cannot afford to be unaware of the ways in which our universities are organising themselves in this area, which this overview has sought to illuminate.

References

DfE (2018). "New Universities Regulator Comes into Force", Department for Education. (online) available from: www.gov.uk/government/news/new-universities-regulator-comes-into-force.

Organisational responses to the employability agenda 139

Bridge Group (2017). *Social Mobility and University Careers Services.* London: Bridge Group..

Browne, J. (2010). *Securing a Sustainable Future for Higher Education, an Independent Review of Higher Education Funding and Student Finance,* Department for Business Innovation and Skills. London: HMSO.

Gilworth, R.B. (2013). *Organisational Responses to the Employability Agenda in English Universities.* DBA Thesis International Centre for Higher Education Management (ICHEM), University of Bath.

Gilworth, R.B. (2017). "Report Launched on Careers Services and Social Mobility", Bridge Group. (online) available from: https://thebridgegroup.org.uk/report-launched-on-careers-services-and-social-mobility/.

Gilworth, R.B., and Thambar, N.P. (2013). *Careers Registration a Data Revolution.* (Conference presentation), AGCAS Biennial Conference, Exeter 2013. (online) available from: www.agcas.org.uk/events/766-Biennial-Conference-2013-Exeter.

Hammersley, M. (2005). *Assessing Quality in Qualitative Research* (Conference presentation), ESRC TLRP seminar series, Quality in Educational Research, University of Birmingham 7 July. (online) available from: www.bhamlive3.bham.ac.uk/Documents/college-socialsciences/education/projects/esrc-2005-seminarseries4.pdf.

Higher Education Funding Council for England (2107). *Catalyst Fund.* (online) available from: www.hefce.ac.uk/funding/catalyst/.

Johnson, G., and Scholes, K. (1993). *Exploring Corporate Strategy* (3rd Edition). London: Prentice Hall.

Kazi, M.A.F. (2003). *Realist Evaluation in Practice.* London: Sage.

Marginson, S. (2004). "Competition and Markets in Higher Education: a 'glonacal' analysis", *Journal of Education Policy Futures, 2*(2): 175–244.

Pawson R, (1996). "Theorizing the Interview", *The British Journal of Sociology, 47*(2): 295–314.

Soy, S.K. (1997). "The case study as a research method" Unpublished paper, University of Texas at Austin. (online) available from: www.gslis.utexas.edu/~ssoy/usesusers/l391d1b.html.

Thompson, J., and Martin, F. (2005). *Strategic Management Awareness and Change.* Andover: South Western.

Universities UK (2017). *Education, Consumer Rights and Maintaining Trust: What Students Want from their University.* London: UUK.

Watts, A.G., and Butcher, V. (2008). *Break Out or Break Up?* Manchester: Higher Education Careers Services Unit.

Willetts, D. (2017). Speech at "A University Education, Past, Present and Future", HEPI London, 21 November 2017.

Wilson, T. (2012). *Review of Business-University Collaboration.* (online) available from: www.wilsonreview.co.uk/.

Zhu, C. (2017). *AGCAS Graduate Labour Market Survey Report.* Sheffield: AGCAS.

11 A new career in higher education careers work

Siobhan Neary and Jill Hanson

Introduction

As has already been reported in previous chapters the role and importance of employability has become central within the context of higher education in the UK. Whilst the conceptualisation, operationalisation and utility of 'employability' has long been contested (e.g., Wolf, 1991, Holmes, 2000), Higher Education Institutions are nonetheless increasingly under pressure from students, government and employers to ensure that students have the skills, behaviours and attitudes that will enable them to undertake an effective transition into the workplace (Artess, Hooley and Mellors-Bourne, 2017). To address this university careers services now offer a portfolio of activities that support students with effective transition. These can include a wide range of activities including curriculum delivery, employer engagement activities, placement support, job search support and advice and guidance (Christie, 2016, Thambar, 2018).

In this chapter we present recent research which aims to better understand the expectations and realities of career development practitioners who have recently transitioned into a careers role within Higher Education Institutions (HEIs), focusing on what attracts them to the profession and how they see their new career. It provides an exploration of the knowledge, skills and experiences of career changers who want to utilise their previous expertise within a new context. This research presents an insight into the backgrounds of many of the new staff that have entered the field over the last five years and what they bring with them that can contribute to graduates becoming better informed about careers and the labour market as well as more empowered in the application of their employability and career management skills. It presents an opportunity to consider issues on how the field is evolving and issues for the HE career development field going forward.

The evolving career development workforce

The focus on metrics including the Destinations of Leavers from Higher Education (DLHE) as evidence of successful transition from Higher Education (HE) to work has become a driver for the employability agenda and the heightened role of careers services. Whilst such metrics *can* misrepresent the reality of students transitioning into work or further study after graduating, the fact remains that universities typically place a great deal of importance on them (Christie, 2017).

This focus on employability has contributed to a rapid and dynamic expansion of careers services in some institutions. This has also resulted in the development of a range of differentiated work roles, for example, curriculum development officers, placement co-ordinators, volunteering officers/co-ordinators, employability advisers, enterprise advisers/co-ordinators, DLHE co-ordinators/statistics officers. The extent to which a range of roles are provided will be dependent on the size of the service and the characteristics of the student body. Many careers services have also adopted a devolved approach providing services within and across faculties and departments offering some, if not all, a selection of these specialist roles.

Research by the Association of Graduate Careers Advisory Services (AGCAS) (2016) suggests that on average, careers and employability services will have 23 staff undertaking a variety of roles, which equates to approximately 20.2 staff delivering these activities (Full Time Equivalents [FTE]). A comparison to a similar staffing survey undertaken by AGCAS in 2008 illustrates that the range of job roles in HE careers services has evolved significantly. Table 11.1 compares how the number and variation of roles has developed.

In addition to the posts identified above other roles were also identified including internship officers, student award officers, marketing officers and enterprise officers. The 2016 research identified over 100 job titles. There is a growing body of research which examines the role, activities and impacts of career development practitioners working in an HE context (Christie, 2016; Thambar, 2016, 2018;

Table 11.1 Comparison of staffing levels between 2008 and 2016

2008[*] – Mean number of staff	2016[**] – FTE number of staff
Head of Service (00.98)	Head of Service (1)
Deputy Head of Service (0.55)	Deputy Head of Service (0.8)
Careers advisers (4.8)	Management team role (2.4)
Employer liaison (1.69)	Careers advisers (3)
Information specialist (1.79)	Career consultants (2.2)
IT specialist (0.44)	Employer engagement officer (1.7)
	Placement Officers (1.5)
	Student engagement officers (including information and statistics) (1.6)
	IT specialist (0.3)
	Admin clerical (2.3)
	Other staff (2.2)

[*] 72 Heads of Service responded
[**] 56 Heads of Service responded

142 *Siobhan Neary and Jill Hanson*

Taylor and Hooley, 2014). However, due to the diverse nature of HE institutions, there has tended not to be universal benchmarks concerning how services are constituted, which means it is difficult to compare services (Christie, 2016; Bridge Group, 2017).

Career transitions

In this section, we explore the literature which details the skills, behaviours and attitudes that support career change generally and discuss the limited findings on transition into careers work, in order to understand the broader context for why people might move into HE careers posts. There is considerable research into career changers, examining theory (e.g., Grzeda, 1999) as well as actual behaviour and the skills that support it, for example, Carless and Arnup (2011), who looked at the determinants and outcomes of career change, and Brown and co-authors who have focussed on career adaptabilities and the processes underlying career identity development and transition (e.g., Brown et al., 2012; Brown, 2015). Factors which underpin a decision to change career can be considered as individual or organisational (Rhodes and Doering, 1983). Carless and Arnup (2011) found that personality characteristics (openness to experience, extraversion), demographics (age, gender, education level and occupation tenure) and attitudes to job security are all determinants of a mid-career change. Haasler and Barabasch (2015) note that mid-career changes may reflect increased self-awareness and personal agency, internal struggles, a need to fully express the inner self and a move against previous restrictions and constraints. It has also been argued that when career transitions are embarked upon out of choice they are driven by personal agency and represent career adaptability, as opposed to forced involuntary transitions which indicate resilience (Damle, 2015).

Movement across roles, professions and sectors, in what are now termed boundaryless careers, requires individual recognition of transferable skills which in turn provides a significant advantage in the scope to change career (Brown et al., 2012). Research from Brown et al. focussed on the role career adaptability played in decision-making and skills development for mid-career changers, highlighting the importance of upskilling and/or re-skilling and the potentially transformative shifts in perspective required for successful change. Research from Bimrose and Hearne (2012) indicated that career resilience and adaptability are important – those moving into the careers sector need to be resilient and anxious to make a positive difference (Bimrose and Hearne, 2012) as well as being highly skilled at decision-making, organisation, time management and counselling (being empathic and able to listen actively) (Patton, 2002). The literature provides some indication of the motivations for moving into careers work and the skills necessary for success, but there remains a significant gap regarding mid-career change to the career development and guidance field, specifically exploring selection and motivation for the field and how previous experiences/skills facilitate the transition.

Methodology

The research was a cross sectional design; data was collected at one point in time using an online survey. The key aim was to better understand the nature of the workforce in the field of HE career guidance, and to illuminate any enablers and barriers for those who had recently transitioned into career development work. The responses were gathered from 175 UK career development professionals working in HE who had moved into the sector from another career. On average practitioners had worked for 4.5 years in a careers related role in the HE sector. The results provide an interesting snapshot of a sample of the HE careers and employability workforce. The majority of respondents (70%) were females aged over 35; 90% of respondents described themselves as white, 3% as Asian, 1% as black and 2% as mixed race. Respondents were primarily qualified to level 7 (post-graduate certificate/diploma or full masters – over 70% were at this level). Sixteen per cent of respondents were qualified to level 6 (undergraduate degree level) and a small percentage (1%) indicated qualifications at sub degree level.

An online self-completion survey was adopted which contained 24 questions that were a mix of closed and open ended questions. It was circulated broadly through iCeGS contacts and adopted a snowball effect, utilising contacts within the professional associations such as the Career Development Institute (CDI) and AGCAS; both are membership organisations in the UK. Survey questions focused on exploring transferable skills, knowledge and experience, career trajectories, the attraction to the sector and views regarding training and progression opportunities.

Data was imported into an Excel spreadsheet and analyses were conducted using Excel and SPSS for quantitative data and NVivo for qualitative data captured through the open questions. Although this was purposive and a convenience sample it was sufficiently large to enable us to make some observations about the sector and the views of the new practitioners within it.

Findings

Demographics

In exploring the demographic data, it is interesting to note that the workforce within careers and employability centres is characterised as white females aged 35 and over, which continues to align careers work with female dominated caring professions (Allan and Moffett, 2015). The age is less of a surprise as it is recognised that the respondents are career changers. However, the data raises issues concerning how representative the careers workforce is when compared with other parts of institutions and the student body. HESA (2017) present that 81% of academic and non-academic staff are defined as white and 57% of professional staff on non-academic contracts are female. When considering student ethnic groups HEFCE (2017) report that 29% of the student body entrants are

144   *Siobhan Neary and Jill Hanson*

BME (Black Minority Ethnic). This presents some interesting considerations concerning the lack of diversity within the careers workforce and what can be done to address this and make the profession more representative of the clients that practitioners work with.

Previous occupations

Through analysing the survey responses, it was possible to identify that new practitioners in HE careers and employability work came from a broad range of job titles and sectors. Over 45 roles were reported; in order to produce a coherent visual representation of this the job roles were collapsed down into broader occupations/sectors. The results show that the most common occupation/sector for respondents to have worked in was education (see Figure 11.1). Of those who had worked in education the range of roles was extremely large, hence collapsing them all down to one broader category. However, the majority of respondents in this category had worked in higher education, which comprised a range of different roles including lecturing, staff development, widening participation and policy development roles. Other roles in education most commonly reported were teaching in secondary level education. This is not surprising as HE careers services often recruit from a range of sectors and train them to undertake careers and employability work for an HE context. Neary et al. (2014) present evidence from an analysis of job adverts that shows that within HE recruitment, experience of working with employers was most highly valued. Other common occupations/ sectors were HR, recruitment and research. In the former case respondents often noted how they had wanted to use their knowledge of the 'other' side of recruitment to help 'young people' (although it is recognised that not all graduates are young people) entering the labour market.

The respondents had worked in their original career area for an average of 11 years and were well established; interestingly 42 respondents had worked for over 20 years in their previous field.

> 'Having a previous career in business has been extremely beneficial to me in Careers. I appreciate the employer perspective and also as a career changer I can support students with their career planning strategy from an empathetic viewpoint'.

This suggests that new practitioners recognise that their experience, networks and understanding of employment sectors and what employers are specifically looking for is central to their new career.

> 'Having changed direction and had a period of career uncertainty involving some unemployment and short term temp work has helped me understand transitions and career decision making from a personal as well as theoretical perspective'.

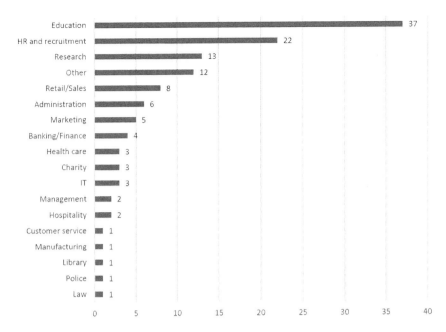

Figure 11.1 Careers staff previous roles/sectors
* More than one occupational area may have been identified

This may provide an extra layer of utility for practitioners, providing this experience of uncertainty, career exploration/decision-making and transition is considered and used empathetically when working with students, in recognition that transition experiences can vary considerably.

The new career in careers

Reflecting the diversification of careers departments in HE we identified 14 primary roles respondents had transitioned to – it should be noted however that it is often not easy to differentiate between the various roles as the nomenclature across services may vary. The majority described their new role as either a consultant or an adviser, however within some services a consultant is seen as a senior role and may have responsibility for other staff or coordinating curriculum activities. However, many other roles were reported; management and leadership, coach, lecturer, researcher, counsellor, facilitator, educator, co-ordinator, strategist and specialist. These roles were often connected to an identifier of which there were several including; employability, development, opportunities, employment; volunteering, information, rewards and placements/internships. This replicates Neary et al.'s (2014) findings, at least in part, they noted that the term employability was identified regularly in relation to jobs and person specifications for HE roles.

The widening range of titles and identifiers may have significance with respect to the development of a professional career identity. The role of nomenclature is an important element of career identity. Neary (2014a) argues that having titles that clearly describe what practitioners do is an important part of being a professional and contributes to the establishment of a professional identity, which is described as 'the concept that describes how we perceive ourselves within our professional context and how we communicate this to others' (Neary, 2014b: 14). This is specifically important for individuals transitioning into a new career in which being able to align themselves with other practitioners in similar roles will contribute to positive assimilation.

What factors attracted individuals in to the profession?

Over 70% (123) of respondents identified themselves within a practitioner role (as opposed to a management role). For many of those who contributed to the study, practice, that is to say working directly with (young) people, was an important element of their decision to move into careers work. A key driver for them was the desire to provide support to or help (young) people (44) to shape their future lives. Respondents identified a general desire for the opportunity to 'help, develop and support people' (49%), and to be engaged in 'varied, practical, work with people', comprised of '1 to 1 interactions', which offered 'security/stability and work-life balance' (37%) and that would be 'making a difference/impacting on people's lives' (27%). As many respondents had come from roles that could be considered 'helping' in the broadest sense it is interesting to note that providing personalised support to individuals attracted career changers to the profession. This was even more apparent in those whose previous roles did not offer the opportunity to work closely with and help others; several reported a need to do something with more personal meaning and impact.

> 'I wanted more opportunity to see a direct impact in what I was doing'.
> 'A light bulb moment, it gave me the opportunity to put something back in and to be authentic'.
> 'Helping people as opposed to selling'.

Eight of the respondents had been inspired by a career guidance professional or had a positive experience of career guidance. Role modelling is an important element in attracting others to the profession (Ibarra, 2004) and underlines the importance of having staff that represent and reflect the client group. Role models need to demonstrate desirable attitudes, behaviours, goals or social status and serve to motivate and inspire aspiration in others (Gibson, 2004).

> 'Having my own career coach, when I got made redundant from a PR job about 6 years ago, was the first thing that inspired me about careers work, as

A *new career in higher education careers work* 147

I think may be the case for others in this field. I was also influenced by my Dad who did a coaching course (NLP) many years ago and really inspired me about this kind of practice'.

Many of the respondents felt that they had experience, knowledge and skills that were transferable within their new role. These tended to focus on two key areas; skills which were related to their original roles such as recruitment practice, management, etc., and a large range of skills that are specifically considered as helping skills such as communication (42), understanding others (29), listening (23), coaching (14), advice giving (11). The skills that individuals already had were felt to have contributed to their selection of career development work as their new career. These findings broadly align with those of Patton (2002), who found that decision-making, organisation and time-management skills are required in addition to those of counselling.

Being able to see alignment between current skills and future careers would seem to aid transition and ensure that there is a stronger fit within the new role. Ibarra (2004) suggests that 'knowing yourself turns out to be the prize at the end of the journey rather than the light at its beginning' (p161). Another way to interpret this is that practitioners have had within their roles the opportunity to reflect upon and compare their current roles with the previous ones they did. As such with hindsight they can make clearer alignment between what they were able to bring to the role and also how they have been able to use it. Again, this type and level of understanding is essential in professional practice helping students to understand their learning and skills and how it transfers to the wider context.

'Communications: – Knowing how to best get messages about our service across and generally present written information in a way that is digestible (which I developed while working in marketing) – Also, communication/ interpersonal skills generally developed through working with a range of people throughout my career'.

'Supporting people within organisations with their training needs, understanding recruitment practices from the employer point of view'.

Satisfaction with new role

We asked respondents about their expectations of their role and the extent to which these had been met. Approximately 42% of the new entrants sought out opportunities for placements, shadowing and work experience prior to applying for jobs. Most found this very or extremely useful. Over half believed it had had at least some influence on their decision to move into careers. Having the opportunity to gain some experience and to observe in practice what the work involves is (as we know) a good way not just for the participant but also as a recruitment activity for the service. These opportunities also helped to explore potential recruits' expectations of the role and to help them to envision themselves within it. Ibarra

(2004) refers to this as exploring possible selves and helps individuals to consider the options of who they might become. Yates (in press) considers that individuals in career transition may have multiple images of their possible self: these can be positive, negative, realistic or fanciful. This is an important element of career change and the transition process where individuals are able to identify congruence between how they have previously seen themselves and what their future selves may look like.

The majority of respondents were happy with their new career. They found that it provided them with opportunities to undertake work on a personal level with indivdiuals and groups, it was rewarding and they had a real sense of job satisfaction. They particularly enjoyed the practical nature of the job.

> 'I find it as satisfying as I'd imagined. The majority of the time I am offering practical help to students who need help to get on in their preferred career, and sometimes I am helping people through some difficult issues which makes it very rewarding'.

When asked to describe how they felt about their role the most common terms used were 'enjoy', 'autonomy' and 'variety'. Repondents focused very much on key elements of the role, specifically providing one:one support and group work, which all enjoyed. For those who were less happy in the role, this tended to be due to lack of one:one/group contact. This predominantly arose because they were in supervisory positions which were less client focussed. Respondents referred to the client-focussed nature of the role and the relationship they have with their colleagues as being important to them in their new career. It is worth recognising that as the focus of the research was on recent career changers, practitioners who have been in the role longer may have different views (Barbour, 2016).

Respondents liked that they had control over the work they did, but some were critical of the universities as being bureaucratic, managerial and target driven. Considering the backgrounds of the respondents this is interesting as it offers up the possibility that HE institutes may be more bureaucratic, managerial and target-driven than the organisations they previously worked in.

> 'HE is very bureaucratic compared to the City and it takes a very long time to make meaningful change'.

Other elements of the work which were valued were variety and diversity within the role. Most respondents felt that the role provided opportunities to engage with different people across the institution and wider afield and contribute to a broad range of activities and to feel they were making a difference to people's lives.

> 'I had originally intended the role to be a stepping-stone, but instead the role has grown to embrace my skills and, to an extent, ambitions. I did not expect the experience to be so diverse and did not expect to gain the influence and reach that I have. It has been much more enjoyable than expected. So, my expectations have not been met – they have been exceeded'.

Autonomy and control over the work was an important element for many, which was often linked to creativity and the opportunity to be innovative with the development of practice. From a professional practice perspective, many felt that they were generally valued within the institution. However, some were surprised at what was perceived as a disparity in how careers practitioners were perceived by academics. This reflects Thambar (2016), who suggests that careers advisers often feel unconfident about the professional identity due to a lack of recognition of their role. The employability agenda has undoubtedly helped to develop the form and visibility of careers services witin HE (e.g., AGCAS, 2008; Wilson Review, 2012) but it may be there is still a lack of understanding by academics of the roles, responsibilities and abilities within them. Given that careers professionals working in HE not only play a central role in supporting performance metrics, and are knowledge workers just like academics (knowledge workers are those 'who access, create and use information in a way that adds value to an enterprise and its stakeholders" [Tymon and Stumpf, 2002: 12]), this lack of understanding is no longer warranted.

A number of respondents had been supported to extend their qualifications and specialist knowledge such as undertaking masters level, guidance qualifications and psychometric testing to enhance their abilities, providing good opportunities for CPD and personal growth. Some responses suggested the work not only developed their knowledge and skill sets but also fed into social and professional cultural capital. They were able to work in projects in other departments, allowing them to develop their own profile, and that of the careers profession within the university.

> 'It has actually been a much broader and richer experience than I anticipated, with more focus on education and learning than I expected (in addition to the one:one guidance I thought I would be doing primarily). I have also found that, working in HE, there has been a lot of focus on issues of policy and approach to employability generally which is really interesting, with more scope than I expected for collaboration with or learning from/about other parts of the university and related student/learner agendas'.

For most respondents, the role met their expectations or in some cases exceeded their expectations; specifically, where practitioners have had the opportunity to influence the direction of the service.

> 'It has exceeded my expectations. I find it a rewarding, challenging and creative job. I keep learning and developing skills. And I'm now in a position of influence over institutional strategic planning'.

Conclusions

Higher Education has become a dynamic and fast paced environment subject to much external scrutiny through a variety of metrics (Christie, 2017). For institutions the concept of employability plays a central role in being able to perform well in these metrics – the need to demonstrate tangible outcomes linked to higher education have rarely been more important. This has led to careers services evolving in form and content. The research here has demonstrated that the careers and employability workforce, although lacking (currently) in diversity in terms of gender and ethnicity, do bring a wealth of relevant experience, skills and knowledge from previous employers. Central to this is their experience of being in transition, assessing their skills, undertaking pre-employment shadowing and experience to test out their new career ideas. These activities reflect the current experiences and anxieties of many of the students they are working with.

The practitioners in this study were passionate about the work they do, hugely enthusiastic about the difference they make and feel a sense of reward, job satisfaction and value. Whilst the new format of HE allows diversity, specialisms and variation in working, allowing expectations to typically be met, HE can also be a bureaucratic, management-heavy place to work. Given that people are intrinsically motivated to work in this sector because the work is meaningful and allows them to make a difference, it may be important for management and the institutions to place less emphasis on quantity and instead place emphasis on quality of service. The data also suggests significant social and cultural capital associated with the role of careers professionals which is hard to measure in job descriptions but of enormous importance in undertaking the role.

References

Allan, G., and Moffett, J. (2015). "Professionalism in career guidance and counselling – How professional do trainee career practitioners feel at the end of a postgraduate programme of study", *British Journal of Guidance and Counselling*, *44*(4): 447–465.

Artess, J., Hooley, T., and Mellors-Bourne, R. (2017). *Employability: A Review of the Literature 2012–2016, A Report for the Higher Education Academy.* York: Higher Education Academy.

Association of Graduate Careers Advisory Services (AGCAS) (2008). *AGCAS Membership Survey 2008.* Sheffield: AGCAS.

Association of Graduate Careers Advisory Services (AGCAS) (2016). *AGCAS Membership Survey 2016.* Sheffield: AGCAS.

Barbour, K. (2016). *Exploring the Impact of Change on University Careers Services: Death of a Service or Thriving and Surviving.* Ed.D Thesis. University of Glasgow. Glasgow.

Bimrose, J., and Hearne, L. (2012). "Resilience and career adaptability: Qualitative studies of adult career counselling", *Journal of Vocational Behavior*, (81): 338–344.

Bridge Group (2017). *Social Mobility and University Careers Services.* London: UPP Foundation.

Brown, A. (2015). "Mid-career reframing: The learning and development processes through which individuals seek to effect major career changes", *British Journal of Guidance and Counselling*, *43*(3): 278–291.

Brown, A., Bimrose, J., Barnes, S.A., and Hughes, D. (2012). "The role of career adaptabilities for mid-career changers", *Journal of Vocational Behavior*, *80*: 754–761.

Carless, S., and Arnup, J. (2011). "A longitudinal study of the determinants and outcomes of career change", *Journal of Vocational Behaviour*, 78: 80–91.

Christie, F. (2016). "Careers guidance and social mobility in UK higher education: Practitioner perspectives", *British Journal of Guidance and Counselling*, 44(1): 72–85.

Christie, F. (2017). "The reporting of university league table employability rankings: A critical review", *Journal of Education and Work*, 30(4): 403–418.

Damle, P. (2015). "Tracing the tangential career transition", *Journal of Management Research*, 15(2): 111–122.

Department for Business, Innovation and Skills. (BIS) (2012). *The Wilson Review: A review of Business – University Collaboration*. London: HMSO.

Gibson, D.E. (2004). "Role models in career development: New directions for theory and research", *Journal of Vocational Behavior*, 65(1): 134–156.

Grzeda, M. (1999). "Re-conceptualizing career change: a career development perspective", *Career Development International*, 4(6): 305–311.

Haasler, S.R., and Barabasch, A. (2015). "The role of learning and career guidance for managing mid-career transitions – comparing Germany and Denmark", *British Journal of Guidance and Counselling*, 43(3): 306–322.

Higher Education Funding Council for England. (2017). *Student characteristics*. (online) available from: www.hefce.ac.uk/analysis/HEinEngland/students/.

Higher Education Statistical Agency. (2017). *Staff*. (online) available from: www.hesa.ac.uk/data-and-analysis/staff.

Holmes, L. (2000). "Questioning the skills agenda", In: Fallows, S., and Steven, C. (Eds.), *Integrating Key Skills in Higher Education*. London: Kogan Page.

Ibarra, H. (2004). *Working Identity, Unconventional Strategies for Inventing Your Career*. Boston: Harvard Business School Press.

Neary, S., Marriott, J., and Hooley, T. (2014). *Understanding a 'career in careers': Learning From an Analysis of Current Job and Person Specifications*. Derby: International Centre for Guidance Studies, University of Derby.

Neary, S. (2014a). "Reclaiming professional identity through postgraduate professional development: Career practitioner reclaiming their professional selves", *British Journal of Guidance and Counselling*, 42(2): 199–210.

Neary, S. (2014b). "Professional identity: What I call myself defines who I am", *Careers Matters*, 2(3): 14–15.

Patton, W. (2002). "Training for career development professionals: Responding to supply and demand in the next decade", *Australian Journal of Career Development*, 11(3): 56–62.

Rhodes, S.R., and Doering, M. (1983). "An integrated model of career change", *Academy of Management Review*, 8(4): 631–639.

Taylor, A., and Hooley, T. (2014). "Evaluating the impact of career management skills module and internship programme within a university business school", *British Journal of Guidance and Counselling*, 42(5): 487–499.

Thambar, N. (2016). "I am just a plain old careers adviser – Recognizing the hidden expert", *Journal of the National Institute for Careers Education and Counselling*, 37: 26–32.

Thambar, N. (2018). "Contested boundaries of expertise in HE careers and employability services", In Christie, F., and Burke, C. (Eds.) *Graduate Careers in Context: Research, Policy and Practice*. Abingdon: Routledge.

Tymon, E., and Stumpf, S. (2002). "Social capital in the success of knowledge workers", *Development International*, 8(1): 12–20.

Wolf, A. (1991). "Assessing core skills: Wisdom or wild goose chase?", *Cambridge Journal of Education*, 21(2): 189–201.

Yates, J. (in press). *The Career Coach's Toolkit*. Hove: Routledge.

12 Contested boundaries of professional expertise in HE careers and employability services

Nalayini Thambar

Introduction

A changed 'employability climate' within Higher Education has emerged following the 2012 increase in undergraduate tuition fees in England and a greater attention to graduate outcomes. The resulting focus on careers services questions established practice and the claims of Careers Advisers as experts in student career development, while also offering the potential for greater recognition, appreciation and support for careers services, their expertise, outcomes and impact. This chapter considers the current challenges that leaders and managers face in organising their careers services and positioning their experts in response to institutional employability agendas, drawing upon the evolution of higher education careers services and literature on professions and professionalism, to provide context and further perspectives. The discussion is informed by a sector-wide study by the author, conducted in 2012, which explored the professional identity of Careers Advisers and proposed recommendations for action by managers and Careers Advisers themselves that would position Careers Advisers, and their services, as experts in this field. It is also informed by subsequent research by the author and their professional experience in large English universities as a Careers Adviser, an Associate Director, and now Director of Careers and Employability. The conclusion suggests approaches to careers service leadership and management that demonstrably support institutional employability priorities, and can (re)establish Careers Advisers as careers and employability experts, who make an essential contribution to the student experience.

The history of higher education careers services

A brief history of Higher Education Careers Services highlights the extent to which changes over the last decade have transformed the expectations of their contribution to institutional outcomes. By the 1950s, every university had a careers service, focussed on helping students to identify vacancies of interest, and introducing them to employers who visited campuses to recruit final year students. Sector expansion in the 1960s grew the range and number of students at university, increasing the need for guidance about choices, information about graduate pathways and group delivery in order to meet demand. From

1985–1996, the Enterprise in Higher Education initiative (EHE), encouraged the development of work-based skills through the curriculum, which gave many careers services the opportunity to engage in teaching and learning or significant co-curricular activity, in line with their institutional approach.

Further sector expansion in the early 2000s led to growth and diversification of careers service activity depending on institutional priorities and the success of Heads of Service in positioning and gaining resources. If supported, services co-ordinated the delivery of skills awards or co-curricular skills acquisition, and delivered accredited curricular delivery, while the growth of the graduate recruitment 'industry' led to an expansion of employer engagement, specialist work placement and internship functions. Simultaneously, more services became involved with, or responsible for, entrepreneurial education and business start-up support, while the increase in technology and opportunities for student engagement introduced functional specialisms, resources permitting, linked to IT and Marketing.

The publication of the Browne Review in 2010, heralding the rise in fees up to £9,000 p.a. for English undergraduates from 2012, brought about significant change, particularly in English institutions. The concepts of 'value for money' and 'return on investment' were even more closely linked, if not equated with, 'getting a graduate job', and employability became a high-profile, strategic, sector-wide priority with careers services in the spotlight. This led to unprecedented levels of institutional enquiry about activity, impact and outcomes, while engagement with employers and the provision of internship and placement opportunities were seen by many as the solution to the graduate employment and league table challenge (particularly following the 2008 financial crash). A growing interest in employability by sections of the academic community has also challenged careers service involvement in curricular delivery. The impact is not uniform: some institutional approaches have led to a splintering of educative, employer engagement and information, advice and guidance functions, placing services, or aspects of them, deeper within student-facing divisions or in business engagement operations. Where a careers service was considered the solution to the employability challenge, their position of expertise has been affirmed with steady or increased investment and a stronger institutional position.

Careers advisers: from core professional to functional specialist

The roles of Careers Advisers and Heads of Careers Services have evolved in response to the changes outlined above. They jointly comprised the core membership at the inception of the Association of Graduate Careers Advisory Services, AGCAS, in 1967 with the head of service commonly a Careers Adviser, but 'first amongst equals'. Until the early 2000s, Careers Advisers continued to enjoy a powerful influence within their service as the core professional role, legitimised by their experience and increasingly by qualification; either the Postgraduate Diploma in Careers Guidance acquired as training to work in a Local Education Authority or, from the mid-1990s, the AGCAS postgraduate diploma in Careers

Education, Information, Advice and Guidance. Careers Advisers engaged in all aspects of service delivery: information, advice, guidance, teaching (where appropriate), destinations data collection, liaison with academic schools and employer engagement. Service initiatives were routinely led by Careers Advisers, even if they fell outside the scope of their training and experience, and Careers Advisers tended to dominate, if not constitute, service decision-making structures.

The management challenge

In the 2000s, diversified service delivery brought in a requirement for functional specialists in, for example, employer engagement, entrepreneurial education and the delivery of skills awards. Those specialists were not necessarily Careers Advisers and service management structures evolved to represent all functions. This, particularly in larger services, limited the voice and influence of Careers Advisers. Meanwhile the 2005 Higher Education Role Analysis (HERA) exercise across the sector encouraged a focus on guidance and (accredited) curricular input to justify the level of the Careers Adviser role. This aligned Careers Advisers with other functional specialists rather than as the primary professional role within the service. During this period, the role of head of service, which had been moving from 'first among equals' to a position akin to a senior or managing partner, became increasingly distinct from that of the Careers Adviser.

Role divergence between managers and professionals

The divergence between management and Careers Adviser roles has been amplified following the publication of the Browne Review. In many institutions, the Head of Service is the institutional careers and employability lead, while all Heads are responsible for meeting institutional priorities by running a high quality service, demonstrating impact, outputs and value for money. League table position and graduate employment outcomes are common indicators of success. Reflecting their institution, services take many different forms:

- comprehensive and integrated
- comprehensive, but comprising specialist functions
- comprehensive and organised to reflect Faculty structures
- focussed on information, advice and guidance only
- organised around employer engagement and placement activity.

The variation in approach has also changed the overall profile of those leading services, with many from graduate recruitment, placements and broader university management experience moving into such roles.

In this context, Careers Advisers have experienced significant change. Some have moved into newly created management roles, while others, depending on their service structure, have found their role changed in emphasis or centrality with their activities and delivery rigorously questioned at an institutional, if

156 *Nalayini Thambar*

not a service level. This is particularly the case with time-intensive one-to-one activity through which careers guidance, the activity at the heart of the role, is practised, yet where direct outcome and impact are traditionally hard to evidence. Meanwhile, in specialised, segmented and functionally stratified services, Careers Advisers are engaging differently – if at all – in areas of activity which traditionally formed a part of the role, raising questions about the nature of their expertise. Is an application adviser, qualified to A level, and focussing on CV, application and interview support now the service expert on job-hunting techniques? How do employer engagement and business development roles align with Careers Advisers' involvement? If academics now deliver career development input in the curriculum, does that make them careers experts as well as subject specialists?

Boundaries of expertise are currently at their most fluid in the history of careers services, with the greatest impact upon Careers Advisers, formerly the core professional role. This has created a need and opportunity for Careers Advisers and Heads of Service to negotiate a new approach to the Careers Adviser role, to ensure that institutions benefit from their expertise and, pragmatically, to optimise resources within careers services. The next section of this chapter considers the management of professionals and individual and collective professional identity as discussed in the literature, as context to explore this issue further.

Professions and their management

A profession is understood to be a group of people in an occupational role, where the purpose of the role is to solve a publicly understood problem through the deployment of specific skills and knowledge (Torstendahl, 1990). Members of that group will control entry, training and standards of practice themselves (Wilensky, 1964), and it is suggested that as well as maintaining high standards the exercising of judgement and autonomy characterise the work of those within a profession (Freidson, 2001). The dynamics between a profession and those who manage them have been increasingly explored as organisational structures have become more established in both private and public sectors. The rise of professional managers within an organisation, who do not have the qualification and experience of core professional groups, creates potential for tension between professional influence and management control. Scott (2008) suggested that as professional service firms move from public to corporate clients, professional groups within such organisations lose influence as they represent one specialist area within a managed business, while managers lead the strategic planning, operations and marketing of the business (Hinnings, 1999). In such settings, Ackroyd (1996) identified 'new model' professions as those who are highly organised through a professional association, and then again, within the organisation in which they work. He suggested that such professional groups become doubly 'encapsulated' – once within their professional association and secondly by their organisation; vertically by management and horizontally by other professional groups. The model is illustrated in Figure 12.1.

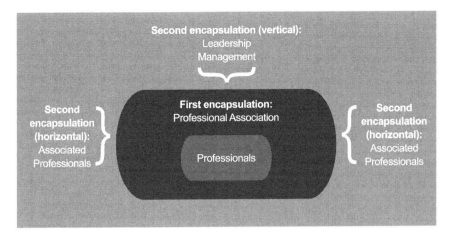

Figure 12.1 Professional Encapsulation (Thambar, 2016a: 32) representing the work of Ackroyd (1996)

Ackroyd suggested that a profession in this situation is likely to become inward looking and act defensively in relation to their organisation, focussed primarily on their professional rather than organisational identity, and that a profession will act defensively towards other professional groups within their organisation to protect their jurisdiction. This can result in a hierarchy as the most dominant groups protect their interests at the expense of others. More positively, Ackroyd suggested that where a profession can see mutual benefit from working with another group, working partnerships will be forged.

Within the public sector, Noordegraaf (2011) acknowledged the neo-liberal agendas which have led to many public service professions operating within organisational structures to deliver services that are value for money, within a market setting. In this context, Noordegraaf noted the emergence of an unhelpful divergence of 'occupations versus organisations' and 'managers versus professionals' (Noordegraaf, 2011: 1350). He suggested that professions should be encouraged to see management concerns and challenges, such as the deployment of scarce resources, as professional issues, thus creating 'management-minded professionals' who practice 'organized professionalism'. Broadbent et al. (1997) suggested that organisational imperatives can be reconciled with professional values and practice, where managers operate as change agents and accommodate professional autonomy. Gleeson and Knights (2006) argued that a process of Creative Mediation could create new knowledge in the public sector as professionals find ways to make external pressures and targets work for the profession. They cited the example of a Further Education lecturer who channelled a need for closer attendance monitoring into a process of maintaining closer contact with their students, which led to greater support and better results for the student

158   *Nalayini Thambar*

while meeting the attendance monitoring requirements. While these pragmatic approaches offer solutions to the potential tensions between management and professionals, collective professional identity will be affected by such dynamics.

The social constructionist view of professional identity formation is that it is developed through social interactions with fellow-professionals which shape individual behaviour (Burr, 2003, Busher, 2005), and studies indicate that the experience of being part of a professional group with shared experience of training, possession of recognisable knowledge and a similar occupation will strengthen a sense of being part of a profession (Adams, 2008; Beck and Young, 2005). Professional identity can be challenged by a lack of definition of the specialist knowledge being deployed, which masks expertise (Crawford et al., 2008) or in multi-professional groups where a group does not feel they have an equal voice when determining the tasks at hand (Molyneux, 2001). Within the academic community, it is suggested that the subject discipline and the institutions within which they work are strong influences on individual professional identity (Jawitz, 2009) and that group identity is weaker amongst academics as they do not collectively use a similar set of skills to solve a common problem (Torstendahl, 1990).

The challenge in context

These broader observations resonate with the changes within careers services in recent years. The role of Careers Adviser traditionally reflected many features of a profession through a shared training experience, and possession of specialised knowledge and skills, used to solve a commonly understood problem. As the role moves towards that of a functional specialist and Heads of Service roles are increasingly oriented towards 'professional manager' rather than a senior partner, conditions have been created that could result in a sense of 'managers versus professionals' and a more defensive and inward-looking approach by organisationally encapsulated Careers Advisers. The introduction of higher tuition fees in England and a greater neo-liberal influence across the sector, with a focus on value for money and outcomes, has the potential to exacerbate this divergence, creating further challenges for both Heads of Service in meeting institutional expectations, and Careers Advisers in demonstrating and deploying their expertise in an institutional context.

The next section outlines the findings from an investigation into the professional identity of Careers Advisers during this period. From these findings emerge recommendations to managers and Careers Advisers themselves to strengthen the position of Careers Advisers – and their services – as experts in their field.

The careers advisers' perspective

A study undertaken by the author sought to understand the professional identity of Careers Advisers in higher education and to address the management challenges and opportunities that their role presents. Twenty-three interviews were undertaken in fourteen institutions across England, Scotland and Wales, the institutions selected through stratified sampling to ensure representation across the sector. The study was approached from a social constructionist perspective, seeking to make sense of the issue by understanding shared experience through individual perspectives (Crotty, 1998). The interviews were analysed using the method of Interpretative Phenomenological Analysis suggested by Smith et al. (2009) which pays attention to the individual accounts while acknowledging the reflexivity of the researcher. The findings of the study indicate that Careers Advisers have a professional identity that can be summarised as Undefined, Locally Focussed, Unrecognised, Unconfident but Dedicated to their purpose (Thambar, 2016b). These facets are outlined in further detail here:

Undefined: The lack of definition is shaped by the range of qualifications and entry to practice, loose induction and CPD structures which do not always help to define the role or affirm the knowledge and skills required to fulfil the role, and a range of unprotected job titles, which don't convey the expertise within the role.

Locally Focussed: This was demonstrated by Careers Advisers appearing not to recognise the broader institutional context in which they work. For example, conceptualising the academic role as primarily about undergraduate teaching, mentioning research secondarily, if at all. This is understandable given the primary context for Careers Adviser interactions with their academic contacts. However, it also suggests a lack of understanding of the academic imperative and identity, closely linked to disciplinary research, with undergraduate teaching, in certain universities at least, traditionally perceived to be a lower status activity. Further indication of a local, rather than institutional focus is that within a range of conceptualisations of the role, there was only one respondent who felt that they were an 'expert', with others seeking to clarify that they were not. To consider oneself 'not an expert', yet seek parity with the academic role, suggests a lack of understanding of academic identity, which is to be a specialist in a particular subject area. There were references to AGCAS throughout accounts of experience indicating a strong affiliation to their profession and professional association, perhaps to the point of encapsulation.

Unrecognised: The Local Focus may relate to the finding that Careers Advisers feel Unrecognised by others, experiencing a lack of recognition of their purpose, skill and professional identity within their institution. In response, Careers Advisers express a desire for 'kudos' and 'credibility', often drawing upon previous, often non-careers- advisory experience, through association with graduate recruiters, or from positive associations with academics. All these routes to credibility involve disassociation from their role, and those who could, reported a greater sense of kudos where they are able to use an alternative job title that includes 'Head of' and 'Director' which they also felt offered a clearer explanation of their role.

Unconfident: Unsurprisingly, given a level of disassociation with their role and working context in order to feel credible, the professional identity of Careers Advisers in higher education is Unconfident. This is conveyed through use of diminutive language such as 'our own little office' and 'my own little part of the careers advisory room' and, strikingly, 'I'm just a plain old Careers Adviser.' This lack of confidence is compounded further where Careers Advisers compare their own qualifications to those of academic colleagues and are conscious of the difference between their Bachelor's Degree even when followed by a postgraduate Careers Guidance qualification, and a Masters or PhD.

Dedicated: Despite this lack of confidence, Careers Advisers are dedicated to their role, driven by the satisfaction of working with and making a difference to students. Despite any frustrations of the role, very few of them think of making a career move, partly due to a lack of appetite for management roles, which appears to be the only way to make career progress, but largely due to rewards reported in their current role.

Such dedication provides an opportunity for Heads of Service to engage with Careers Advisers and explore ways to maintain the rewarding aspects of the role, while collectively addressing management challenges. Such balanced routes may also provide opportunities for Careers Advisers to derive greater kudos and credibility from their role, rather than from alternative sources. The final part of the study confirmed that while Careers Advisers may (thankfully) consider themselves distant from broader institutional and management issues, they are aware of the changing climate; the risks and the opportunity presented by a greater degree of visibility and accountability, the challenge of meeting greater demand, a risk that existing services will be duplicated, as other parts of their institution 'discover' employability, and a concern that new employability models will challenge the position and expertise of their service. These are precisely the issues that Heads of Service continue to face.

A more recent study, as yet unpublished, has been conducted with a number of Heads of Service, whose Careers Advisers were interviewed for the study above, in order to understand their experience of their role over the last ten years. The position of Careers Advisers within their services ranged from fulfilling a highly specialised, student-focussed role, to operating as the senior colleagues within the service, taking responsibility for key challenges. One Head of Service expressed concern for the future of the Careers Adviser role, noting that the theoretical underpinning of vocational guidance makes it a 'unique and valuable role'. Another describes the role as 'a really important job', but comments that 'the university itself isn't that interested in the role of Careers Adviser.' This suggests that despite tensions between traditional delivery and current demands, Careers Advisers and Heads of Service share common ground. Constructive approaches will help to (re) establish and confirm Careers Advisers as careers and employability experts who can contribute to institutional outcomes and service success while they continue to make a difference to students' futures.

Recommendations

These recommendations reflect the approaches of Organized Professionalism (Noordegraaf, 2011), Creative Mediation (Gleeson and Knights, 2006) and top management of professionals as change agents, not definers of the professional task (Broadbent et al., 1997). They are offered as approaches that will enable Careers Advisers to (re-)establish their expertise and give Heads of Service greater support and capacity to extend their influence across the institution and strengthen the position of their service as the institutional careers and employability experts.

1. Connecting careers advisers to their institutional context

Careers Advisers are most effective and relevant to their institution when they understand their service and role in the context of the institution's priorities, structure and culture. As these forces are the context for the head of service role, heads are ideally placed to help Careers Advisers to understand the contribution and balance of undergraduate and postgraduate teaching income and of research income and the financial impact of knowledge transfer and business engagement activity, which will help to put an undergraduate focus in context. Institutional understanding in the context of close peers or competitors will also contextualise broader aspirations and challenges. Given the primacy of league tables, and the impact of graduate outcomes scores, such understanding will enable Careers Advisers to find increased areas of common ground when working with colleagues in schools and faculties.

Critical to institutional understanding is a clear appreciation of the academic role – arguably the core professional role within any university, and the most common background for senior and executive leaders. This will involve understanding the nature of an academic career: the forging of an individual and collaborative research path, institutional expectations of publication and the balancing of 'administrative roles', i.e., leadership and management. Careers Advisers will therefore be better able to see the employability agenda through the eyes of academics and tailor their approach so that it is more likely to resonate and align with academic priorities. This will strengthen the impact and reach of the careers service as a whole.

If Careers Advisers are sufficiently encapsulated then they may not fully appreciate their careers service as a resource unit. Helping them to understand the service in financial terms will also enable them to contribute to the configuration of service delivery and consider ways in which their practices could adapt to meet available resources and expectations.

2. Defining the role, expertise and capabilities of careers advisers to embed them in a higher education setting

Alongside the recommendation above, it is suggested that Heads of Service and Careers Advisers work together to define the Careers Adviser role as being 'of the sector', rather than as from a professional group that happens to be working within a particular institution. This does not need to compromise the principle of impartiality, fundamental to the practice of careers guidance, but will enable Careers Advisers to be seen, and to express themselves, as part of the solution to the institutional employability challenge and a key contributor to the student experience. This will increase the agency of the service as a whole. To achieve this, it will be important to define, create and build a body of expertise and knowledge that Careers Advisers can own and describe in terms that are commonly understood, comprising relevant employer and sector knowledge as well as deep insights into student engagement, behaviour and aspiration in order to effectively deploy their careers education, advice and guidance skills. Possession of expertise will also align Careers Advisers and therefore services with the core principle of academic endeavour.

To support this expertise, an evidence-based approach to practice should be encouraged through the development of practitioner-research. This will further support the claim by Careers Advisers, and therefore the service, to be a professional group with a distinct and current body of knowledge. Such an approach will strengthen Careers Advisers' capacity to make a difference to students' futures, and so will not conflict with their core motivations. Conducting research to inform practice and disseminating findings will provide further alignment with academic endeavour and increase the confidence in the careers services and the confidence in, and of, the professionals within. Further and related association to the institution's research agenda will be achieved where Careers Advisers do not focus on undergraduate students alone; support for research students, if not those at a post-doctoral stage (resources permitting) will help Careers Advisers to gain a deeper understanding of the academic career experience and, over time, lead to more academics understanding the skill and expertise of the careers service through personal experience. Careers Advisers will demonstrate greater relevance to their institutions by engaging with more elements of institutional activity, extending to, for example, widening participation, and alumni engagement where the application of the expertise and skill of Careers Advisers adds important value.

3. Creating a professional development framework

The recommendations outlined above could be incorporated into a Continuing Professional Development (CPD) framework which would help to strengthen the professional identity of Careers Advisers in their institutional setting, and enable them to support the profile and influence of the careers service. Such a framework could include a robust induction to help those either new to higher education or to the particular institution to fully understand their professional setting. Structured CPD to support the recommendations outlined above would extend beyond 'traditional' areas such as guidance skills, group work skills and updating of labour market knowledge to include work shadowing to increase the depth of knowledge and insight around graduate opportunities; research skills to facilitate practitioner research and project management; and negotiating and influencing skills to enable Careers Advisers to fulfil a broader role than one which focuses purely on student-facing delivery. The contextualisation of such skills will be achieved where Heads of Service share with their colleagues approaches that they take to their institutional role, particularly in the building of effective, strategic networks. Development of these latter skill areas may also help Careers Advisers to appreciate the approaches used by Heads of Service and de-mystify 'management' in a way that makes such roles more appealing.

AGCAS also has a role to play here, supporting services through the provision of relevant learning and development opportunities for Heads of Service and Careers Advisers, within a robust quality assurance framework which supports the expertise and professionalism of careers services within higher education.

Conclusion

This chapter has explored the roles of Careers Advisers and their service leaders and managers which have often diverged in response to increased sector interest in employability. A tension, perceived or actual, between student outcomes and institutional priorities has resulted in an encapsulation of expertise and experience which has not always supported the institutional position of careers services as career development and employability experts. However the current climate affords opportunities for Careers Advisers and their managers to work together to optimise the position and influence of the role and the wider service in support of institutional interests. This opportunity should be seized to avoid further professional encapsulation which will limit careers services' potential to be institutionally relevant thus increasing their vulnerability; services are at risk of fragmentation, marginalisation or absorption into larger administrative structures if their services are not clearly identifiable or can easily be replicated through an absence of specialist knowledge, professional skills and expert delivery. Working to identify and articulate Careers Adviser expertise, through the development of a distinct body of knowledge, evidence-based practice, engagement with research and a definition of the role to situate it within an institutional context is critical for the success of Careers Advisers. It is also critical for the sustainability of their profession, for leaders and managers to create effective and relevant careers services, for the institution and, most importantly, the students and graduates who need sustained expert, impartial career development support in order to realise their potential.

References

Ackroyd, S. (1996). "Organization contra organizations: Professionals and organizational change in the United Kingdom", *Organization Studies, 17*: 599–621.

Adams, K. (2008). "What's in a name? Seeking professional status through degree studies within the Scottish early years context", *European Early Childhood Education Research Journal, 16*(2): 196–209.

Beck, J., and Young, M.F.D. (2005). "The assault on the professions and the restructuring of academic and professional identities: a Bernsteinian analysis", *British Journal of the Sociology of Education*, 26(2): 183–197.

Broadbent, J., Dietrich, M., and Roberts, J. (1997). *The End of the Professions? The Restructuring of Professional Work.* Abingdon: Routledge.

Burr, V. (2003). *Social Constructionism*, 2nd edition. London: Routledge.

Busher, H. (2005). "Being a middle leader: Exploring professional identities", *School Leadership and Management*, 25(2): 137–153.

Crawford, P., Brown, B., and Majomi, P. (2008). "Professional identity in community mental health nursing: A thematic analysis", *International Journal of Nursing Studies*, (45): 1055–1063.

Crotty, M. (1998). *The Foundations of Social Research: Meaning and Perspective in the Research Process.* London: Sage.

Freidson, E. (2001). *Professionalism: The Third Logic.* London: Polity Press.

Gleeson, D., and Knights, D. (2006). "Challenging dualism: Public professionalism in 'Troubled Times'", *Sociology*, 40: 277–295.

Hinnings, C.R., Greenwood, R., and Cooper, D. (1999). "The dynamics of change in large accounting firms in restructuring the professional organization", In: Brock, D.M, Powell, M.J., and Hinnings, C.R. (Eds.), *Accounting, Health Care and Law.* London: Routledge, pp. 131–153.

Jawitz, J. (2009). "Academic identities and communities of practice in a professional discipline", *Teaching in Higher Education*, 14(3): 241–251.

Molyneux, J. (2001). "Interprofessional teamworking: what makes teams work well?" *Journal of Interprofessional Care*, 15: 29–35.

Noordegraaf, M. (2011). "Risky business: How professionals and professional fields (Must) deal with organizational issues", *Organization Studies*, 32: 1349–1371.

Scott, W.R. (2008). "Lords of the dance: Professionals as institutional agents", *Organization Studies*, 29: 219–238.

Smith, J.A., Flowers, P., and Larkin, M. (2009). *Interpretative Phenomenological Analysis: Theory, Method and Research.* London: Sage.

Thambar, N. (2016a). "What is the professional identity of careers advisers in higher education? Challenges and opportunities for careers service leaders and managers", Doctor of Business Administration, Bradford School of Management.

Thambar, N. (2016b). "'I'm Just a Plain Old Careers Adviser' – Recognising the hidden expert", *Journal of the National Institute for Career Education and Counselling*, 37: 26–32.

Torstendahl, R. (1990). "Introduction - Promotion and strategies of knowledge-based groups", In: Torstendahl, R., and Burrage, M. (Eds.). *The Formation of Professions.* London: Sage.

Wilensky, H.L. (1964). "The professionalization of everyone?", *American Journal of Sociology, 70* as cited in Collins, R. (1990). "Changing conceptions in the sociology of professions", In: Torstendahl, R., and. Burrage, M. (Eds.), *The Formation of Professions.* London: Sage.

Part 4

Careers professionals evolving into researchers

13 The rise of the practitioner-researcher

How big data and evidence-based practice requires practitioners with a research mindset

David Winter

Introduction

The growing attention paid to graduate employability and the increasing capability of universities to track and measure the activities of students are converging to drive a change in the nature of careers work within higher education. This chapter provides a brief introduction to the concept of big data and how it is starting to have an impact on higher education institutions. It then explores how the availability of data on students' career thinking has the potential to transform the practice of careers and employability support in universities. These pressures are making it increasingly important for careers service staff to be willing and able to engage with robust evidence-based practice. Ultimately, this is driving a change in the fundamental skills and identity of careers professionals. This chapter looks at how an individual service and the profession as a whole is responding to these changes.

The era of big data

Every time you click a link on a website, make an online purchase, use contactless payment, use a smartphone app to plan a journey or post an update to social media, you are leaving a trail of data. This data is being captured and analysed in order to provide you with recommendations for books to read, films to watch, music to download, things to buy and places to go on holiday. It allows advertisers to target your tastes and search engines to predict what you will type next and researchers to predict film box office revenues from Twitter mentions (Asur and Huberman, 2010).

In addition to examining individual datasets, organisations are combining data from different sources in order to make useful predictions about people's behaviours. For example, some supermarkets are correlating meteorological data with sales data to predict what products customers will buy in particular weather conditions.

168   *David Winter*

In the early days of big data, the characteristics and challenges it presents were summarised succinctly by Laney (2001) as:

- Volume. The amount of information being gathered is vast and is increasing as more aspects of our life are automated.
- Velocity. With increasing connectedness across the globe and the availability of processing power, it is possible to collect, share and analyse information in real time.
- Variety. As well as connecting together fields in structured databases from different disciplines, sophisticated algorithms can now analyse unstructured information sources such as free text records.

However, as well as producing useful predictions, data mining can throw up some nonsensical correlations. For example the number of people drowned in a swimming pool in the US each year correlates surprisingly well with the power output of US nuclear power plants (Vigen, 2015) even though there is unlikely to be any causal relationship between the two.

Megahed and Jones-Farmer (2015) have proposed two additional considerations that users of big data need to be mindful of:

- Veracity. How trustworthy is the data being used? Is it accurate? Is it representative?
- Value. Do the findings from the data truly add to creating knowledge about a particular topic? Does it tell us anything useful?

In higher education (HE), a similar growth in the use of data about student activities has been happening. Instead of just monitoring test scores, the advent of online learning technologies and virtual learning environments has made it possible to assess student learning at more regular intervals with online tests and automated scoring and feedback. Tracking the use of electronic library resources allows academics to monitor what materials students are reading, in what order and for how long. With swipe cards it is possible to track students' attendance at lectures, their movements on campus and their use of resources.

This real-time, 'fluid' data can be combined with existing sources of 'static' data, such as student records to identify particular patterns of behaviour and correlate them against other factors. Such learning analytics are being used to attempt to predict student performance and retention or to redesign academic courses in order to enhance learning with varying degrees of success (Conijn et al., 2016; Shacklock, 2016).

The need for data on graduate employability

With the introduction of student fees and the Teaching Excellence Framework (TEF) (Department for Education, 2016) there has been increasing pressure on higher education institutions to demonstrate the benefits that a university education brings to enhancing an individual's subsequent career prospects. This 'employability' agenda has focused attention on the ways in which university prepares students for careers beyond their course and, in particular, on the effectiveness of higher education careers services. The primary dataset which has been used for assessing this effectiveness has been the Destinations of Leavers of Higher Education (DLHE) survey, which takes place six months after graduation. However, every head of careers knows that DLHE is a flawed indicator of the effectiveness of an HE careers service. The measure of 'success' of graduates (indicated by the proportions in roles classified as 'graduate level' employment) is dependent on a whole range of factors linked to the individual, the subject of study, the institution and the wider economy (Britton et al., 2016). The fact that the impact of careers and employability activities on this measure of success is hard to determine has not stopped it being used to decide the fate of many HE careers services. The ability to manage the collection, analysis and presentation of the DLHE data is, therefore, a critical skill for careers practitioners. Apart from the DLHE, the only other way to evaluate the effectiveness of employability interventions has been through the collection of direct feedback and evaluation from participating students. Data collected in this way is patchy and subject to selection bias. In addition, it only measures the students' subjective perceptions of the usefulness of the intervention rather than effects on subsequent behaviours and outcomes.

The review of the DLHE undertaken by the Higher Education Statistics Agency between 2015 and 2017 has led to a proposal to change the survey (Hewitt and Barnard, 2017), moving the collection point from six months to 15 months after graduation. In the new survey graduates will be asked to indicate their reason for deciding to take up their current job, whether their current activity fits in with their future plans and whether it is meaningful or important to them. Whilst these developments mean that the information collected from graduates will allow for a subjective determination by the graduate as to whether their outcome is successful for them, it further separates the measurement of outcomes from the point at which anything can be done to help those individuals. Therefore, it becomes even less useful as a tool for providing timely feedback on the effectiveness of employability-related activities undertaken while at university.

Big data comes to HE careers

However, a number of relatively recent developments have the potential to change this situation dramatically. An increasing number of HE careers services are implementing careers service management systems (CSMS). These systems (such as TARGETconnect, CareerHub, Abintegro, Symplicity, etc.) allow for the collection and management of information about careers appointments and events, employer relationships, vacancies and placements, as well as providing a platform to provide career learning resources to students. These systems can be used to improve the collection of immediate and more longitudinal feedback data from interventions through the use of automated messaging.

Many of these CSMS packages link to the student records system, providing real-time, fluid data which can be used to identify which students are engaging

170   David Winter

or not engaging with career development activities. For those who do engage, it is possible to track their involvement across their time at university and to evaluate their progress. It is also possible to use CSMS systems to identify those individuals and courses who do not engage with the careers service, but the systems enable us to learn very little else about the unengaged. Even this limited information, when linked to DLHE data, might make it possible to explore the extent to which engagement with careers activities has an impact on graduate outcomes.

Alongside this development, in 2012 the University of Leeds Careers Service was able introduce two questions into the mandatory registration data collection that students complete when they join the institution and each time they re-enrol for the duration of their programme (Gilworth and Cobb, 2017). The original version of Careers Registration (CR) consisted of two questions. The first is a self-reported assessment of the student's level of career decidedness in which they choose from a range of statements the one which best describes their current state of readiness to engage with career planning. For the purposes of analysis, the statements were grouped into four categories:

- *Deciding* – statements that indicate the individual has not yet identified specific career options
- *Planning* – statements that indicate the individual has identified options and is now engaged in researching and preparing themselves to pursue those options
- *Competing* – statements that indicate the individual is actively engaged in pursing their chosen options
- *Sorted* – statements that indicate the individual has secured a job or further study, or is establishing their own business

---

Box 1 – Question 1 from the original University of Leeds version of Careers Registration

Please select the statement which best represents your current careers position:

- ☐ I am not ready to start thinking about my career yet
- ☐ I have no career ideas yet but want to start thinking
- ☐ I have some ideas about my career & am ready to start planning
- ☐ I have a career in mind & intend to gain relevant work experience
- ☐ I know what I want to do but not sure how to get there
- ☐ I want to spend a year gaining experience
- ☐ I am ready to apply for graduate level/professional opportunities
- ☐ I am ready to apply for further study
- ☐ I have been applying for opportunities & have not been successful
- ☐ I have a job, further study or my own business plan confirmed

---

The second question attempted to collect information on the extent to which a student had undertaken work experience activities aimed at enhancing their career development and their attractiveness to employers.

Box 2 – Question 2 from the original University of Leeds version of Careers Registration

I have gained work experience through (select all that apply):
- ☐ a placement year during my degree
- ☐ a summer internship with an organisation
- ☐ a vacation internship (not summer) with an organisation
- ☐ work shadowing
- ☐ a short placement as part of a University module (e.g. 10 or 20 credit module)
- ☐ part time work alongside my studies
- ☐ a holiday job
- ☐ volunteering
- ☐ a position of responsibility in a club or society
- ☐ full time work prior to my course (two years or less)
- ☐ full time work prior to my course (more than two years)
- ☐ self-employment/running my own business
- ☐ I have no work experience to date

The number and complexity of the questions was limited by the constraints of the registration process and an understandable reluctance on behalf of the registry department to burden students with too many questions during enrolment. However, they presented a unique opportunity to gain a snapshot of the thinking and activities of every student in the institution and to track their progression through each subsequent year. Since its introduction at Leeds, an increasing number of HE institutions have implemented versions of CR. Some have managed to introduce extra questions to capture students' interests in particular employment sectors.

In 2015, Careers Registration was identified as an item of interest in the RAND Europe research on learning gain (McGrath et al., 2015) commissioned by the Higher Education Funding Council for England (HEFCE). Learning gain is defined as 'the "distance travelled', or the difference between the skills, competencies, content knowledge and personal development demonstrated by students at two points in time' (McGrath et al., 2015: xi). Subsequently, a consortium of 16 HE careers services led by The Careers Group, University of London, obtained HEFCE funding for a three-year pilot project to investigate the potential use of CR as a measure of learning gain in relation to work readiness and employability.

172 David Winter

The aims of the project are:

- To establish the progression of student responses to the CR questions over their time at university and to identify any distinctive patterns in the progression of various student groups by discipline and student characteristics.
- To correlate CR data with DLHE data and other information in the student record in order to establish whether CR can act as a predictor of graduate outcomes, academic success, retention, etc.
- To evaluate the impact of variations in the implementations of CR on the validity and usefulness of the data obtained and to provide recommendations for future iterations of the survey.
- To explore how CR data is being used to inform employability strategies and service provision within institutions.

One of the earliest findings from this data is that a fairly consistent proportion of students (over 40%) entering their final year of study characterise themselves as still within the *Deciding* phase of career readiness. A lot of the investment in HE careers services over the last decade has gone into providing more work experience opportunities for students and enhancing the development of workplace skills. Whilst this is valuable, if such activities are not supported by efforts to enable students to develop some form of career plan, then they run the risk of only helping the students who have already progressed to the *Planning* stage of career thinking. This finding is backed up by research which shows that one of the top three factors which predicted whether graduates were able to achieve successful employment outcomes was having a career plan upon leaving university (Shury et al., 2017).

Linking CR data with information from management systems could make it possible to investigate whether engagement with the careers service has a differential impact on a student's career development. Analysis of data from one of our partner institutions seems to indicate a correlation between engagement and progression in career decidedness measured by question 1. However, it is too early to say whether this correlation is significant. It is also not possible to say whether the progression results from interaction with the careers service or whether students who are naturally more likely to progress are also more likely to engage. Nevertheless, this does provide some hope that this data can be used to provide a much more direct and timely measure of the effectiveness of HE careers services than anything currently available.

One of the most useful aspects of the project so far is the opportunity to catalogue and share best practice in the use of the increased understanding that CR data gives us into student career thinking to inform strategy and operations within HE careers. In some institutions, CR has been used to feed into institutional-level employability strategies. Other careers services have used the data to engage individual academic departments, often using the data to challenge unfounded assumptions about the employability needs of their students. Still other institutions have used the data to implement tailored marketing campaigns to students, promoting events and services most appropriate to the student's stage of career readiness.

The challenges of becoming a data-driven careers service

At the time of writing we have over 300,000 student responses being analysed. Aside from encountering several technological challenges around sharing and storing the data, the project team has also had to grapple with both legislative and ethical concerns linked to sharing and processing data linked to individuals. This has been complicated by trying to anticipate the constraints that the forthcoming European Union General Data Protection Regulation (GDPR) might place on our activities (Blackmer, 2016). This is something that anyone who handles student data will have to wrestle with.

One strand of the Careers Registration research project is to explore the capability and confidence of careers staff in understanding and using CR data. To examine this, we are developing a tool based on the Researcher Development Framework (Vitae, 2011). The need for such an audit of research competence of careers staff has been emphasised by some of the additional challenges encountered by the project team when dealing with our project partners.

One such challenge has involved trying to reconcile the variations in the statements introduced as each institution implemented its own particular version of the CR questions. In some cases, this was just a minor change of wording; in others new items were added to capture information relevant to a particular institution. However, some of the new statements were worded in such a way that it made it impossible to include them in the categorised ranking of statements needed to map progression. For example, one institution introduced the statement 'I thought I knew what I wanted to do but I have changed my mind'. Not only does this statement not include any indication of the student's current state (only their former state), it completely misses the point of CR that you can track changes of mind by comparing one year's data with the next.

Even more fundamental issues were encountered in the variations introduced into the second question around employability-enhancing experiences. Only one institution specifically asked students about their experiences within the previous year, meaning that students could potentially register the same experiences in each year they answered the question, leading to multiple counting of the same data. Another institution allowed students to select multiple experiences alongside statements expressing opinions about the value of those experiences. This made it impossible to identify which experiences the evaluations related to. Many of these mistakes were driven by a desire to gather as much information as possible within the small number of questions allowed, but they demonstrated a lack of understanding of how such information might need to be organised and analysed.

Since starting the project, the team has been approached by a number of institutions which have implemented or are considering implementing CR. It has become obvious that some of them have not given proper consideration to how they will use the data they are collecting. Nor have they always properly considered whether they have the capacity or capability within their service to analyse and prepare the data for use. HE careers services are beginning to face the classic challenges of big data – dealing with volume, velocity and variety. A certain level of naivety in the fundamentals of good research design and project management in careers staff is not surprising. It is not something that HE careers services have had to engage with to such a level in the past. Despite working in a research-intensive environment in which subject expertise is highly prized, careers professionals have been slow to embrace the need for developing and demonstrating their own expertise (Thambar, 2016). Many of the services involved in the Careers Registration project have found some of their careers staff reluctant to engage with CR and lacking confidence in how to interpret the data.

There has traditionally been a perceived divide between practitioners and researchers in the area of careers and employability. There are certainly a vast number of practitioners who engage with theory and research during their professional qualification but rarely, if ever, think about it again afterwards. From the literature it is also clear that there are some academics who are out of touch with modern practice. However, there has always been a range of people exploring the boulder-strewn valley in between these two extremes. There are practice-engaged researchers and teachers, practitioners-turned-academics, practitioner-researchers and academically-engaged practitioners – some of them are contributors to this book.

Developing research self-efficacy in careers staff

The growth of careers education programmes and credit-bearing employability teaching modules in the HE sector has led to an increasing emphasis on the need for career practitioners to have teaching and learning qualifications such as Higher Education Academy Fellowships alongside or instead of one-to-one guidance expertise. In a similar way, it is likely that the increasing importance of data in HE careers will lead to the need for research and analysis expertise within careers teams. Some of this expertise is coming through the creation of special analyst roles within careers services or the redefining of more traditional careers information roles. However, this does not remove the need for careers practitioners to develop greater confidence in understanding and applying the outputs of research, as they are the people likely to be using the data to transform practice and influence stakeholders.

Recognising this need, The Careers Group has established a dedicated research unit. The purpose of this small team is not just to conduct and disseminate primary and secondary research but to support the whole organisation in developing greater awareness, competence and confidence around research, evidence-based practice and scholarship in the field. We organise an annual 'festival of research' where we encourage staff to share their own research ideas and experiences. This is not just aimed at those individuals undertaking a research project as part of a

The rise of the practitioner-researcher 175

masters or PhD, but employees who are collecting data as part of their day-to-day activities and are beginning to explore how to use that data to gain a better understanding of student needs and what constitutes best practice. We have supported one member of staff in turning such data into a published article (Roberts et al., 2017). We have also delivered a series of research and evidence-based staff development webinars on topics such as: *Introduction to data analysis*, *Data collection for careers services*, *Choosing your research topic and formulating your research questions*, *How to find and read a relevant research paper*, *Conducting a literature review* and *Writing for publication*.

The Careers Group has been able to pursue this approach because of its size and unique structure. It is possible that other large HE careers services could do something similar. However, the varied sizes and levels of resourcing for HE careers means that this approach would not be possible everywhere. If the profession as a whole is to be able to respond to these changing times, it is important that the development of practitioner research and scholarship self-efficacy is coordinated nationally.

In 2016 the Association of Graduate Careers Advisory Service (AGCAS), the professional association for HE careers services, published its new strategy (AGCAS, 2016). One of the five core strategy areas identified was 'Research and Knowledge' with the aim to be 'experts in HE student career development and graduate employment' (2016: 2). At the time of writing, AGCAS has organised two research conferences, focusing on the use of research to strengthen practice. It has instigated an award to recognise research-informed practice and is exploring ways in which all AGCAS members can be encouraged to undertake and share research. The Higher Education Careers Service Unit (HECSU) provides funding for small-scale research projects in the area of graduate employability. The majority of these projects are undertaken by AGCAS members (HECSU, 2017). In addition, at 'Rethinking Career Development for a Globalised World' (a conference organised by the National Institute for Career Education and Counselling in September 2016), at least 25% of the presenters were current practitioners engaged in their own research.

These developments are moving the profession in a direction in which, whether they are involved in conducting primary research or not, every practitioner will be expected to have:

- an awareness and understanding of basic research principles and methods – even if they are not conducting research themselves, to understand how research data is produced by others
- the ability to identify, understand, critically evaluate and synthesise research information from various sources and to apply the learning to practice
- the ability to construct arguments based on research findings and to present them appropriately to a range of audiences
- an awareness of ethical and legal considerations linked to the handling of personal data

176 David Winter

In addition, those involved directly in conducting research should have:

- the ability to formulate research questions and to construct appropriate research methodologies
- an understanding of the fundamentals of quantitative and qualitative data analysis
- the ability to manage research projects effectively
- an awareness of the channels for communicating research output and their requirements

If the use of big data within HE careers lives up to its potential it is likely that such requirements may be incorporated into the selection requirements, standards of professional practice and frameworks of continuing professional development for HE careers practitioners across the UK.

Conclusion

Whilst some questions remain about the extent to which big data can enable greater understanding and facilitate evidence-based change within higher education, big data is not going away. There is little prospect of there being a reduction in the amount of data produced and the number of claims made that it will provide transformative insights. Driven by the commercial and political pressures outlined in chapters three and ten, institutional senior managers will always be drawn towards accessible 'hard' data which seems to provide them with an opportunity to increase organisational efficiency and effectiveness even if the content quality of the data is questionable (Popovič et al., 2012). If careers professionals do not take an active role in gathering, analysing and interpreting this data, they will be at the mercy of anyone else who is willing to do so.

The introduction of Careers Registration in a growing number of HE institutions provides an unparalleled opportunity to use a big data approach to gain an evidence-based insight into the career development needs of current students and to prioritise and target support accordingly. It is a positive sign for the profession that this initiative is being led mainly by the careers service in those institutions. However, there is still a deficit in the confidence and capability of careers staff to deal with such data. There are signs that individuals, services and the profession as a whole are taking steps to address this deficit. The following chapter provides an insight into the barriers and enablers for individual practitioners attempting to develop expertise in research and scholarship.

Beyond the issue of developing practical skills of data handling and interpretation, there exists a more fundamental challenge of developing and projecting an appropriate professional identity for career practitioners within higher education. The research presented in chapter eleven illustrates the struggle that careers practitioners have in gaining acceptance for their expertise within their institutions. Chapter twelve hints at an even more worrying reluctance of careers practitioners to claim their identity as experts in employability. If careers professionals are to

The rise of the practitioner-researcher   177

rise to the challenges presented by big data, they need not only to work more closely with those already involved in the study of careers and employability but also to develop their own identities as practitioner-researchers.

References

AGCAS. (2016). AGCAS Strategy – 2016/17 to 2018/19. Association of Graduate Careers Advisory Services.

Asur, S., and Huberman, B.A. (2010). "Predicting the future with social media", In: *Web Intelligence and Intelligent Agent Technology (WI-IAT), 2010 IEEE/WIC/ACM International Conference*. IEEE, pp. 492–499.

Blackmer, W.S. (2016). *GDPR: Getting Ready for the New EU General Data Protection Regulation*. (online) available from: www.infolawgroup.com/2016/05/articles/gdpr/gdpr-getting-ready-for-the-new-eu-general-data-protection-regulation/.

Britton, J., Dearden, L., Shephard, N., and Vignoles, A. (2016). *How English Domiciled Graduate Earnings Vary with Gender, Institution Attended, Subject and Socioeconomic Background*. Working Paper No. W16/06. Institute for Fiscal Studies. (online) available from: www.ifs.org.uk/uploads/publications/wps/wp201606.pdf.

Conijn, M.R., Snijders, C.C., Matzat, U.U., Kleingeld, P.A., and Bijvank, W.W.N. (2016). *EXCTRA-EXploiting the Click-TRAil Assessing the benefits of Learning Analytics*. Eindhoven University of Technology.

Department for Education. (2016). *Teaching Excellence Framework: Year Two Specification*. (online) available from: www.gov.uk/government/uploads/system/uploads/attachment_data/file/556355/TEF_Year_2_specification.pdf.

Gilworth, R., and Cobb, F. (2017). *Where Are You Right Now? Using Careers Registration to Support Employability in Higher Education*. Presented at the HEA Surveys Conference 2017. (online) available from: www.heacademy.ac.uk/knowledge-hub/where-are-you-right-now-using-careers-registration-support-employability-higher.

HECSU. (2017). *HECSU-funded Research*. (online) available from: www.hecsu.ac.uk/current_projects_hecsu_funded_research.htm.

Hewitt, R., and Barnard, M. (2017). *NewDLHE: The Future of Graduate Outcomes Data: Synthesis of Responses to Our Second and Final Consultation*. Cheltenham, UK: HESA. (online) available from: www.hesa.ac.uk/files/NewDLHE_second-consultation-synthesis.pdf.

Laney, D. (2001). *3D Data Management: Controlling Data Volume, Velocity, and Variety*. META Group. (online) available from: http://blogs.gartner.com/doug-laney/files/2012/01/ad949-3D-Data-Management-Controlling-Data-Volume-Velocity-and-Variety.pdf.

McGrath, C.H., Guerin, B., Harte, E., Frearson, M., and Manville, C. (2015). *Learning Gain in Higher Education*. Santa Monica, CA: RAND Corporation.

Megahed, F.M., and Jones-Farmer, L.A. (2015). "Statistical Perspectives on 'Big Data'", In *Frontiers in Statistical Quality Control 11*. Cham: Springer.

Popovič, A., Hackney, R., Coelho, P.S., and Jaklič, J. (2012). "Towards business intelligence systems success: Effects of maturity and culture on analytical decision making", *Decision Support Systems*, 54(1): 729–739.

Roberts, R., Brammar, L., and Cobb, F. (2017). "Experiential work-based learning as a social mobility mechanism for widening participation students", *Journal of the National Institute for Career Education and Counselling*, 38(1): 44–51.

Shacklock, X. (2016). *From Bricks to Clicks: The Potential of Data and Analytics in Higher Education*. London, UK: Higher Education Commission.

Shury, J., Vivian, D., Turner, C., and Downing, C. (2017). *Planning for Success: Graduates' Career Planning and Its Effect on Graduate Outcomes*. Department for Education/IFF. (online) available from: www.gov.uk/government/uploads/system/uploads/attachment_data/file/604170/Graduates__career_planning_and_its_effect_on_their_outcomes.pdf.

Thambar, N. (2016). "'I'm Just a Plain Old Careers Adviser' recognising the hidden expert", *Journal of the National Institute for Career Education and Counselling*, 37(1): 26–32.

Vigen, T. (2015). *Spurious Correlations*. New York: Hachette Books.

Vitae. (2011, April). *Researcher Development Framework*. Careers Research and Advisory Centre (CRAC) Limited. (online) available from: www.vitae.ac.uk/rdf.

14 Making connections through practitioner research

Gill Frigerio

Introduction

This chapter focuses on the role of the career development practitioner integrating theory with their practice through engaging in practitioner research. It is built around three case studies of practitioner research, each explored from the author's perspective. The chapter uses the systems theory framework developed over the last twenty years by Mary McMahon and Wendy Patton (McMahon and Patton, 1995; McMahon, 2017; Patton and McMahon, 2014) as a way of visualising complexity of the individual in context when considering career development. This is used to consider the practitioner researcher in context and identify barriers and enablers to practitioners engaging in research and speculate as to some of the consequences of such engagement.

So far, this volume has explored the space between theory and practice in higher education career and employability provision from various angles. We have problematised increasingly instrumental approaches to employability in response to the policy context, lamenting the commodification of the higher education experience and effect on professional practice. In this chapter, however, I want to subvert the notion of a gulf between theory and practice and explore instances where they are integrated.

I write from my own perspective as an educational researcher who became a careers practitioner, then manager and now is an educator in the field. I am trying to understand my experiences, presented here as three case studies, to see what can be learned. My contention is that practitioner research, informed by career development theories, develops criticality and helps all involved to unpack contested concepts like 'career', thus can assist us in bridging that gap.

Everyone has their own more or less tacit and assumed theories of career which they use to draw conclusions and take actions in relation to their own careers, the careers of others and even how career and employability can best be supported for higher education students. Career development practitioners' professional training provides a grounding in a range of extant career development theories: a transdisciplinary body of work drawing on fields such as vocational psychology, sociology and organisational and cultural studies. Coming from varying disciplinary backgrounds, these theories vary in their focus and underpinning

180 *Gill Frigerio*

assumptions about the way that new knowledge can be generated. These extend from scientific processes of rational judgement (logical positivism) to emergent constructions of subjective meaning.

As a means to accommodate and extend the convergence of this wide theoretical base, a 'Systems Theory Framework' (STF) developed by Patton and McMahon proposes an integrative framework to represent the wide range of influences on career development, capturing both content and process considerations at the level of three systems: the individual, the mid-range social context and wider societal and environmental factors. The parts of these systems, nor the systems themselves, are not static and a mutual, recursive process sees aspects shift and change over time, influencing one another. The framework is summarised in Figure 14.1.

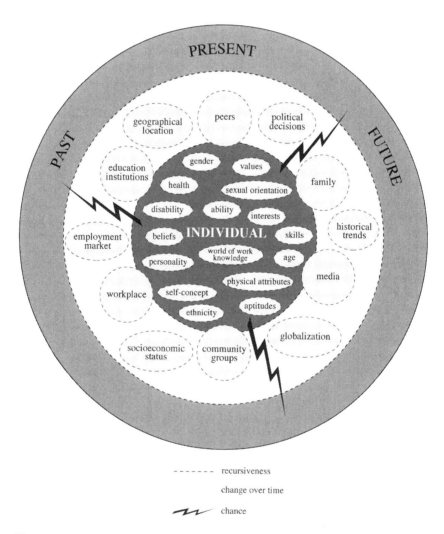

------- recursiveness

change over time

chance

Figure 14.1 Systems Theory Framework – change over time

Making connections through practitioner research   181

In outlining the potential for the framework's use in career development practice, Patton and McMahon show how each system is open, allowing for the elements within to recursively influence one another. The interconnecting systems allow individuals to see themselves in context and facilitate their narration and construction of their career story. Learning, story and connectedness are foregrounded. The STF has influenced research and practice in career counselling, education and assessment and now contributes to discussion of the role of context in career development and work with diverse clients.

A further feature is that the framework makes clear the connections between multiple individuals involved in career development. Patton and McMahon describe this as the 'therapeutic system', referring specifically to career counselling (Figure 14.2). An alternative conceptualisation is that the counsellor role can be played by anyone supporting the career development learning of another. For the purposes of this chapter, this enables us to see the end-user of a career and employability service, career development practitioner, service manager, educator and researcher. It highlights the commonality between all these identities: we are all individual 'careerists' in our individual systems, recursively influencing

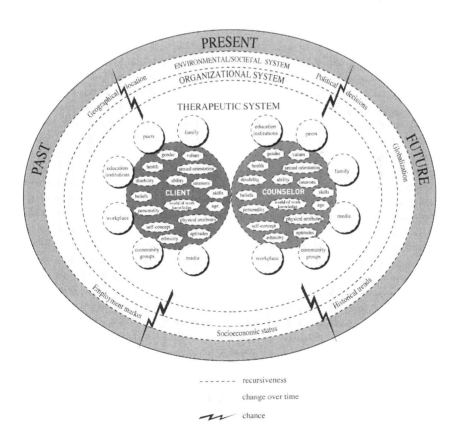

Figure 14.2 Systems Theory Framework – therapeutic system

182 *Gill Frigerio*

one another in social and organisational systems and operating in the same wider geo-political and environmental context. Change over time, and chance events, will also influence all the components.

The approach this chapter takes is to present three case studies, recounted from my own perspective, of experiences with practitioner research over a ten year period. Whilst each case study is presented as a bounded unit, the experiences have run alongside various roles in careers work. They are presented as what Hamilton and Corbett-Whittier (2013) term an 'instrumental case study' captured with a focus on enablers for practitioner research.

In each case study I focus on research processes rather than detailing findings and there is an auto-ethnographic dimension to the work, which remains my own reflexive interpretation of experiences. After the case studies I will return to the systems theory framework to integrate the cases and consider the barriers and enablers for the engagement of higher education career and employability practitioners in 'insider research' (Costley, Elliot and Gibbs, 2010) and further integration of theory and practice.

The story told by linking the case studies is one of my own professional learning and demonstrates the links between practitioner research and the social learning processes at the heart of career development. There are multiple connections to be made: between reflexivity in research and reflective practice in professional development, between service innovation and evaluation, between professional standards and status and more nuanced understanding of how career development practice supports graduates' employability.

Case study 1 – Researching the effectiveness of guidance practice

In 2009, as Manager of Career Education and Guidance at the University of Warwick, I secured a practitioner research grant from the Higher Education Career Service Unit (HECSU) to explore the effectiveness of career guidance. The stimulus for this was a context where service impact was moving rapidly up the agenda of career service managers with studies beginning to grapple with how it might be measured (Nijjar, 2009). Destination data (pivotal to league tables), usage data and reported student satisfaction via feedback surveys were all in use as potential indicators, serving as 'strong surrogates' (Markless and Streatfield, 2006) for effectiveness. At the same time, questions were being raised within the higher education careers world about the role of one to one guidance within wider career service provision (Martin, 2012; Watts and Butcher, 2008). As our most resource intensive activity, too costly to scale up for all potential users, services were moving beyond a focus on managing and meeting demand to one based on assessing and responding to need. As a former researcher, I was fascinated by the methodological complexity of assessing impact. Usage trends and patterns conflate effectiveness with demand without illuminating the process of providing information, advice and guidance services to clients or the outcome(s) of that work. Assessment of client satisfaction becomes embroiled

Making connections through practitioner research   183

with complexities around the meeting of client expectations, whether those be mutually agreed and contracted or not.

The project was inspired by a five-year longitudinal study carried out by Warwick's Institute for Employment Research (Bimrose et al, 2004) evaluating the effectiveness of guidance in a variety of settings. Our study scaled down the IER methodology to follow six first-time student service users through a 20-minute career guidance interview to two months later, seeking rich and deep insights into the way clients approach and make use of a career guidance appointment (Frigerio, 2010).

In October 2008 six participants were identified who had made a first-time booking to see a careers consultant. With a small incentive offered, consent was secured to participate in a three-stage study as follows:

Stage 1: Shortly before their guidance consultation, semi-structured interviews with each participant explored their expectations of a guidance appointment and how these had been informed.

Stage 2: The subsequent consultation was digitally recorded, and feedback sought immediately from client and practitioner. External review by an 'expert witness' was sought and comments built into analysis.

Stage 3: Two months later, the researchers re-contacted clients and interviewed them again to explore what, if any, follow-up actions had been taken and assess developments in their understanding of career management. A £20 payment was made following completion of this stage.

Reflecting on the impact on the research process of service provision being researched from within highlights two salient points.

The first relates to the experience of carrying out the research as the manager of the team whose work was being researched. Some might argue this compromised the process so far as to make it worthless. Groundwork, including staff development and peer review, was essential to create an environment where our own guidance practice, often invisible to colleagues, was transparent and discussable. Power dynamics were inevitably at play through the research and in purposive sampling I did exclude two members of staff: as their line manager I judged that the stress of being recorded was likely to distort the practice itself. I made it as clear as I could to careers consultants that their performance was not being assessed. Outweighing these factors were the advantages of the cost-effective nature of the research being done in-house, the professional learning for everybody that came from involvement as well as the resultant ownership of the findings throughout the service.

Secondly, the situated nature of practitioner research led us to recalibrate the generic methods the IER team had followed, given that they were researching guidance in their variety of contexts, to develop something tailored to our own service provision. Through staff development activities we had identified that our service model of short guidance appointments emphasised an action-oriented, goal-directed approach to guidance and our own process and interview

184 *Gill Frigerio*

framework was developed. This was then built into the research design as used as an evaluative framework for the project, rather than simply seeking the client definition of useful.

Findings of the study helped us understand the process of guidance and how students viewed its contribution to their development of an individual career story. The study made a contribution to the development of service strategy at the time. Beyond that, as a small-scale study in a context seeking a justification for continued investment in resource-hungry one to one services, it suffered from the weight of expectation. As I moved on, the work had no further internal champion. However, the sense of story and the primacy of students' own 'narratives of employability' (Tomlinson, 2007) remained significant in strategic planning for the new service.

Case study 2 – Working with career adapt-abilities in practice

The second case study considers the process of integrating a new theoretical approach to career development and considering how it can be operationalised into career service provision through a process of pilots in various higher education contexts.

'Career Adapt-abilities' form part of a theoretical model developed by Mark Savickas based on his work in the field of vocational psychology on career construction theory. In response to increased change in the labour market, Savickas laid out an interpretation of the process by which individuals respond to this need to adapt to change. He defines four psycho-social adaptabilities as: 'the readiness to cope with the predictable tasks of preparing for and participating in the work role and with the unpredictable adjustments prompted by changes in work and working conditions' (1997: 254). The model posits that these can be developed so that individuals are ready, willing and able to respond to labour market change when required. The adapt-abilities themselves are articulated as the four Cs:

Concern: developing a positive optimistic attitude to the future
Control: exerting a degree of intra-personal influence on their situations
Curiosity: broadening horizons by exploring social opportunities & possibilities
Confidence: believing in yourself & your ability to achieve your goal

The development of these abilities renders an individual ready, willing and able to adapt to change when needed. The suggestion for practice is that by focusing on the learning of these 4 adapt-abilities, adaptive response to the outcome of graduation transition would be improved, along with ability to adapt to future labour market change. In the search for meaningful performance indicators, career practitioners may view as oppositional a focus on *either* immediate transitions *or* long-term career development. The focus here on change 'when needed' can be seen as reframing the either/or nature of this debate. Instead, it provides space to consider 'both/and' immediate transition (measured by post-graduation destination data) and lifelong career management (perhaps unmeasurable).

Making connections through practitioner research 185

Central to the development of this strand of Savickas's work was a 24-item scale which would assess levels of Career Adapt-abilities (Porfeli and Savickas, 2012) and an international programme to amend as necessary and validate the scale for use in diverse country contexts (Savickas and Porfeli, 2012). This coincided with collaborative research endeavours in the UK to explore potential and available scales for measuring employability. A group of UK HE Career service managers and researchers convened to consider the possible use of a UK-based CAAI (Career Adapt-abilities Inventory) as an appropriate measure for use in practice. We began by amending and validating a UK version of the scale (the CAAI-UK). Whilst this work was ongoing, discussions were stimulated with practitioners about how this could be integrated with practice through publications (Frigerio, 2013) and at events.

Once the validated scale was available, funding was secured from the Higher Education Academy to pilot its use in practice. A steering group of the original parties involved in the validating study invited bids to be involved in pilots and secured participation of a diverse group of six HE organisations to conduct different pilots. These included:

- Three Pilots investigating the feasibility of using the CAAI-UK to target interventions in groups of students who had already been identified by other means, e.g.,

  - A course of study showing a lower level of graduate employment than the institutional average in the DLHE survey.
  - One programme within a particular adviser's caseload where small group access within the curriculum had already been earmarked for career development activity
  - Mature learners on a bespoke programme in a partner college

- One pilot investigating the possibility of using the CAAI-UK in an institutional context as the basis for a reworked employability strategy, gathering benchmark data for a whole cohort, and particularly investigating the institutional processes (e.g., linking with student records and IT systems) which might be involved in such an endeavour.
- One pilot exploring the feasibility of producing an online version of the CAAI-UK which could be used autonomously by students, giving feedback on scores, and to what extent this might be perceived as useful by students and careers services.
- One pilot explored how the CAAI-UK might be used in conjunction with a work placement to help students to reflect on learning, career development and transitions between university and the world of work.

Funding was restricted to one financial year and was confirmed in autumn 2013, with all pilot sites agreed by January 2014. Hard copy and electronic PDF forms of the CAAI-UK were provided to the lead researcher-practitioners in each pilot site, along with briefing notes and support from the research team throughout the duration of the pilots. Along the way, the research team had generated

186 *Gill Frigerio*

a lot of interest in CA in 2013–14, culminating in a symposium event attend by over 30 delegates.

To summarise the learning resulting from the pilots about using career adapt-abilities in practice, pilot sites found that the adapt-abilities can offer an appropriate framework to unify discussions with academic and administrative colleagues. Researchers in a number of pilots found that colleagues outside career and employability work responded with interest to the accessibility of the concepts and welcomed the use of such a theoretical framework. We concluded it was therefore feasible in principle to use the Career Adapt-abilities Inventory on an institution-wide basis, along the same lines as the career registration process described by Winter in this volume. The integration of both short- and long-term perspectives was judged relevant to both the current policy context and the underpinning professional values of career practitioners.

However, pilots were hindered by the short timescales available and the difficulty in engaging students, particularly when the window for fieldwork came at a pressured time of the academic year. Completion of a hard copy inventory and manual scoring is cumbersome and outside contemporary expectations of online service delivery. However, the pilot developing an online tool for unmediated use found this to be too complex a task for the resources of the project. Challenges included how to render the underlying concepts readily understandable, so that the purpose of the Inventory was clear, which in turn would help to manage student expectation, and how to signpost appropriately to both local and national services, dependent on scores.

Wider findings relating to practitioner research also emerged. The motivations of the research practitioners for participating in the pilots varied. These included an innate desire to innovate, an interest in solutions to address challenges of the changing practice context, an interest in research, a desire to extend professional networks or a response to the interest or encouragement of a manager. However, the combination of pressured professional roles, a lack of protected time for involvement in the pilots and operational difficulties in reaching student participants hampered pilots, in spite of these motivations. Moreover, concepts are quite distant from practice in how they are presented in academic literature and can be hard for practitioners to grasp on the run. More detailed briefing of practitioners that allowed for critical engagement with the underlying concepts, and even a chance to consider them in relation to their own career development, would have created a more secure basis for the pilots. These difficulties are even more acute for student users, who may approach services with expectations of matching and directive approaches and find Career Adapt-abilities to be conceptually challenging.

Findings from all six pilots suggest that, as well as providing a constructive and valued activity for students as part of career support services, career adapt-ability offered a promising framework for structuring conversations between higher education career development practitioners and other colleagues. The theoretical rigour evident in the development of the career adapt-abilities scale can be viewed positively by colleagues in a context which values academic output. Career adapt-ability can therefore provide a foundation for an institution-wide discussion on career development services. For example, trend data for the CAAI-UK collected over a number of years may show useful patterns in student perceptions of their adapt-abilities over their course of study, which could inform career development planning at an institutional level (Wright and Frigerio, 2015). However, there is a danger in assuming linear development of the adaptability dimensions and directly correlated increases in scores, which are based on self-perceived ratings. Ratings may decrease initially as self-awareness increases, thus direct use of scores as a measure of change may produce misleading results in the short term.

Despite the value of a theoretical construct which can be used at all levels of practice, from strategic prioritisation to one to one development work, the momentum needed to continue to disseminate this work is hard to maintain. For example, the functioning online version is no longer available and despite interest from a number of individual practitioners and institutions separately, there is no collective resource to pursue it at a national level. At the time of writing, the most positive development is the inclusion of one strand of the HEFCE Learning Gain programme, the Legacy project. The focus here is on looking at its potential use as a measure, consistent with career registration data as opposed to how it can be used in guidance practice.

Case study 3 – Supporting practitioner research through a 'research project' module

The final case study draws upon my experiences as co-leader of a module on the suite of professional development programmes in career development and coach-ing in the Centre for Lifelong Learning at the University of Warwick. A signifi-cant proportion of these students are higher education career and employability practitioners pursuing our collaborative programme run in partnership with the Association for Graduate Career Advisory Services (AGCAS). This module, and indeed the programme as a whole, has integration of theory and practice as its DNA, aiming to support learning about the research process through practical experience of a research project. It can serve as a capstone project for those com-pleting Postgraduate Diploma level, as well as providing the necessary grounding for dissertation work for students going on to pursue a Master's.

This 20-credit module is taught via a blended approach of online resources, a two-day workshop and individual supervision, and assessed via completion of a 5000-word research project. Since moving into teaching from a practitioner/manager role I have supervised around 50 students' work exploring a range of research questions, all identified from their practice contexts. Relevant examples include:

- Students' definitions of career success
- Variations in engagement and destination by faculty and gender

188   *Gill Frigerio*

- Stimulating student reflection on learning through employability awards
- Experiences of students from different social classes and potential influence on placement decisions
- Learning outcomes of an enterprise placement year
- Tensions between medical students' aspirations and NHS workforce needs and implications for practice

The online materials, developed by my colleague Phil McCash, seek to orient the student towards key concepts in social research and guides them through the research process, covering different epistemological positions that research might take, the establishment of research questions, exploring existing literature, identifying appropriate research strategies, sources and how to identify and evaluate them, reflexivity and ethics in practitioner research, triangulation and dissemination.

The two-day workshop is designed to respond to the concerns of those new to practitioner research, devoting considerable time to exploring researcher identities and previous experiences of research, often based in different disciplinary contexts. This often informs consideration of differing epistemologies and typically sees scientific and objective assumptions about the nature of research put alongside understandings of the concept of career being contestable and playing out in differently constructed social worlds. For practitioner researchers whose workplaces might be seeking generalisable findings on which to base solutions to real problems, this attention to an individual's own construction of meaning and the challenges it creates in establishing universal truths can lead to some frustration. I often find that it is through reflexive consideration of their own perspective and how this differs from others that students are able to arrive at an interpretivist position. This allows for a level of ownership of any resulting recommendations for practice, grounded in the professional competence and confidence needed to see them through.

Research strategies covered in our teaching include literature review, case study, action research, surveys, (auto)ethnography and narrative enquiry. Students select the strategy best placed to answer their research questions and identify sources such as a range of literatures, focus groups, secondary data, reflective diaries or semi-structured interviews.

One to one supervision supports students in preparing a research proposal, ensuring ethical approval through the University's procedures conducting the research and writing up, over a 5-month period. One of the threshold concepts we address early on is the scoping of a study of manageable size. When so many questions are posed in our day-to-day practice, it can be hard to identify the ones that can be answered and to hold lightly the perceived pressure to produce a definitive work on the topic. It can help to reframe outcomes in terms of the students' own professional learning with the research process a stimulus for further theoretically informed reflective practice and ongoing curiosity. We also pay attention to the process of recognising insider status – that being a practitioner who is providing a service to the researched gives a particular stake and perspective which can be harnessed in interpretation of data.

Students commonly report experiencing this module as challenging – perhaps the most challenging of their overall programme – although also one where they are particularly able to consider a workplace problem in some depth and make self-directed use of key concepts covered in previous modules. The opportunity to craft research-informed recommendations gives tangible outcomes. Along the way students negotiate many of the challenges known to insider researchers considering their own practice such as managing expectations of colleagues and managers as to the scope of the research, negotiating access, particularly given the vagaries of the academic cycle, where many students are either fully engaged in their academic studies or absent from the university and finding appropriate chunks of time to devote to their project alongside busy jobs.

Making connections between the cases

At individual level, the practitioner-researcher might be at any stage of career development, taking part in initial in-service training or pursuing research as part of their continuing professional development activity. The link to CPD activities reminds us that it is scope for reflective practice which enables the questions to be identified which are then addressed through research. This can be a disruptive experience for practitioners, and the confidence and ability to engage both with career development theories and research processes and terminology are critical here. Practitioner-researchers need to be able to carve out time and space for their research, processing questions that can be raised about policy and practice. For many, I notice that their experience is that this is a factor both at work and outside of working hours, where the writing stage of projects tends to spill over.

So, very early in our consideration of the enablers of practitioner research we find ourselves considering the social contexts in which it is taking place. Identifying time requires the support of others – colleagues and managers – and they will also need to manage the discomfort that can be raised by asking questions.

Here I also lay down a challenge to researchers. As Ali and Brown (2016) argue, integration of theory and practice implies 'bidirectional relationships between each of these concepts' (p. 73), not simply application of one to the passive other, ready to receive. In the same volume, Sampson, Bullock-Yowell, Dozier, Osborn and Lenz (2016) note the existent difficulty in communication among theorists, researchers and practitioners as a key impediment to achieving greater integration into practice. This may be an overly gloomy assessment of the UK context: I have certainly personally benefited from the support of researchers who were generous with their time and expertise and encouraged me. It is positive to see the practitioner research bursary which funded case study 1 has been recently re-established. There is a need for researchers to develop resources that practitioners can use based on their findings. The curriculum resources developed by the Irish career development organisation AHECs (2014) and by Frigerio, Mendez and McCash (2012) are positive examples. It is to be hoped that career adapt-abilities resources will soon follow suit.

190   *Gill Frigerio*

The Systems Theory Framework reminds us that practitioner researchers are individuals in the midst of a long tradition of both career development practice and social research. They are engaging in practitioner research as part of their work: work which is done by them as individuals but located in social contexts. These individual systems then connect through social and societal systems with their participants and contexts, and with each other. As well as sharpening criticality in ways that will disrupt and recursively affect other aspects of their system, this will also bleed out into affecting those around them as they construct their own career development and foster their own learning through their research.

Stepping out into the wider sphere of the systems theory framework, we can see societal factors such as higher education policy and technological change recursively influencing the micro-level experience of the practitioner-researcher. The sector and its institutions, themselves in the grip of marketisation, can pay more attention to the small-scale studies typical of practitioner research. There is something of a paradox here. On the one hand we have the positivist paradigm through which we view large scale destination surveys and other metrics which inform exercises like the Teaching Excellence Framework. On the other hand, any understanding of career development which acknowledges that it is ultimately about the actions and perceptions of the individual will share the same constructivist epistemology which underpins reflective practice. As we make connections we find ourselves holding these tensions.

In my introduction I reiterated the connection between learning, career development and practitioner research. In his work *The Courage to Teach* Parker Palmer (2007: 76–80) writes of supporting learning through the creation of 'paradoxical spaces'.

These spaces should:

1) Be both bounded and open
2) Be both hospitable and charged
3) Invite both the voice of the individual and of the group
4) Both honour 'little' stories of those involved and the 'big' stories of the disciplines and tradition
5) Both support solitude and surround them with the resources of the community
6) Welcome both silence and speech

These paradoxes seem to me to be evident throughout the case studies and valuable in considering how the sector can encourage and support integration of theory and practice through practitioner research. Within the open space needed for questions to emerge, we provide structure, such as the research project module, to follow. We bring scholars and practitioners together, acknowledging that there will be differences of perspective, both for individuals and for professional and disciplinary groups. Given space, within interlocking systems, practitioners can develop confidence in their own perspective through research and through this make connections with other higher education professional communities.

References

Association of Higher Education Career Services (2014). *Crafting the Present for Future Employability: An AHECS Employability Module*, Cork, Republic of Ireland: AHECS.

Ali, S.R., and Brown, S.D. (2016). "Integration of theory, research, and practice: Using our tools to address challenging times", In: Sampson, J.P., Bullock-Yowell, E., Dozier, V.C., Osborn, D.S., and Lenz, J.G. (Eds.), *Integrating Theory, Research, and Practice in Vocational Psychology: Current Status and Future Directions*. Tallahassee, FL: Florida State University.

Bimrose, J., Barnes, S.A., Hughes, D., and Orton, M. (2004). *What is Effective Guidance? Evidence from Longitudinal Case Studies in England*. DfES/Warwick Institute for Employment Research.

Costley, C., Elliott, G., and Gibbs, P. (2010). *Doing Work Based Research: Approaches to Enquiry for Insider-researchers*. London: Sage.

Frigerio, G. (2010). *Narratives of Employability: Effective Guidance in a Higher Education Context. A Qualitative Evaluation of the Impact of Guidance*. Coventry: University of Warwick (online) available from: https://www2.warwick.ac.uk/study/cll/about/cllteam/gfrigerio.

Frigerio, G. (2013). "Career adaptabilities: A new approach", *Graduate Market Trends*, Spring 2013.

Frigerio, G., Mendez, R., and McCash, P. (2012). *Re-designing Work-related Learning: A Management Studies Placement Module*. Coventry: Career Studies Unit.

Hamilton, L., and Corbett-Whittier, C. (2013). *Using Case Study in Education Research*. London: Sage.

Martin, A-M. (2012). "Employer engagement and impact measurement: AGCAS Impact Agenda", Keynote speaker at AGCAS Scotland Biennial Conference 2012, St Andrew's University, 28 June 2012.

Markless, S., and Streatfield, D.R. (2006). *Evaluating the Impact of Your Library Service: The Quest for Evidence*. London: Facet.

McMahon, M. (2017). "Work and why we do it: A Systems Theory Framework *Perspective*", *Career Planning and Adult Development Journal*, 33(2): 9–15.

McMahon, M., and Patton, W. (1995). "Development of a Systems Theory Framework of Career Development", *Australian Journal of Career Development*, 4: 15–20.

Nijjar, A.K. (2009). *Stop and Measure the Roses: How University Careers Services Measure their Effectiveness and Success*. HECSU: Manchester.

Palmer, P. (2007). *The Courage to Teach: Exploring the Inner Landscape of a Teacher's Life*. San Francisco: Jossey-Bass.

Patton, W., and McMahon, M. (2014). *Career Development and Systems Theory: Connecting Theory and Practice* (3rd edition). Rotterdam, Netherlands: Sense.

Porfeli, E., and Savickas, M. (2012). "Career adapt-abilities scale – USA form: Psychometric properties and relation to vocational identity", *Journal of Vocational Behavior*, 80(3): 674–679.

Sampson, J.P., Bullock-Yowell, E., Dozier, V.C., Osborn, D.S., and Lenz, J.G. (Eds.) (2016). *Integrating Theory, Research, and Practice in Vocational Psychology: Current Status and Future Directions*. Tallahassee, FL: Florida State University.

Savickas, M.L. (1997). "Career adaptability: An integrative construct for life-span, life-space theory", *The Career Development Quarterly*, 45: 247–259.

192 *Gill Frigerio*

Savickas, M.L., and Porfeli, E.J. (2012). "Career adapt-abilities scale: Construction, reliability, and measurement equivalence across 13 countries", *Journal of Vocational Behavior, 80*: 661–673.

Tomlinson, M. (2007). "Graduate employability and student attitudes and orientations to the labour market", *Journal of Education and Work, 20*(4): 285–304.

Watts, A.G., and Butcher, V. (2008). *Break Out or Break Up?* Cambridge: HECSU.

Wright, T., and Frigerio, G. (2015). *The Career Adapt-Abilities Pilots Project.* York: Higher Education Academy. (online) available from: https://www2.warwick.ac.uk/study/cll/about/cllteam/gfrigerio.

15 Conclusion – editorial reflections and a call to action

Fiona Christie and Ciaran Burke

Although this is an academic book firmly situated in a vast body of relevant literature, at its heart it is a call for action to explore new territory in thinking about graduate careers that can inform research, policy and practice. In making this argument, we are acutely aware of the challenges that current graduates face in carving out meaningful careers; and it follows that considerable responsibility lies with researchers and practitioners in this field to produce research and knowledge, which can be of practical impact for society and specifically students and graduates as they embark on a hoped-for graduate career.

The changing graduate labour market

Chapters in this book present the case for a more nuanced perspective on graduate transitions out of university and into their careers. Ball highlights valuable macro-level trends which dispel some myths about the graduate labour market, while Vigurs et al., Crew and Scurry and Blenkinsopp explore qualitatively early experiences of the job market. The findings of these authors are of relevance to policy-making as they highlight diversity in the graduate job market especially around geographical domicile and social class. Scurry and Blenkinsopp also provide a valuable illumination upon graduate underemployment and how this can represent an ordinary stage of adjustment from university life for some, but also risks being something that individuals may get stuck in. Unfortunately public policy which needs to defend tuition fees forces attention too narrowly on the return on investment of a degree. University responses have followed the direction of government, and courses can be sold which idealise graduate destinations and ignore the more subtle and slower ways that graduate careers develop. There is a strong case for practices in universities that relate to employability and careers advice to pay due attention to contextual factors that affect transition and be candid with students about the challenges they may face along the way, while providing enabling support for graduates on their journeys to find meaningful and fulfilling work. A consideration of the relationship between wellbeing and employability is also important. Graduates are subject to competing perspectives which highlight individual responsibility and competition while also raising consumerist expectations about the employment outcomes of a degree. Such an

194 *Fiona Christie, Ciaran Burke*

environment can adversely affect the wellbeing of students and graduates who compare themselves unfavourably to idealised notions of being a graduate.

Policy context

Graduate career destinations are of consistent interest to policy-makers. The use of graduate outcomes in TEF suggests that policy attention will increase. We are not naïve about the highly charged political context that surround graduate careers and public policy in universities. The neo-liberal university context demands swift reactions to the latest government policy. It also gives priority to marketisation, efficiency and management processes which can militate against new research and scholarship about careers and employability that does not offer quick wins.

Careers advisory practice in universities faces a difficult hinterland with regard to the removal of a publicly funded careers service in schools and colleges in England. Provision has been partially retained in the other nations of the UK. However, this does mean that what advice students get before coming to university is patchy, which can impact on career clarity of those starting university (the importance of which is highlighted in Artess's chapter). The removal of a statutory public service pre-HE also adversely affects the pipeline of practitioners working in this field in higher education and may contribute to wider doubts about the point of a careers service at all. Neo-liberal ideology which advocates competitive individualism certainly casts a shadow over many brokerage and helping services in wider society. It is no surprise that professionally this is a field experiencing considerable turbulence as both Thambar and Gilworth explain in their chapters, creating new challenges for careers practitioners and managers.

Boundaries between practitioners and academic researchers

There has been some evidence that the scope for non-academic staff such as careers practitioners to engage in research and scholarship is reducing as boundaries between academic and professional staff appear more demarcated. This trend is in opposition to what many authors in this book recommend; in fact, many argue that more research and scholarship should underpin practice, or that practice risks failing to adapt to new contexts.

We would argue that the space at the boundary between academic researchers and practitioners is a fertile one, which should be embraced for the benefit of all, not least the current generation of students and graduates. Many of the authors of this book operate in this grey space drawing together the policy and practice implications of research and scholarship, and could be described as boundary spanners. They explore issues about careers and employability that appear obvious and taken-for-granted but are actually complex, and in so doing illuminate important issues. It follows that the topics raised in this book invite staff in universities who are connected to careers advisory and employability practices

Conclusion – editorial reflections and a call to action   195

(including careers professionals, employment researchers, education developers and academics tasked with employability-related teaching) to think critically about their own assumptions about employability, e.g., in relation to the balance between individual characteristics, personal circumstances, labour market conditions and the role of enabling systems provided by a university, e.g., careers services, careers modules, etc.

The role of practitioners in relation to research

Careers services are increasingly under the spotlight as illustrated by the recent Bridge Group report 'Social Mobility and University Careers Services' which explored them as a proxy for how universities support social mobility. That report highlighted the differential resourcing of careers services which Gilworth's chapter outlines as being reflective of varied organisational responses to employability. The chapters in this book written by those in management positions like Gilworth, Thambar and Winter showcase careers service managers who actively promote the development of research and knowledge in practice, which can be responsive to organisational and policy demands. The benefits of research to practice are also illustrated by chapters from Alexander, Winter and Frigerio who are actively involved in research from a practitioner perspective.

University careers services are in a unique position as they are positioned between many different stakeholders, including students, graduates, employers and academics and other university staff. Their engagement with cross-sector professional bodies such as AGCAS (of which some of our authors are leaders), NASES and ASET give them a rich perspective. It is perhaps no surprise that Neary and Hanson's chapter depicts people moving into this work as highly motivated and satisfied – this is an important and interesting field of work, but rarely easy. Professional bodies such as AGCAS can have a significant role in enhancing the quality of this field of work by fostering shared values and knowledge which can create new ways of thinking. Careers staff continue to collaborate across universities widely; however, this co-operation requires commitment and determination by careers service managers to see beyond short-term organisational drivers. Notably, the AGCAS strategy (2016–2019) has objectives around research and knowledge, learning, community, quality and advocacy which this volume endorses. The contribution of AGCAS members as authors to this book can be considered part of the development of the body of knowledge that critically underpins the work of careers services.

The role of researchers in relation to practice

However, we also recognise that many practitioners are not specialist researchers, and it is here that researchers can seek to conduct work that is accessible and useable by those in practice. As such we would argue for greater collaboration between careers services and employment researchers, not to mention other university staff with an interest in employability as part of their job. Notably, there appears to be scope for a renaissance in relation to sociologically informed educational research, around practice issues. Historically, sociological writing has been considered to question what careers advisory practice and employability interventions can really achieve as employment outcomes are largely socially determined by social background. However, the researchers presented in this volume represent a new turn in sociology which tackles structural issues but does not negate the hope for change. This book brings perspectives together; however, there is scope for academics and practitioners to work more closely on projects in the future. One of the challenges of careers work has been its ability to prove its value. Perhaps with the onset of big data and more research collaborations, the time has come to create new evidence about what works in careers work. Researchers can also delve into difficult topics, evocatively illustrated by Scurry and Blenkinsopp in their discussion of graduate underemployment, which practitioners who are subject to organisational constraints may steer clear of.

Our volume has also invited consideration that new ways of thinking through theory are needed in the uncertain times in which we live. Burke and Hannaford-Simpson consider the theoretical value of Bourdieusian ideas, whereas Morrison draws upon Fraser's ideas about social justice. Crew employs the language of capitals to consider how employability can vary across regions which disrupts normative assumptions about employability. Alexander's chapter, with the use of theory, skilfully illuminates taken-for-granted approaches to practice in her depiction of mobilisers and integrators. Many authors are searching for a space between theories of the individual, the organisational and the social which can help understand current contexts. Frigerio makes a case for the untapped value of Patton and McMahon's systems theory framework to do this. Arguably theory has been much neglected in careers practice as criticality is hard to maintain in a marketised HE context. But this volume illustrates that there is appetite for more probing research into practice, and theory can provide useful thinking tools to make this happen.

Index

abductive research 127
Aberdeen 89
Abrahams, J. 19, 42, 43, 47, 73, [27, 51, 52, 83]
absolute employability 31–32
abstract theory/analysis 37–38
Alexander, R. 8, 87–90, 92, 195–196, [94]
Allan, G. 143, [150]
Annual Population Survey (APS) 58, 60, 61, 63–64
Artess, J. ix, 4, 8, 18–19, 26, 41, 86, 92, 96, 99, 140, 194, [10, 27, 51, 94, 108, 150]
Arthur, M.B. 3, [10, 11, 12]
aspirations 6, 18, 22, 24, 79, 91, 100, 111, 146, 161–162, 188
Association of Graduate Careers Advisory Services (AGCAS) 8, 63, 141, 143, 149, 154, 159, 163, 175, 187, 195

Ball, C. 3, 7, 47, 67, 86, 193, [10, 53, 70, 94]
Barley, S.R. 119, [121]
Bathmaker, A.M. 5, 19, 36, 42, 47, 49–50, [10, 27, 38, 51]
Becker, G.S. 3, [10]
Behle, H. 3, 32, 96, 100, 103, 106, 110–111 [10, 12, 38, 109, 121]
Bell, D. 17–18, [27]
Bimrose, J. 5, 93, 142, 183 [10, 94, 150, 191]
Black and Minority Ethnic (BME) 33–35, 50, 101, 103, 143–144
boomerang transitions 72–73
Boundaryless Career, The 3–5, 142
Bourdieu, P. 4, 7, 19–20, 24, 26, 35–37, 42, 196, [10, 27, 38, 51];

capital 3–7, 17–26, 30, 35–36, 38, 41–51, 74, 82, 87, 90, 111–112, 149–150, 196; dispositions 20, 42, 50; field 19–20, 24, 26, 38, 42–43, 47, 50; "field of the possibles" 20, 42; habitus 4–5, 19–24, 42–43, 47; misrecognition 37
Bradley, H. 3, 19, 43, 73, 81–82, [10, 27, 51, 83]
Break-Out or Break-Up? 135
Bridge Group 19, 130, 141–142, 195
Britton, J. 4, 29, 32–33, 169, [11, 39, 177]
Brown, A. 142, [150]
Brown, P. 4, 18, 30–32, 35, 110, [11, 28, 39, 121]
Browne Review (Department for Business, Innovation and Skills) 129, 154, 155
Burke, C. 5, 7, 21–22, 36, 42, 47, 50, 85, 86, 90, 120, 196 [11, 27, 39, 52, 94, 121]
Burris, B.H. 111, 112, 116, [121]
Butcher, V. 135–136, 182, [139, 192]

capitals 3–7, 17–26, 30, 35–36, 38, 41–51, 74, 82, 87, 90, 111–112, 149–150, 196; career 90; cultural 20, 35, 38, 42, 44, 49–50, 74, 87, 149, 150; economic/financial 20, 36, 38, 42, 50, 74, 82, 87; educational/scholastic 17, 20–21, 26, 35–36; human 3, 17, 18, 26, 30, 111–112; institutional 20, 42; regional 7, 41–51; social 18–21, 23–24, 25–26, 35, 36, 38, 42–43, 47, 50, 74, 149, 150
career adapt-abilities 184–187, 189
Career Adapt-abilities Inventory (CAAI) 185–186

198   *Index*

Career Development Institute (CDI) 143
career development practitioners 2, 6,
8–10, 140–150, 163, 169, 175–176,
179–190, 195
career management skills 42, 99, 131, 140
careers adviser 9, 87–88, 92–93,
137–138, 141, 145, 149, 153–156,
158–163
careers adviser identities 159–160
Careers consultant 103–104, 137, 141,
145, 183
career scripts 119–120
career success 91, 112, 120, 131, 187
Carless, S. 142, [151]
Case, J. 1, 17, [10, 11, 27]
Centre for Cities 65–66
Christie, F. 42–43, 100, 140–142,
149–150, [52, 108, 151]
community activist 87, 91
*Community Interaction and Its
Importance for Contemporary
Careers Work* 5
concrete analysis 37–38
continuing professional development
162–163, 176, 189
co-production - student and institution
128, 131

Destination of Leavers from Higher
Education (DLHE) xii, 30–31, 58,
63–64, 66, 88, 97, 129–130, 133,
140–141, 169–170, 172, 185
Diamond Review of Higher Education
in Wales 41
dispositions 20, 42, 50
Downing, C. 172, [178]

effectiveness of guidance 169, 172, 176,
182–184
Elias, P. 2–3, 31–32, 62–63, 82–83,
100, 110, 115, 120, [10, 11, 12, 38,
39, 70, 83, 108, 109, 121]
*Embedding Employability Into the
Curriculum* 99
employer engagement 136, 140–141,
154–156
*Employment and Earnings Outcomes
of Higher Education Graduates by
Subject and Institution: Experimental
Statistics Using the Longitudinal
Educational Outcomes data* (DfE
2017) 97
employment mismatch 18, 57–58,
64–65

Enterprise in Higher Education initiative
(EHE) 153–154
Environment, Values and Resources
(E, V, R) 128–133
Evandrou, M. 86, [95]
expectations 17, 20, 22, 24–26,
114–120
extra-curricular activities 19, 35–36, 98

Falkingham, J. 86, [95]
Feldman, D.C. 111–113, 119, [121,
122, 123]
field 19–20, 24, 26, 38, 42–43, 47, 50
field of the possibles 20, 42
financial crash of 2008 1, 154
Finn, K. 5, 45, 85–86, 90, [11, 52,
94, 95]
Fraser, N. 7, 29–30, 33–35, 36–38,
196, [39]; James, D. on 37, [39];
justice 7, 29–30, 33–35, 36–38;
misrecognition 37; moral worth 38;
parity of participation 34–35, 36–37;
perspectival dualism 34, 37–38
Frigerio, G. 10, 183, 185, 187, 189,
195–196, [191, 192]
*Fulfilling Our Potential: Teaching
Excellence, Social Mobility and Student
Choice* (BIS 2015) 3–4, 98
Futuretrack 4–5, 8, 96–97, 100–108

gap year 7–8, 42, 71–83, 114–120, 170
gender 4–5, 9, 21, 29, 32–35, 44,
73–75, 77, 82, 92–93, 100–101,
103, 105, 114, 142, 143, 150,
187–188
Gilworth, R.B. 8, 130, 134, 138, 170,
194–195, [139, 177]
globalisation 11, 30, 73, 175
graduate attributes 4, 7, 17–19, 26,
31–33, 45, 50, 99, 105, 113
graduate destinations xii, 29–31, 58, 64,
66–67, 88–90, 97, 110, 140–141,
154–155, 169, 182, 184, 187, 190,
193–194
Graduate Outcomes (GO) xii, 97,
129–131
graduate premium 4, 32, 63, 64, 120
graduate resilience 18, 26, 31, 35,
99, 142
graduate transitions 3, 6–8, 24, 71–83,
93, 98–100, 105, 107, 111, 116,
140–150, 184–185, 193
Green, F. 3, 63, 110, 111–112,
[11, 70, 121]

habitus 4–5, 19–24, 42–43, 47
Hall, D.T. 3, [11, 13]
Hammersley, M. 127, [139]
happenstance 5
HEA Framework for Employability 41–44, 99
Hearne, L. 5, 142, [10, 150]
HE finance reform 82
Hesketh, A. 4, 31–32, 35, 110, 115, [11, 39, 121]
Heslin, P.A. 112, [122]
Higher Education Academy (HEA) 31, 35, 41–44, 99, 174, 185
Higher Education and Research Act (2017) 129–130
Higher Education Careers Service Unit (HECSU) 63, 67, 96–97, 175, 182
Higher Education Funding Council for England (HEFCE) 9, 32, 129, 143, 171, 187
Higher Education Funding Council for Wales (HEFCW) 41, 49
Higher Education Role Analysis (HERA) exercise 155–156
Higher Education Statistics Agency (HESA) 58, 97, 108, 110, 120, 143, 169
Higher Education: Students at the Heart of the System (BIS 2011) 3–4, 18
Highlands and Islands Enterprise 85, 88, 89
Hodkinson, P. 5, [11]
Holland, J.L. 5, [11]
Holmes, L. 1, 4, 5, 140, [12, 13, 151]
Holton, M. 90, [95]
Hooley, T. 4, 6, 18–19, 26, 41, 86–87, 88, 90–92, 99, 140, 141–142 [10, 12, 27, 51, 94, 95, 108, 150, 151]
hyper-reality 20

impact measurement 6, 97–99, 130–131, 167, 169, 172, 182
Ingram, N. 5, 19, 36, 42, 47, 49–50, [10, 27, 38, 51]
Institute for Employment Research (University of Warwick) 4–5, 64, 96, 183
Institute of Student Employers/ Association of Graduate Recruiters (ISE/AGR) xi, xiii, 31, 35, 67–68
institutional identity 128, 133–135, 158–160, 162, 176

institutional strategy 128, 132–133, 135, 149, 172, 185
integrators 8, 91–93, 196
internships 36, 43–44, 73, 75–77, 78, 79, 113, 135–136, 145, 154, 171

job-crafting 113
Johnson, G. 132, [139]
Johnson, W.R. 111–112, [122]
Jones-Johnson, G. 111–112 [122]

Kazi, M.A.F. 127, [139]
Kent 86–88
Key Information sets (KIS) 129
Knight, P. 99, [109]
knowledge economy 1–2, 17, 19, 129–130
Krumboltz, J.D. 5, [12]

labour market information xii, 69, 92, 100–101, 103, 132, 135, 145, 153–155, 169–172, 174–175, 182–183
Law, B. 5, [12]
league tables 129–130, 132, 154–155, 161, 182
learning gain 98, 103, 171, 174, 187
Levin, A.S. 5, [12]
Lindsay, C. 4, [12]
Longitudinal Education Outcomes (LEO) 97, 129, 130
Loveday, V. 92, [95]

Marginson, S. 131–132, [139]
marketisation of higher education 1, 6, 17–18, 26, 31, 69, 97–98, 129–132, 133, 140, 162–163, 190, 194, 196
McCash, P. 5–6, 188, 189 [12, 191]
McMahon, M. 6, 10, 179, 181, 196, [12, 191]
McQuaid, R. 4, [12]
Mellors-Bourne, R. 4, 10, 18–19, 26, 41, 86, 92, 99, 140, [10, 27, 51, 94, 108, 150]
misrecognition 37
mobility 8, 42–43, 45, 49, 67, 85–93; home islands 89; migration 67, 85, 86–91; youth depopulation 85, 90
Moffett, J. 143, [150]
moral worth 38
Mosley, E. 86, [95]

200   *Index*

Neary, S. x, 6, 9, 98, 140, 144, 145–146, 195, [12, 109, 151]
NOMIS 58, 69

objective underemployment 111, 120
Office for Students 11, 129–130
Office of National Statistics (ONS) 31, 58, 110
ordinary work 71, 75, 76, 78–83
Organisation for Economic Cooperation and Development (OECD) 1, 2, 17, 30, 33, 62–63, [12, 28]
Orkney and Shetland Islands 85, 87–90

parity of participation 34–35, 36–37
Patton, W. 6, 10, 142, 147, 179–181, 196, [12, 151, 191]
Pawson, R. 127, [139]
Pennington, M. 86, [95]
perspectival dualism 34, 37–38
placements 87, 132–136, 140–141, 145, 147, 154–155, 169, 171, 185–188
Planning for Success: Graduates' Career Planning and Its Effect on Graduate Outcomes (Department of Education) 172
positional/status competition 128, 131–133
Post-1992 university 21, 71, 74–82, 134
Postgraduate Diploma in Careers Guidance 154–155, 187
post-industrialisation i, 1, 17
practitioner research 1, 2, 6, 9–10, 26, 140–141, 143–145, 148, 150, 162–163, 167–177, 179–190, 193–196
pre-1992 university 21, 134, 135
precarious employment 71, 73, 86
professional encapsulation 157, 159, 163
professionalism 6, 12, 153–163; boundaries of expertise 9, 153–163; role divergence 155, 158
protean career 3, 4
Purcell, K. 2–3, 4–5, 31–32, 62–63, 82–83, 96, 100, 101, 103, 104–106, 110, 113–115, 120, [10, 11, 12, 39, 70, 83, 108, 109, 121]

race and ethnicity 4–5, 33–35, 44, 100, 101, 103, 105, 142–144, 150
Reay, D. 20, 26, 47, [28, 53]

reflective practice 182, 188–190
regional economies 41, 50, 60, 87, 129–130
relative employability 32
Roberts, K. 5, [12]
Rousseau, D.M. 3, [10]

Sage, J. 86, [95]
Savage, M. 87, [95]
Savickas, M. 5, 184–185, [12, 13, 191, 192]
Sayer, A. 37–38, [40]
Scholes, K. 132, [139]
Schultz, T. 18, [28]
Scotland 50, 60, 85, 87–90, 158–159
Shepherd, N. 4, 29, 32–33, 169, [11, 39, 177]
Shury, J. 172, [178]
Sinclair, R. 86, [95]
skills provision 18, 50, 58, 86–87, 98–99, 107, 132, 137, 138, 154, 179, 182–184, 194
Small Business, Enterprise and Employment Act (BIS 2015) 97
social advantage 32, 35–38, 42, 43, 45, 47–51, 63, 72, 77, 80, 82–83, 86, 100, 111, 131
social class 3, 4, 5, 17, 20, 21–22, 24, 26, 29–30, 32–38, 42–43, 47, 49–50, 69, 72–73, 82–83, 85–86, 90, 92, 99–100, 111, 120, 131, 187–188, 193; middle class 21–22, 47, 50, 86; working class 21, 24, 42
social justice 6, 7, 19, 29–38, 41, 50–51, 90, 196; distribution 30, 33–34, 36, 38; recognition 30, 33–34, 37–38; restorative 38; two-dimensional 7, 29–30, 33–35, 37
social mobility 1, 17, 19, 29, 36, 43, 85–87, 99, 130, 195
Social Mobility Commission 1, 36
Soy, S.K. 127, [153]
student debt 8, 33, 41, 65, 71–74, 82, 100
subjective careers 119–120
subjective underemployment 111–112
Sultana, R.G. 6, 90–91, [12, 13, 94, 95]
Super, D.E. 5, [13]
systems theory framework 10, 179–182, 190, 196; therapeutic system 181–182

Teaching Excellence and Student Outcomes Framework (TEF) xi, 29, 31, 96–98, 107, 129–130, 133, 168, 190, 194
Thambar, N. 9, 138, 140–141, 149, 157, 159, 174, 194–195, [139, 151, 164, 178]
Tholen, G. 1, 3, 18, 32, [13, 28, 39]
Tomlinson, M. 1, 4, 19, 184, [13, 28, 192]
tuition fees 4, 7, 18, 29–33, 41, 73–74, 79, 81–82, 98, 129, 153–154, 158, 168–169, 193
Turner, C. 172, [178]

underemployment 8, 17, 58, 62–64, 110–120, 193, 196
Unistats 97, 129
Universities and Colleges Admissions Service (UCAS) 96, 100
Universities UK 11, 131
university careers service xiii, 5, 9, 103–104, 128, 133, 135–136, 153–154, 161–162, 167, 169–172, 173–176, 194–196
University of the Highlands and Islands 88

Vivian, D. 172, [178]

Waller, R. 5, 19, 42, 43, 47, 49–50, 73, 81–82, [10, 27, 36, 38, 51, 83]
Watts, T. 5–6, 135–136, 182, [12, 13, 139, 192]
Welsh devolution 41, 43, 45–46, [53]
widening participation (WP) 74, 75–82, 130, 144, 162
Williams, S. 4, 31–32, [11, 39]
Wilson Review (Department for Business, Innovation and Skills) 129, 132, 149
work experience 9, 43, 64, 73, 75, 79–80, 81, 82, 87, 112, 147, 170–172

Yates, J. 147–148, [152]
Yorke, M. 99, [109]